Jed,
Connection!!
LOVE

Advance Praise for
One Choice, One World

"A brilliant guide for navigating today's turbulent waters by a fourth-generation family business entrepreneur, inspired by traditional Chinese wisdom as well as informed by avant-garde quantum science. Essential insights for today's leaders both young and old, in business and in all spheres of civic life."

    —ERVIN LASZLO, philosopher and systems scientist, author, co-author, and editor of 107 different books translated into twenty-four languages

"Frederick Tsao has brought together his Eastern heritage and Western upbringing, his experience of business leadership and his practice of personal meditation to create this important book on the well-being and happiness economy. Every section contains rich insights that stimulate the reader's imagination about what is possible at this critical moment in human history. I recommend it to everyone concerned about the future."

    —PROFESSOR PAUL DALZIEL, lead author of *Wellbeing Economics: The Capabilities Approach to Prosperity*

"Fred Tsao shows that business experience fused with a desire for lifelong learning opens new perspectives. In this book he aptly describes his contemporary economic model to achieve a "Well-Being and Happiness Economy," anchoring his reflections on the state of the global economy on his own evolution as a world-renowned business leader and advocate of the consciousness movement.

Beginning his adulthood with a Western education in the USA and participation in the American business world, Fred integrated his Eastern roots of traditional Chinese spiritual practices to offer new economic leadership pathways from his vision of what a future well-being and happiness economy would look like.

This book is for everyone curious and open to pondering the extraordinary opportunities to contribute meaningful solutions to ease our turbulent world."

    —CHANDRAN NAIR, founder and CEO of The Global Institute for Tomorrow, author of *Dismantling Global White Privilege: Equity for a Post-Western World*

ONE CHOICE, ONE WORLD

ONE CHOICE, ONE WORLD

The Rise of the Well-Being and Happiness Economy

Frederick Tsao

SelectBooks, Inc.
New York

This edition published by SelectBooks, Inc.
For information address SelectBooks, Inc., New York, New York.

First Edition

ISBN 978-1-59079-554-5

Library of Congress Cataloging-in-Publication Data

Names: Tsao, Frederick, author.
Title: One choice, one world : the rise of the well-being and happiness economy / Frederick Tsao.
Description: New York : SelectBooks, [2023] | Includes bibliographical references and index. | Summary: "Fourth generation family-business steward Frederick Tsao shares his vision of a new consciousness of life in the quantum era. To confront global challenges and create an economy of well-being and happiness, he believes we must forge a common worldview grounded in the recognition that humanity is part of one holistic system for all life on Earth" -- Provided by publisher.
Identifiers: LCCN 2022055235 (print) | LCCN 2022055236 (ebook) | ISBN 9781590795545 (hardbound) | ISBN 9781590795552 (ebook)
Subjects: LCSH: Well-being. | Happiness. | Consciousness. | Leadership.
Classification: LCC BF575.H27 T746 2023 (print) | LCC BF575.H27 (ebook) | DDC 158--dc23/eng/20230124
LC record available at https://lccn.loc.gov/2022055235
LC ebook record available at https://lccn.loc.gov/2022055236

Manufactured in China
10 9 8 7 6 5 4 3 2 1

Dedicated to

Those who are awakening to the calling for well-being...

The sages for their timeless wisdom...

Modern science that boldly meets consciousness...

Economists who can build new economic models in this new era...

Entrepreneurs who have the capacity to act and serve humanity's purest wishes of love...

And humanity who trusts that the future is in our hands!

Contents

Chapter 3

A Vision of Quantum Leadership 85

Preface

For a long time, I have been trying to fathom how much the world has changed in my lifetime. Sometimes it seems as if my generation of baby boomers has experienced the greatest and most radical shifts in the history of humanity.

After my hippie college years, I found myself suddenly plunged without warning into an entirely new world of globalization. With the constant technological advancement and complex economic systems based on a "market economy," I had a sense of the proverbial rug yanked from under my feet. Everything I used to know—everything that my parents taught me—was melting into the ether.

In our current era, we continue to live with the effects of the Covid-19 pandemic, and this has thrown my occasional meditations into deep focus. Being unable to travel as freely as I was accustomed to, and needing to adjust to the new normal of online business meetings, meant I was like many others who spent most of our time at home. My home had become my world. Long periods of solitude gave me abundant space to reflect on how I would like to lead my life.

I grew up as a child of the sixties and am a true-blue product of that time. I have witnessed the massive changes wrought by the advent of globalization and the challenges of sustainability that resulted. During my more than forty-five years in business as a fourth-generation steward, I have seen a lot more—good things and also starkly negative things. I've experienced the invisible hands that manipulated global systems, the duplicity of bankers, the insidious ways in which corruption can devour a business alive from within.

These decades also featured a truly formidable rise of Eastern countries, from Japan to the Four Asian Dragons (Singapore, Taiwan,

South Korea, Hong Kong) and most recently, China. At the same time, I have been privy to the disintegrations and failures of systems built in the industrial era. I saw firsthand the damage that irresponsible and unchecked economic growth can inflict on society and the social inequalities that it could exacerbate. Many of humanity's old structures that served us well in the past can no longer retain their relevance today. They must be rebuilt to accommodate the important concept of the new era of well-being and the happiness economy.

My reflections during the pandemic confirmed that we are witnessing the occurrence of something profound on a universal scale. In the past we took for granted that things existed in isolation. We believed that what mattered was material—it was tangible, visible, and perceptible through our sensory organs. But the worldview of a mechanistic, utilitarian paradigm of reality that held sway over mankind's imagination is being displaced by something utterly different: the quantum paradigm.

The quantum paradigm defines life as the universe being present in everything and everything being present in the universe. It regards all things as holistic and formed out of the clay of consciousness. This new paradigm connects us to our past epistemologies of mysticism, faith, and spirituality as they converge into a new unified worldview of old and new, and East and West.

Rather than believing the world can be grasped and reduced to sensory perception, the quantum paradigm instead foregrounds the invisible. These are evolutionary forces that circulate and reign over our lives without our being able to see or pinpoint—much less control—what they are. At the same time, somewhat paradoxically, it is our consciousness, the collective consciousness of humanity, that gives rise to these forces and makes them possible. It is our thoughts—humanity's capacity for thinking—that creates our worldview, culture, economics, politics, technology, and everything we know. In short, humanity's consciousness brings into being the very systems that govern our existence.

If we were to unravel the manifold implications of the quantum paradigm, how would we live our lives differently? If we saw consciousness as an experience without knowing its true depths, would we understand reality beyond what we currently imagine it to be? How can we rethink our own relationships to the whole so that we each know our role in serving and relating to the holistic system?

These are some of the questions I have grappled with. In a world where perception becomes our reality, and where the nature of reality itself can no longer be a stable certainty, I needed to search for an alternative footing to ground myself in life. For guidance, I turned to ancient and classical systems of Chinese wisdom, reflecting deeply on the spirit of Chinese values that persists to this day. I reasoned that there must be something behind the nascent rise of China in this quantum age.

My story is one of perpetual movement and evolution. I was steeped in a materialist mindset when I was younger. At an early age, I started asking myself existential questions; I continually pondered the reason for my being in this world and tried to understand what I was born to do. Later as an entrepreneur, I became one of the actors in the capitalist economy that created all the ethical issues and sustainability challenges associated with it.

In 1993, by coincidence, I started meditating. This practice sparked a significant personal change. I journeyed inward and began to access collective wisdom and receive information from the universe. This allowed me to perceive the world differently. The more I meditated, the more deeply I connected with the most profound recesses of my inner world. My journey did not start with the intention to find a new way forward; I simply sat down and meditated, and my purpose eventually became apparent to me. The process invoked an internal authority that lay deep within me. I no longer needed to rely on sources of external authority that distracted me from my true calling.

Only in retrospect, did I realize what I felt then was love, a desire to reshape the world in the direction of coherence. What others might perceive as risk, I learned to see as a precious opportunity to build a future I aspired to have. Although I was not sure why I felt that way, I distinctly saw the possibility of fulfilling a deep desire within me. I followed this calling, a response that might be called wisdom. It was a feeling of connection with wholeness and a longing for coherence. Only later did I understand that such feelings can arrive in any form: as love, sadness, connection, or inspiration. Once acknowledged, these feelings cannot be pushed away, ignored, or extinguished.

I could not unsee what I had seen.

In accessing my calling and understanding the purpose of my life, I contemplated the evolution of humanity across the whole of its history. One of my discoveries was the bridge between physics and metaphysics. This offered me insights into a new worldview: the new quantum paradigm in which life is everything and everything is life. I started to change as my worldview changed, and I was led out of my habitual comfort zones. Slowly, I accepted what I had initially considered a curse and grew to see it as a possibility for creativity—the revelation with which I had been entrusted. This, for me, marked the tipping point of *bifurcation*, an important concept that will recur throughout this text.

This book is conceived at a time of a momentous crossroad of modern thought—when the field of quantum mechanics has shifted our scientific thinking to the quantum paradigm, now in the process of displacing our era of dualistic worldviews. What readers hold in their hands are my reflections on both personal and collective levels on a wide range of topics. I focus mainly on the subjects of consciousness, sustainability, and economics and include observations on science, culture, business leadership, and business management. It is a consolidation of what I have learned when witnessing the trends of a tumultuous world, and how I believe these insights will lead to actions that in the future will benefit all of humanity.

I draw on my experience of Eastern origins and my Western upbringing. As I inhabit this intersection, I hope to show the total compatibility of the Western science of consciousness with traditional Eastern wisdom of life. Together, the merging of these worldviews will result in a common language and purpose for all of humanity. By recognizing our similarities and tackling common challenges and celebrating our diversity, we can collectively integrate what we have learned from the past and more readily evolve into the future.

For me, this has been a journey of awakening—discovering that our true nature is to love and connect with each other. This is a journey of "stewardship" defined as the responsible, ethical management of entrusted resources to achieve a set of common objectives. Joseph Campbell, an expert in comparative mythology, once discussed the archetype of the hero with a thousand faces, so named because the myth is widely applicable, regardless of social, historical, and cultural context. It is my hope that my own journey—one of deep meditation that drove me to become, for myself, the hero of a thousand faces on a quest for wholeness and coherence—can take this on by offering some wisdom and guidance for everyone invested in building a sustainable future for the collective well-being of humanity.

I address this book to all who engage with economics in their lives, whether they are governments, nongovernmental organizations, businesses, entrepreneurs, individuals, or communities. In it I present the vision of *one world, one humanity*—the dreams of a flourishing life for all—and the belief that the fundamental purpose of economic activity is to serve life. To this end, I offer ideas for solutions to the problems of sustainability and globalization that plague our world today. I think of this book as a kind of experiment in advocacy, to take seriously what the UN terms "the paradigm of well-being" and extend it to its logical conclusions. What might this look like in our daily lives? How can we reflect on it and respond to this urgent call? How would our desires driving economics, change with an awakening to our true nature and inner calling?

For some people, this book will succeed in outlining a vision or suggesting a mission; for others, what I present may seem a crazy

xviii ONE CHOICE, ONE WORLD

idea. My intention is not to establish a hierarchy of worldviews or to prescribe just one way forward. There is no right and wrong when it comes to culture, only different vantage points from which we interpret the world and filter our viewpoints through the level of consciousness that serves us. On the contrary, it is my belief that we can draw on the strength of this extraordinary diversity to build a common culture. At the core of our being, we have much in common in the life that binds us all, as well as having our shared responsibility to protect the one planet that we all inhabit.

At this crossroad of the receding of Covid-19, I call on all of us to make the choice to move from the self-centered, atomized *I* to the expansive, collective *we*. Let us all undertake this inward journey of stewardship to discover the true nature of our being so that we, who are united by our humanity, can thrive in coherence with everything around us and redefine a new well-being and happiness economy that serves all life. Together we can create this new era, distinct in human history, founded upon a common worldview that contributes to the flourishing of all. We all have the freedom to choose to be great; let us exercise our extraordinary abilities to rise upward, united as one.

Introduction

In our search for purpose and meaning in life, we often unduly neglect the fact that real purpose and meaning rest within *us*—as individuals, as biological beings—and also as a *collective* species. Everything in our life is inherently systemic. From the universe to human society, from the body to the cell, we are reminded that layers of systems exist within the broader system. At its core, well-being is an interconnected and systemic concept—one that expands like fractals from the most minuscule to the most macroscopic.

The only constant observable truth in the world is change. Everything in the world evolves in accordance with evolutionary energy, which is a creative kind of energy-in-formation. Evolution is always generating more energy and moving toward changes and integrating systems: large systems like the universe, galaxies, and beyond; medium systems like planet Earth and international politics; and small systems like our bodies and cells. This evolutionary movement has taken us through many phases and states to arrive where we are today. It is this movement that increased its rapidity, that make us feel like we are travelling at breakneck speeds.

Today, humanity stands at the cusp of a new era. This quantum era is a time of awakening. But the real awakening and transformation can come only when we go with the flow that defines our epoch, the recognition and development of our relationship with the cosmos inside us and the external universe. For centuries we have evolved our way of living, from a life oriented primarily toward survival to one focused on fulfilling our pleasures. Now our tendency to prioritize our existential purpose to have a purposeful life in coherence within the systems—to achieve the essence of well-being. For all to experience well-being, there is one choice to be made: to follow the beacon of life on an inward journey within to locate our calling and meaning. To make sense of where we stand and where we are headed, we need a philosophically guided economic paradigm—a new paradigm that becomes a quantum era worldview premised on oneness and holistic well-being—one that draws together the personal and public dimensions of economic and social theories to cultivate a cogent set of rules governing economics and our society across all levels and scales.[1]

In this book, we begin with the premise that humanity plays a critical role in the creation process. We are a unique and distinctive species who is in the forefront of consciousness, and as highly self-aware, motivated change-makers and agents, we contribute to the continued evolution of the universe. The universe and humanity are constantly changing in an orderly manner. Underpinning this order is holism—the notion that everything comes together as parts of the whole. In my discussion about the evolutionary history of humanity and a new change theory, I hope I have arrived at a cogent account of the trajectory of human civilization throughout time and identify the pathways of change as society evolved and developed. Change in every era has begun with a shift in consciousness and worldview that informs humanity's choices and in turn initiates an observable series of social, economic, political and environmental shifts. From surveying great events in history in both the East and the West to drawing upon nascent accounts of consciousness in phenomenology and metaphysics, this book aims to clarify and elucidate the mechanisms of the fluxes and shifts of our universe and their effects on the direction of humanity and civilization.

What makes these changes meaningful to almost everyone on Earth? What makes a single life purposeful? How can we live good lives without allowing this objective to be resolute to become a fixation?

This is where our *theory of well-being* comes in. Happiness and well-being are both synonymous terms that capture the most robust and advanced state of welfare that ought to matter to humanity. We can take a leaf or two from Maslow's hierarchy of needs theory—acknowledging that a good life requires far more than just the most carnal and primordial of desires. He labels this the stage as self-actualization, requiring us to shift our consciousness and from that space respond in synchronicity to the universe's natural flow, oriented by a holistic sense of purpose and meaning. Everything is fundamentally unified, regardless of the scale of the system; human beings are themselves systems within systems. Well-being, then, is when a system achieves coherence, internally, with itself and, externally, with all the systems that surround it. Thus, when I am well, everything is well; and when everything is well, I am well. All of us are gathered within one collective, inseparable interdependent system.

To genuinely come to grips with the contemporary effects of changes, and to awaken our consciousness to this transformation, we need a vision of quantum leadership. Quantum leadership anchors itself in our *sui generis* relationship with the universe as human beings and encourages us to *lead through purposeful leadership and meaningful followership*. It is this movement of the evolutionary energy that is continuously recalibrating back to harmony. This is a process that disrupts, and then self-adjusts and self-organizes, in order to transform itself naturally and seamlessly into equilibrium. Quantum leadership is a property that you and I, anyone and everyone, could cultivate and harness with mindful practices.

This quantum leap happens when we are in coherence with our bodies, when our minds and spirits are conjoined in unity, and when our consciousness shifts—thereby enabling the oneness of our inner world. Consciousness is the mother of capital and is embodied in quantum leadership that strives to achieve coherence among the systems of humanity and nature. Coherence is diversity flowing in harmony, integrated into each other to create a state of well-being. Expressed as joy and bliss, it produces real happiness.

Chapter 5 sketches, in detail, how a "Renewed Economic Model of Social Transformation and Integration" can occur only through our recognizing and embracing quantum leadership. Our inner intention—our true calling—needs constant guidance. *Open your heart, follow your gut.* This is the message I have arrived at through meditation and communicating with many of my fellow like-minded journey-mates on this path. Respecting the cosmos is key. A new economic paradigm has emerged to actualize this transformation—one that prioritizes well-being in its purest form, with precise and conscientious forms of self-regulation in order. This new quantum paradigm—where human desires are aligned to our true self that has a natural inclination to be well, to collaborate, and to constantly create—is best reconstructed through the amalgamation and synergy of insights from East and West, ancient and modern. Such a paradigm where pure intention rules will guide and determine the ethical boundaries that will hold humanity responsible and accountable for our decisions and actions.

What do I mean when I refer to the cosmos, the universe, and us?

The cosmos and the universe are distinct from one another. The cosmos has no form; it is pure energy and the source of all material creation, including humans on Earth who are conscious beings. The universe has form as a construct of the cosmos, which makes up the field of consciousness. Only in the cosmos are we all at one. In the universe, we are constantly moving to seek connection and coherence.

The human body is a wondrous and complex system composed of about fifty trillion cells.[2] Mirroring the evolutionary movement of the universe, cells function as independent members of the community, communicating and collaborating with each other within one cohesive system—a human being. This movement is reflective of the nature of evolutionary energy, a continuous process of integration, disruption, and reintegration to form a cohesive microcosm of humanity at large.

What is unique in my argument, however, is the recognition that humanity is a microcosm of the entire universe, its cycle of creation mirroring that of the universe. Humanity is the most creative and conscious species on the planet. This constant movement of creative disruption appears chaotic, but it is nothing more than cycles of creation reflecting the nature of evolutionary energy. The process may also be perceived as conflictual—we clash, we disagree, we bicker and fight over what is real, right, and true—as the system shifts between the separate part of *I* and the collective system of the *We*. In these shifts, humanity can choose our responses that synchronize with the collective reality or otherwise. Whatever choice we make in our response, the order of the cosmos will calibrate all systems naturally back to oneness; this is the cycle of creating, sustaining, deconstructing, and reconstructing. These are cycles of harmony, collaboration, and evolution as nature is constantly moving toward integration.

My Change Theory

So how exactly does change come about in the universe, on Earth, and in our everyday lives? In my view, change is inevitable and interconnected. The evolutionary energy is constantly in movement, creating, moving, and transforming. Humans serve as an integral part of that creation process because of our freedom to choose how we respond. My change theory is systemic. With a consciousness shift, we perceive the world through a new lens that informs how we think and feel as well as how we act. Eventually, this is solidified through interactions with each other, finally forming our culture.

In 1974, psychologist Clare W. Graves published an 8-level system called "Spiral Dynamics"[3] to model human evolution and life. Twenty-five years later, the concept was refined by Don Edward Beck and Christopher C. Cowan. The Spiral Dynamics model is conceptualized as a color-coded eight-level system, beginning in subsistence and moving through degrees of human societies' sophistication and evolution. Graves subsequently proposed another tier beyond the current level of human evolution. He showed this as an open spiral.[4] He posited that every value system arises as a response to the problems and questions about values posed in the former system. The era that we live in is an open spiral. A new value system will emerge that will allow us to respond appropriately to the multitude of new global challenges.

We might question how we have evolved according to these values. How have we responded, and how should we respond? Evolutionary biologists have said that evolution is not about the survival of the fittest but is instead about those living beings and organisms who are most responsive to the integral systems in their environments.[5] Responsiveness, indeed, is a form of responsibility. It is no coincidence that the words "responsive" and "responsible" share the same etymological roots. To respond to one's own needs and the needs of the outside world at the same time are the qualities that have enabled humanity to survive and thrive throughout its history. We use our natural capabilities to synchronize, integrate, and add value to vastly different environments.

I propose that this change theory be viewed as one big cycle with two distinct yet interconnected systems: our internal and external systems. The internal system features shift in our consciousness, the journey of discovering our true identities and realizing our full potential, which leads to shifts in our worldview and culminates in shifts in the fundamental nature of our desires. Eventually, desires inform our choice of action. As for the external world, it is through our shifting choices that we kickstart changes to the larger systems, such as the supply and demand within the economy, which engenders changes in our society, culture, and political ethos. These changes are constant, nonlinear and mutually reinforcing—they can come ahead or before one another, or occur at all at once.

Being responsible requires us to co-create with the environment—to be in coherence with larger systems, such as the systems of *We* (as opposed to *I*) that inform our actions as members of broader collectives. The vision of responsibility we espouse here is one where the intention and purpose underpinning individual actions are collective and coherence-seeking, even though they are performed by free individuals. The value of life rests in collaboration and harmony. We are born with a moral need and a natural prerogative to seek harmony and wholeness—regardless of whether we call it conscience, god, or morality. We know, deep in our bones, that there is a bigger system beyond us. The whole of our universe—and our humanity— shifts towards dynamic harmonization. It continuously evolves in a loop of creation. When the system is disrupted, it deconstructs and reconstruct itself. What we thus need to do is to awaken to our deeper self-consciousness to find our calling; listening and responding to this calling would enable us to expand our creativity to its fullest potential.

The Evolutionary History of Humanity

We have come a long way since the dawn of humanity. In many ways, our evolutionary directions are largely consistent with Maslow's hierarchy of needs.[6] Maslow observes that the physiological needs lie at the base of our pyramid of needs. These are followed by safety needs, love, and belonging. Then comes esteem, and finally, perched above all tiers of needs, is the highest level of self-actualization. We may not consciously and intentionally crave it, but we are fundamentally underpinned by a common desire to become the most that we can be. As Maslow aptly put it, well-being is self-actualization. However, here I argue that self-actualization, as we shall see shortly, requires *connecting* with the cosmos and *responding* to the rhythms of the universe. Well-being is in fact already our natural state in the cosmos—we need not try bringing it about; instead we only need to embrace what we already have.

We have not always conceived of the world in this manner. Our current paradigms are the result of a long history of evolving worldviews, each generated to deal with the challenges of a specific era. Since the time *Homo Sapiens* first walked the earth, human development has resulted from changing needs and desires of the new era. In the earliest ages of humanity, humans were afraid of threatening natural phenomena—such was the *Shamanic era*. Their orientation toward the natural world was, at its core, one of primitive fear.

Hunter-gatherers in the early periods of civilization shifted away from fear and became precipitously occupied with conscious moves for survival.[7] As hunter-gatherers created settlements and formed agrarian societies, they organized themselves into groups bound together by a new worldview. They developed communities that lived, worked, and played together. They began to structure, plan, and organize their social system to include the future beyond the immediate present; the concept of wealth accumulation soon developed. They also cultivated prototypical religious beliefs and values throughout the Axial Age (500–300 BCE) during the emergence of religiosity in Eurasia.

The Renaissance and subsequent Age of Enlightenment were succeeded by an era of rapid growth and expansion in the global economy. Through the Industrial Revolution, major changes in social needs intensified human civilizations' drive to acquire capital and wealth. Competition fissured the bonds between people. Specialization increased, displacing unity and creating communities in silos as the new order. Consequently, social inequalities and wealth disparities widened. The belief systems and spiritual practices that once connected humankind to nature lost their relevance and were replaced by scientific advancements and rationalism. Biologically and neurologically, humans evolved to prioritize their rational faculties and the pursuit of pleasures over their intuitive capacities. This is why in our time, many people no longer trust our instincts as we once did.

It is undeniable that we have made great strides forward and achieved substantial progress in the material arena over the past 500 years. We are affluent, and science has achieved many breakthroughs while technology continually evolves and enables innovation in products and services to serve our new social needs. Yet we also have a widening of economic and social inequalities around the world. Different worldviews, beliefs, and cultures were naturally formed as more reliance was placed on our own rationalism and science. The affluent urban communities created in the industrialized era are focused on comfort, pleasure, and material satisfaction. The insatiable greed that spearheaded this change has turned out, unsurprisingly, to be a detriment for both humanity and our planet. Indeed, like many generations before us, we face a series of unique challenges in this era.

Much of our contemporary thinking about reality can be attributed to the fact that until now we have lived in a time of materialism that espouses a system of ethics based on hyper-individualism and foundational estrangement. As a result of the excessive valorizations of individual success, many of us feel detached from the collectivism of life. In the industrialization era, we have been conditioned to focus on ourselves, often ignoring the welfare of the people around us. Individualism served us well, but there are costs when individual needs consistently take precedence over collective needs. From a systemic perspective, individuals can flourish only when the collective is well. It is because of our reckless actions that sustainability and climate change are such urgent and pressing issues today. The diminishment of biodiversity and the degradation of the natural environment has promoted discord all around the world.

Indeed, the Covid-19 pandemic truly exposed the steep human price of individualism in many societies; too often individuals refused to take the necessary precautions to prevent the spread of the disease as they held on to the notion of protecting individual freedom. This pandemic has served as a wake-up call for us all. Given the monumental challenges we are confronted with today—climate change, wealth inequality, breakdowns in social structure, and wars, just to name a few—we need to decide if we want to participate consciously in creating a desired future or allow Earth's systems to descend further into destruction and possible extinction.

Ervin Laszlo,[8] in his book *The Upshift*,[9] describes the state of crisis in a system as a point of "bifurcation," a forking in the trajectory of the system's evolution. Importantly, this point of bifurcation can be the passport to the system's continued evolution. Scientists of system theory have concluded that although the process of bifurcation is one-way and irreversible, it leaves room for choice. The greater the chaos, the closer we are to a tipping point, to an ontological divide that we must cross to reach the next level of consciousness.

As the relevance of the material and dualist world expires, a new collective order—the era of well-being and happiness—emerges in its place. When we remove the "I" from ourselves and embrace collective coherence in the new era, we can partake in the ultimate dance among all systems and comprehend that humanity is choreographing every move of the systems.

A Theory of Well-Being

When I am well, everything will be well; when everything is well, I will be well. This is a state of well-being when systems are in coherence and have the full spectrum of flourishing. The self is perfectly created, whole, joyful, sufficient unto itself, and suffused with love, creativity, and intelligence. We may regard human beings as born complete with all necessary knowledge and existence encoded into our DNA. But we must learn how to awaken to our true nature and harness these gifts. In critiquing present-day society, popular accounts of world history and social sciences often neglect the more foundational, first-order question: What does a good life entail, and what are the characteristics of well-being?

My theory of well-being is rooted in harmony and collaboration in the evolutionary creative process. Happiness and well-being are vested in harmony, which requires comprehensive coherence across all dimensions of our being. And what is being? Philosophers and thinkers ranging from Aristotle to Confucius and from Immanuel Kant to Anton Wilhelm Amo reflect that humanity is unique because of its ability to reason, think, imagine, and create. We can construct and theorize all realms of concepts about our nature. We consider ourselves special beings that are infinitely creative and loving at our very core. However, we need to let our true selves emerge from behind the shackles and impositions of our ego—which is nothing more than a projection of our desires. Realizing we are spiritual beings authentic to our nature means we follow our calling and allow our being, rather than distortions of the ego, to guide our living.

To be harmonious, or coherent, then, requires us to live authentically—to actualize ourselves and pierce through the distortion of ego. When we awaken to our true nature and live life in accordance with our purpose, we can hear the impetus of the cosmos and respond to the rhythm of the universe—that is constantly calibrating all life towards coherence. Life is all there is, no more and no less; it is the entire universe encompassing us within it. When we awaken to our interconnectedness with the universe, we will naturally align to the evolutionary force and collaborate to create a state of oneness with all life. This flow gives rise to a continual stream of happiness and joy that reigns supreme when life is flourishing. A consciousness shift is needed for us to get to this state.

The Vision of Quantum Leadership

The big question is about how we can make a transition to shift our consciousness. This brings us to the question of quantum leadership. How do we define this kind of leadership? At the core of quantum leadership is a holistic conception and understanding of our relationship with the cosmos as the source of our calling. We are the broadcasting transducer receiving and interpreting these signals. At the core of all events and situations that we experience is information from the quantum field. Quantum leadership denotes the quality of our ability to "vibe," to connect and to accurately translate these messages to our broadcasting screens, our awakening to new levels of consciousness. Our ability to align with these messages and collaborate with one another to create is our response to this calling. As I discuss in my co-authored book with Chris Laszlo in 2019, several tenets underpin this experience.

Quantum leadership picks up on some of the embedded truths we set out in our book *The Cosmos, The Universe, and Us*. To begin with, there is no matter—but only clustering of energy, co-created and further assembled through consciousness. The creation process is a cycle: As our structures become more complex, we are increasingly driven to reconfigure and recreate from deconstructed parts before the next cycle begins again.

The driving premise behind quantum leadership is self-cultivation. Everything is there in us already, but we must awaken to it. We can then naturally align and synergize with others as we are continually collaborating and creating with them. The work we do, of course, unites us in our purposes to create humanity—to evolve humanity toward its natural holistic state. This awakening is an awareness of our true selves to our true calling—and is what gives rise to what I term the *evolutionary energy for change*.

This awareness will inform the practice of stewardship, which is the ethical and responsible management of life. Such stewardship distils the creative evolutionary energy we receive and interprets it through the mind to arrive at a collective response in the direction of coherency and a full-spectrum flourishment.

Ervin Laszlo has written that when there is sufficient instability in our systems "even a small group of dedicated people can critically influence the way the system evolves."[10] Fundamental change seldom comes from the top; it usually originates at the bottom. For bifurcation to happen and take effect in the human system, a critical mass and a shift in mindset is required so that humanity can evolve when we make that quantum leap. Even a shift in consciousness in a small group of people who have awakened their inner selves to their calling can provide the necessary potent push for the systemic shift. Quantum leadership is needed to reach this critical threshold that will provide the catalyst and kickstart the quantum leap into the new era of well-being and happiness.

A Renewed Economic Model of Social Transformation and Integration

A new worldview of our relationship with the cosmos, universe, and life itself is emerging. We are ushering in both a collective shift and a shift towards the collective, a move toward a paradigm for the flourishing of all. Because humans are gifted with the highest self-awareness and consciousness, we are created to always add-value to the system, so it is always growing and expanding as opposed to merely recycling what it already has. The former is a positive-sum process, while the latter is a pure zero-sum game. Humanity needs to reconnect with our core purpose and our calling. Through conscious action and deliberation, human minds have become increasing integrated and interconnected—we have evolved to be more cognizant and aware of one another.

Covid-19's wake-up call has urged us to focus on our well-being and happiness. We must use this time to discover the very meaning of well-being. We have the power to find the tools and resources to deal with the stress that threatens our wellness and build the structures required to ensure our sustainability.

In moments of extreme crisis, people tend to recognize the strength that comes from unity. It may appear that the pandemic has merely been a polarizing experience, creating division and exacerbating problems, but its appearance may well be the tipping point that has ignited the next stage of humanity's evolution. By extending our communities in the direction of unity, we must now come up with new modes of working together, integrating our worldviews, and creating one humanity on Earth.

Even the United Nations (UN) has acknowledged that things are not the same as they were a decade ago. They have conducted numerous studies since the conferences on "Sustainable Development" in April 2012 in Bhutan and other countries. At that time the UN defined the reality of our current humanity on Earth as one with the potential to become a paradigm of well-being and happiness. According to the UN, "Governments should measure the happiness and well-being of their people and use the determinants of happiness and well-being to guide public policy." The thinking was that many cultures have achieved such sufficient levels of affluence and capability that most people no longer need to worry about everyday survival. Instead of a basic drive to accumulate capital and material wealth, wide swathes of human society are now fueled by a drive to achieve well-being.

Many companies have adjusted their working models to fit the post-pandemic new normal. Corporations are rewriting their mission statements. Environmental, social, and governance criteria and impact investment are gaining momentum. Countries have begun rethinking how to be self-sufficient while being a valuable part of the globalized world. Nations have had to reevaluate the meaning of harmony, citizenship, and collectivity in a time of crisis. Concepts like freedom, human rights, and democracy have been redefined to suit the adaptive circumstances in which we find ourselves.

In moments of extreme crisis, people tend to recognize the strength that comes from unity. Our worldviews—whether self-centered or based in collective collaboration—are the foundations for our actions. When our worldviews differ, we will develop different beliefs, values, and philosophies of life. Consequently, different cultures and identities can sow disunity. History has taught us that when the world's narrative of itself is incoherent, when disagreement is rampant, and when there is a rigid refusal to adapt ourselves to an evolving world, dispute mutates into conflict, which then metastasizes into war.

The risk of war has always been a perennial concern. But this fear has been heightened as China continues to grow and climb in economic and political might; its interactions with the proverbial West (a loosely defined collective of states including the United States, the United Kingdom, and some European states) have become precipitously fraught with tensions. Compared with their Western counterparts, Eastern cultures tend to be more top-down, centralized, and focused on developing a careful relationship of pastoral management and guidance between the state and the economy. The West could learn from the East the virtues of collectivism and communitarianism, just as the East would benefit from the infrastructure and institutions that the West has adopted. We should not throw the baby out with the bathwater; both the East and the West are dealing with the same sustainability challenges that define our era and include common defects and merits that are worthy of comprehensive and fair acknowledgment. We explore this in sections dedicated to *The Particular Example of China.*

On the subject of the East, it is imperative that we differentiate between China's political system and the overarching cultural paradigm in which we operate. We are less interested in critiques and arguments centered around and rooted in our political structures. Instead, we are intrigued by what makes the Chinese approach to governance distinct from that of the West. Throughout the many past millennia, rulers of China—whether across the dynasties or in contemporary China—have come to earn their mandate through delivering substantive results to their population: ensuring stability for the creation of prosperity and affluence. We are interested in people-centered nature of the way China governs as opposed to any particular regime that presides over it.

The future is in our hands. Today's disruptive energy will be quantum leadership's evolutionary energy for tomorrow. This is the one choice for us—to continue our externally oriented way of living accumulating external material wealth—or choose a life journey inward to actualize the self and accumulate non-material spiritual wealth to lead life according to our calling. By actualizing the qualities of quantum leadership that have always been vested in us, we find solutions to our challenges. If we desire to foster unity across the whole of humankind, we must find a coherent narrative of life and a common worldview of values and principles premised on adding value to life. This is the One Choice to reclaim our place in our One World!

The new economic model in the quantum paradigm is actually a renewed economic model based on social transformation stemming from the very views on the nature of ethics and market that were penned by Adam Smith in his theory of moral sentiments over 250 years ago. Smith's views that morality is inherently part of our being will guide the way we live our lives. In its true form this will draw us toward holism.

What I am presenting is a philosophy of economics in a new well-being and happiness era—a revised version of Smith's model with a theory of consciousness and change. The transformation from a free-market economy built on self-interest to a well-being and happiness economy is one that liberates humanity to lead the best life possible in a flourishing world—one based equally on freedom of the inner self and the outward expression of collective well-being.

PART ONE

The Global Awakening

If you see our awakening as chaos,
you will only feel turbulence.

If you see it as a transition,
you will be blessed with excitement and hope.

We are awakening to the fact that we have choice.

The future is in our hands!

CHAPTER ONE

The Evolutionary History of Humanity and a Change Theory

I would like to invite the reader to engage in a holistic reflection on the historical changes in humanity. How do these changes occur? When have changes shaped our economic, social, and political orders and shift us from one era to another? The seismic paradigm and structural shifts that have shaped our history—stretching from the days of the shamanic and primordial to the pivotal industrial and digital revolutions—offer valuable clues and information on how we evolved.

The Emergence of a Common Worldview Integrating Western Science and Eastern Traditions

Since the Age of Enlightenment and the First Scientific Revolution in the eighteenth century, humanity was dominated by a materialist, deterministic, and mechanistic worldview of reality in which a utilitarian logic reigned. Newtonian science relied on a protocol of empirically observable and measurable proof. However, we are currently witnessing the emergence of a new quantum worldview grounded in the quantum paradigm and substantiated by the findings of quantum physics. Within this paradigm, matter does not exist; there are only clusters of energy that give an appearance of solidity. What we call consciousness is a process engaged in creating that appearance. As the physicist David Bohm suggested, consciousness is coextensive with the creation of matter.[11] In other words, the way we see the world shapes the way we think, feel, and create.

The three iterations of the Industrial Revolution were anchored in Newtonian science. As summarized by Klaus Schwab, Founder and Executive Chairman of the World Economic Forum, "The First Industrial Revolution (1765) used water and steam power to mechanize production; the Second (1870) used electric power to create mass production; the Third (1969) used electronics and information technology to automate production. Now a Fourth Industrial Revolution is building on the Third. It is the expanded digital revolution that has continued since the middle of the last century."[12] This era, powered by new developments in quantum science, is characterized by technologies that have blurred boundaries between physical, digital, and biological existence.

A new science of consciousness and evolution of living systems merging toward oneness has arrived, challenging the founding precepts of Newtonian science. A whole new science of consciousness and evolution of living systems has arrived that is challenging the founding precepts of Newtonian science.

Science has always played an instrumental role in human evolution. Developing in tandem with human desires, science enables shifts in our lifestyles and cultures and ultimately the ways in which our civilizations evolve. Scientific advancement leads to technological progress to meet evolved human needs, which changes economics.

The quantum paradigm, based on our inter-connectedness and the belief in our oneness, has united the material and the spiritual. In the words often attributed to French philosopher Pierre Teilhard de Chardin, "We are not human beings having a spiritual experience. We are spiritual beings having a human experience."[13] While the belief systems of human society transitioned from spirituality into science during the industrial era, today we are witnessing the seamless reintegration of scientific and spiritual knowledge through quantum science.

As machines increasingly took over repetitive manual labor, humans reconnected with their creative selves. The Newtonian worldviews dominated the world for centuries with a focus on specialization, while rewarding efficiency. This has created silos in our mindsets, processes, and structures and has separated us from one another. What we now need is unity. Creativity is only possible when we are whole and coherent, listening to the impetus of the universe and evolving into alignment in order to have coherence with larger systems. Although the world is becoming more and more interconnected as a function of technology, the present state of our collective consciousness represents the weak link. We are still engaged in ruthless, internecine conflicts with one another, and we are the largest contributors to environmental degradation. Until humanity develops new consciousness in life, we will not be able to tap into the creative power latent in all of us.

Quantum science has presented the perfect opportunity for us to reshape and elevate our consciousness. Bridging physics and metaphysics, the new science of consciousness represents a scientific breakthrough. In recent times, science has made progress by discovering the essence of matter; the prime discovery being that there is no matter, only energy.[14] Driven by this revelation, a new era has emerged, carrying with it a new awareness that physics and metaphysics are inseparable and that metaphysics is the essence of physics.

Western quantum science shares an intimate kinship with many traditional cultures—in particular, with ancient Chinese culture. Some might ask why is it worth our time to pay attention to Chinese cultural wisdom. The answer is that not only has Chinese civilization enjoyed an immense longevity, lasting thousands of years, but China is also home to one and a half billion people, nearly twenty percent of the global population. As one of the oldest and longest surviving traditions, it merits closer study. Information is readily available since traditional

Chinese culture and wisdom has been preserved with a remarkable degree of consistency over millennia and continues to inform policy-making in the twenty-first century.

It is clear that the new generation of leaders is learning from the victories and failures of the past and applying their insights to the present. In our era, China's ascent is undeniable, and its economic performance in recent years is nothing short of a miracle in the history of humankind. It is soon to become the largest economy in the world. We need to learn and understand the Chinese people and system—we can begin by examining their cultural worldview.

It is no coincidence that Western quantum science and ancient Chinese culture share a common ground. After all, we share one earth and one evolutionary process. Both quantum science and ancient Chinese culture view the cosmos as a web. The dynamic movement of the evolutionary force arises from within the cosmic web and constantly moves toward coherence and harmony. Whenever coherence is attained, the whole system begins shifting, and the cycle of evolution is renewed, progressing into ever greater complexity.

Quantum scientists discovered that all forms of matter in this physical world are quantum entities, clusters of coherent vibration formed from energy. Our observations of this phenomena constitute the illusion of our reality. Consciousness, borne of observation, affects what we perceive as reality.

This is a constant movement of expansion and contraction creating a spiraling geometry that defines the complexity and wholeness of the universe. The universe is expanding at a high speed into infinite dimensions; and it is also contracting into the zero dimension. From moment to moment, the universe perpetually calibrates itself into coherence and harmony. This is the principle of evolution shared by both quantum science and the Dao.

Quantum science calculations have shown that it is extremely unlikely for chance events to have produced the universe as we know it in the available timeframe of 13.8 billion years. Rather than coming into being as a result of chance, scientists have posited a factor called directional information that functions like a holotropic attractor,[15] a term coined by Ervin Laszlo that means a statistically revealed direction. This determines that the universe is, on the whole, consistent rather than random. It contains all things and holds together everything in the same field of connection, preventing disintegration. It is in this way that the universe leans into consistency rather than randomness.

The field in which this is happening is the holographic universe, created from our projection of what we know to be reality or nature. Our holographic universe morphs into the state of oneness of the holotropic attractor[16] For humans, the holotropic attractor is present on the level of instinct and intuition. Each time the holograph reaches oneness, it morphs into the next moment again as it is drawn by the holotropic attractor striving to construct and reach the next level of coherence and oneness. Each moment the holograph projects itself, the whole cycle begins again, creating an interconnected universe in which everything is linked by quantum entanglement. Quantum physicists believe that entanglement is nonlocal, traversing temporal and spatial boundaries so that despite everyday appearances, we live in a deeply holistic and interconnected reality.

In quantum entanglement, linked particles share a common, unified quantum state. Regardless of the distance between them, information about one can tell us about another.[17] This is similar to the Buddhist-influenced conception of dependent origination or *yuanqi* (緣起).[18] According to this concept, phenomena co-exist and are inter-dependent. Eastern and Buddhist thought uses the concepts of origin *yuanqi* (緣起), destiny *yuanfen* (緣分), cause *yinyuan* (因緣) and cause-effect *yinguo* (因果) to expand on quantum entanglement into a worldview of interdependent origination. The forces of *yuan* (緣) are influences that extend through time and space, organizing coherent patterns and systems. A deep kinship exists between the Chinese concept of *yuanqi* and David Bohm's idea that there is a deeper, hidden, and underlying physical appearance, an *implicate order*.[19]

These concepts describe the original force that directs and orients our movements, producing constant oscillation and calibration from moment to moment. Creation happens precisely in this dance. Given the interconnectedness of everything, each movement that occurs displaces another, thus necessitating constant movement and adjustment.

Wuji (無極) refers to the origination of creation held in the quantum field, a field of emptiness where all information is stored. In Chinese cultural traditions, the universe is seen as arising from this *wuji* an "ultimate nothingness" in which the energy of the *Dao* (道)[20] or the universe's natural impetus creates all things from movement, from the *wuji* to the *taiji* (太極).[21] When we live in alignment with the evolutionary impetus of the Dao, we will flourish. In the field of movement, the *taiji*, all forms of matter are created from a binary of *yin-yang* (阴阳), which constantly oscillates and vibrates in the shape of a sine curve in a perpetual movement of expansion and contraction. Rather than seeing the movements of the universe as a matter of right and wrong, *yin-yang* are cycles of evolution that partake of the energy of the Dao. When we synchronize with the rhythms of the universe, we create anything and everything.

One implication of this is that everything in the universe is interconnected. A central tenet of the *Daodejing* (道德經), one of the foundational doctrines of Chinese cultural practices, describes the interconnected forces—and humanity is one of the forces—that affect the evolution and creation process.

> The Dao is great, Heaven is great,
> Earth is great and Humanity is also great.[22]

Even with everything naturally moving in the wider process of evolution, human beings have free will, the power to choose how we interact with these grand movements. It is in this way that we influence and shape creation. When our choices are aligned with the Dao, everything flows and flourishes as it should. In the absence of such alignment, chaos would take the place of order. Humanity has an active role to influence the direction of such movement, whether it returns to order or create more chaos.

Everything is related to each other, weaved together like threads into the same intricate tapestry. When there is quantum entanglement or interdependent origination, it might be difficult for us to fathom cause and effect. Rupert Sheldrake's work on the morphic field has shown us when something happens in one place, it can simultaneously affect the evolution of another, totally unrelated part of the world.[23] There is a deep underlying patterning to the organization of the universe, a profound entanglement of all things, even if we do not know its exact contours.

A similar dynamic is observable in Abrahamic religions where an omnipresent god watches over us and determines the nature of everything that exists. Fundamental reality is not random but "informed" by what spiritual and religious doctrines would identify as "divine," whether in the shape of the Divine Matrix, the Akashic Records, the Cosmic Ground, or simply The Source.[24] These interconnections between mystical, religious, and philosophical traditions of East and West furnish us with a kind of common ground, a common language in which vastly different cultures can communicate and resonate with one another.

To a remarkable extent, quantum science coheres and resonates with the core concepts of the Dao in Chinese culture. There are striking parallels between their conceptions of the universe and life. Both quantum science and Chinese culture view consciousness and evolution as the fundamentals of life. The difference perhaps lies in their history. Quantum science, a recent development in the history of human civilization, provides us with empirical evidence, whereas Chinese culture, having survived for over 5,000 years,[25] offers a tried-and-tested framework for living from a deep repository of wisdom.

The numerous resemblances between quantum science and Chinese culture present an opportunity to build a symbiotic relationship between culture and science and tradition and modernity. Both can learn from each other and be repurposed by one another. While quantum science can borrow from the wisdom of Chinese culture to ground itself in the art of living, Chinese culture can be made contemporary and relevant through the science of consciousness.

The new quantum paradigm is a bridge that connects physics and metaphysics. Materiality meets spirituality and encompasses within it religious and mystical traditions as well as the emergent life science of consciousness encapsulated in such disciplines as neuroscience, contemplative science, and epigenetics.

This bridging is essential; it is a transformation unique to our quantum era, as it enables the development of common interpretations across differing worldviews. Irrespective of what these worldviews are grounded in, the quantum paradigm provides an everyday foundation for mankind to interface and communicate with one another. Given that humanity at the present time faces prevalent challenges of sustainability and the fact that our world is globalized from the extent of our access to information and technology, this universal ground is all the more necessary.

The quantum era calls for us to collaborate as one community and to be unified in identifying and addressing our common problems. When and where entanglements arise, how will we respond? In effect, all things we now see as challenges in our world are merely consequences of interdependent activities. We must take advantage of our entanglement as an opportunity to evolve and to choose the right response to our difficulties. This is the locus of humanity's gift.

The time is right, and the time is now. All the conditions of our new quantum worldview present this truth. All the wars, conflicts, natural disasters, and pandemics of our contemporary reality are signs that we have reached a tipping point. Cosmic energy is guiding this transformation from one era into the next. Ancient calendars like the Mayan calendar already predicted this spiritual awakening of humanity, pointing to the accelerating movements of the universe as it grows into greater complexity, unification, and harmony. The Mayan calendar designated December 12, 2012, as the beginning of a new age, a cycle that first commenced on August 11, 3114 BCE.[26]

This state is captured by the Greek word *Kairos*, a moment in which all is aligning into oneness. In astrological terms—where the positions of heavenly bodies and constellations influence human events and are correlated with human behaviors—we might designate this era the Age of Aquarius that refers to a period thought to bring increased harmony and oneness to the world. Or we might even call this the Second Axial Age. The First Axial Age was a term first coined by Karl Jaspers to refer to the *pivotal age* characterizing the period of ancient history from about the 8th to the 3rd century BCE when the intellectual, philosophical, and religious systems emerged to shape subsequent human society and culture. In that period, the spiritual leaders Buddha, Confucius, Socrates, and Jesus all came into being as a response to the destructive conflicts of that epoch. The First Axial Age, in other words, was another *Kairos* with its own quantum entanglements.

Modern science today is merging with the science of consciousness, a fusing of ideas and cosmologies from East and West that will have implications for our mind, body, and spirit. From the trillions of cells that compose the human body—organized and refined over eons of evolution—humanity is evolving into a new entity, a biosocial ecosystem of collective consciousness. Humanity is undergoing a metamorphosis in which all the parts of its immense system are learning to communicate smoothly with one another.

All these different frameworks, cosmologies, and trends bear the same truth. They are helping us to realize that the time is now for the emergence of a new and common worldview for humanity. Because of the sheer rapidity of technological advancement, in recent years we have witnessed the increasing globalization and interconnectedness of humanity. We are edging into another pivotal age. How this pivotal age will emerge hinges upon humanity's decisions and choice of actions. With a common worldview, we will have the power to shape the Second Axial Age.

All systems must be integrated and coordinated for the health and coherence of all life. Just as a caterpillar dissolves its body into liquid before its rebirth, human civilization must disintegrate to transmute itself into the butterfly that will break out of its cocoon, beautifully and gracefully aflutter. As with any process in nature, this transmutation will be painful and difficult but ultimately necessary if we are to build a new future for ourselves. The emergence of this era represents humanity awakening to our purpose of life, a time to explore, review, and develop answers to the existential questions.

Our Change Theory

Our change theory arises at the intersections of quantum science and ancient wisdom, in particular Chinese wisdom that traverses physics and metaphysics, past and present, science and culture, and time and space.

Most other change theories are concerned with projected appearances, comparable to transient images flashing on a wall. Our change theory seeks to penetrate the true nature of things—to go to the source, the projector from which those images originate. Change is the shifting of consciousness from within: Change yourself, and everything will change around you.

This "change theory" is based on the process of our ability to elevate humanity's consciousness to form our worldview of beliefs, desires, and choice of action. This informs our culture and organization of systems in this world—such as economic, political, social, technological, or environmental systems that are inextricably intertwined. The elevation of our consciousness will precipitate the arrival of a new age with the ultimate goal of bringing into being the new well-being and happiness economy. It rests on the assumption that a shift in humanity's consciousness will precipitate systemic change.

The change theory is ultimately grounded in our understanding of human consciousness and is based on the following principles:

1. Everything is an interconnected system in a state of oneness.
2. From moment to moment, everything is evolving and calibrating itself in the direction of alignment with coherence and harmony.
3. Evolution is the energy driving the creation of new, more complex living systems.
4. Our human challenges direct our evolution.
5. Existential questioning is the awakening beacon to this reality.
6. We will evolve our consciousness in our journey of finding who we are.

Comprehending the change theory is necessary for us to share a common worldview and understanding of what needs to change in existing global systems, structures, cultures, and beliefs. With this common ground, a new awareness will make it possible for us to make a united effort to solve a common challenge. Economic, political, social, technological, and environmental systems cannot be separated—a shift in one system prompts shifts in all the others to find new coherence and harmony. The democratic system, now pressured by a bottom-up movement, will merge with a top-down, centrally planned communist system. Practices like impact investment and Environmental, Social, and Governance investing will redirect capital and rewrite governance in the well-being and happiness economic era. The definition of wealth will broaden and will be redistributed to create for everyone the ability to thrive and flourish. In this new era, businesses will be at the forefront of integrating nonprofits, philanthropy, and government to encourage all of them to practice stewardship.

As we move into spiritual reality and consciousness, we will be guided by our natural calling that informs our material desires.

Having moved past survival and indulgence, we progressed toward asking ourselves existential questions and seeking our purpose. We will arrive there through the process of awakening to the reality that we are part of one holistic system and want to align ourselves with this system to create life in tandem with the rhythm of the universe. The expression of love for the greater whole will be the primary driving force of economics in order to manifest a new economy of well-being and happiness.

As we listen to the deep rhythms of the cosmos or the Dao, we realize we are fundamentally spiritual beings, drawn to oneness and coherence. Our true nature is love, and our true purpose is to evolve. With love, we can truly be at one with the greater system and add value to the well-being of the whole. After all, to evolve and sustain our alignment with the coherence of oneness is the purpose and meaning of human existence. If we change ourselves, everything will change around us.

Experiencing Chaos As We Evolve to a New System

We find ourselves poised on a momentous cusp of time. With industrialization, machines mechanized production work and built production capacity. Today, many are enjoying material abundance because humanity transcended the chaotic period of brute survival and moved to a time of affluence. However, at the other end of the spectrum, new challenges and new chaos are emerging.

We need to identify our current challenges so that we are able evolve beyond them. Humanity's awakening is an essential part of the evolutionary process—this is a natural, continuous, and ceaseless movement of energy. The Chinese call this *yin-yang*, while modern science[27] refers to it as a moment-to-moment calibration of the universe toward coherence and harmony. These movements of energy surround us and emanate from deep within us at the right time and in the right place. As a natural process, everything is just as it should be; chaos is an invitation for the evolution and creation of new living systems. Humanity can choose specific responses to these challenges and forge new connections that seek to string chaos into coherence and harmony. Our choices will determine how we add value to this evolutionary process.

Our worldview today is conditioned by the tenets of industrialization, which is built on dualistic paradigms of Newtonian science. Over the last 250 years of industrialization, social gaps emerged and inequalities widened, gradually separating whole systems. Today, the fractures are more apparent than ever with the advent of human rights movements and globalization. The Covid-19 global pandemic has only amplified popular discontent. People all around the world are awakening to these widening inequalities and will no longer meekly accept the status quo. Conflicts are intensifying not only between nation-states; the inequities affect our family life and disrupt individual inner peace—anxiety and stress are everywhere. These challenges have largely been the result of a crisis of consciousness. Humans and institutions have lost the purpose and meaning of their existence.

Our growing affluence has also translated into a renunciation of our former connections with the natural world. In the earlier stages of our history, we were more in touch with the environments we inhabited. In our time we recklessly sacrifice nature in exchange for economic growth and wealth accumulation. We have forgotten that we all live on the same planet—that we only have one world to share with one another.

The chaos we experience today is the result of human choices. We have disturbed the natural evolutionary process to the point that we now must face sustainability challenges. Climate change looms over us, wealth inequality divides people, sparks from these conflicts threaten to mutate into war, and pandemics are likely to become more frequent and more severe as social structures break down. These challenges will only accelerate and intensify in coming years and decades, rendering peace and harmony all but impossible.

In addition, two major events have further destabilized an already chaotic world. This is the tipping point for an awakening and a shift in consciousness, a signal that the larger movements of evolutionary energy in the universe are accelerating our era's systemic shifts. The first is the emergence of China as a major player in the global system with its market of nearly a billion and a half people constituting approximately twenty percent[28] of the global population. China's rise has also introduced a culture that is more collectivist in nature than anywhere else in the world. This collectivism has often led to China being labelled reductively as communist and perceived as authoritarian. China's formidable size and unfamiliar culture have rocked the boat, breaching our comfort zones and causing great fear.

The second event was the Covid-19 pandemic that swept across the globe, leaving no corner untouched. It disrupted the natural rhythm of life and forced a busy world into a standstill. During this time of the slow-down, many of us became reflective. We questioned our existential purpose and reconsidered our options in a troubled world. The necessary isolation of people during the pandemic gave us opportunities to practice meditation and engage in our spiritual interests. Ironically, this difficult time had a positive effect of enabling us to reach a different, higher state of consciousness to access greater wisdom.

However, these waves of chaos that disturbed the organization of our systems has reached a fevered pitch, threatening us with the possibility of self-destruction if left unchecked. In our human history, we have successfully evolved from one era to another, and this time should be no exception. We must search for new ways to evolve and sustain ourselves. What we need is nothing less than a common ground and a mutual language that will unify us.

The world is awakening to the fact that sometimes more is not necessarily better, and less can be more. The pandemic has reinforced the urgency for all of us to take seriously the challenges of sustainability we all face by reflecting on how we got here and assessing what it will take to forge a worldview to unify us all.

The world is questioning the role of business in building humanity's future. Businesses are the most efficient institutions for deploying resources in service of the human desires that drive our economic activities. Transformation of businesses will be a core factor in the creation of the well-being and happiness economy. It is clearly observable that with the progress of advanced industrialization, the economy shifted from a market driven by consumer needs to an economy driven by marketing. Consequently, business enterprises today prioritize growth over all else and focus on financial returns as their defining purpose. This mindset has contributed to current sustainability challenges.

The marketing economy aims to generate profits by capitalizing on human greed and ignorance and inflating identities built on ego and desire. As technology democratizes information, making it accessible and available to the masses, businesses are now being called into question about the sources of their profits and how they are generated. Business practices and the foundations on which they are built have been taken to task. Markets are now more informed, and standards like environmental, social, and governance (ESG) criteria and impact investment are gaining traction in directing capital allocation and driving economic focus.

While the production systems of the industrial era served us well, today's more sophisticated production capabilities that resulted from rapid technological development have taken off in a separate trajectory. Modern systems of production no longer cohere with their original purpose of benefiting all humanity. Our age of great affluence differentiates consumers and divides us rather than bringing us together.

Just as economics and business are mutually intertwined, governments and politics also share a symbiotic relationship; the study of one cannot be accomplished without considering the other. Politics can be traced back to its ancient Greek etymology, meaning "affairs of the cities,"[29] which refers to activities that organize decision-making to consolidate power within a group of people. Governments were set up as institutions to exercise authority and serve this need. In ancient China, such values and principles were espoused in the organization foundations of *fumuguan* (父母官) simply translated as "parental officers," an informal moniker given to county magistrates and their stewardship of power. The comparison of officers to parental figures demonstrates how they were seen to simultaneously embody discipline and love.

The chaos and sustainability challenges we are experiencing today are signs of a massive misalignment of global systems. The current purposes of business and economics and our roles in governments and politics need to be examined and redesigned to serve humanity's well-being. Advancements in technology that have enabled us to deal with globalization by establishing new physical and virtual connections are often experienced as disruptions rather than opportunities. Globalization, rather than fueling evolutionary energy for global integration, has instead escalated misalignments into sustainability challenges.

What we truly need is an elevation in our consciousness and the wisdom to choose the best response to this chaos. What we do affects not only our world but ultimately the entire universe. We hold the power to transition to a new era of well-being. Amidst today's seemingly unending turbulence—from the pandemic to ongoing sociopolitical conflicts—there are many observable positive trends evolving in the areas of economics, politics, society, and emerging technologies. There is hope for the betterment of our world if we ride the wave of this global awakening to build our future.

Awakening to Humanity's Evolutionary Energy

An awakening, unprecedented in scope, is taking place at all levels within ourselves and within cultural, regional, global, and cosmic systems. It is a movement based on our natural energy toward evolution and momentum from the encounter between the new science of consciousness and existing repositories of wisdom, often referred to as "spirituality." The predicted new era of well-being will be a systemic reconfiguration of all systems for the next level of evolution. The biosocial system of humanity is constantly reconstructing itself to respond to the changing needs and demands of the times.

As already stated, this systemic, self-organizing reconfiguration originates from widening gaps that result in conflict. Nowhere is this more evident than in the phenomenon of growing rumbles in response to wealth inequality. Wealth and power are concentrated in the hands of a small group of elites while large swathes of the world's population are denied access to basic needs of food, water, shelter, education, and healthcare. The marketing economy, and the businesses that contribute to it, have also been overtaken by its quest to maximize consumption and profit at the expense of social good. We have awakened to the incoherence in the social system of wealth redistribution. Wealth is redefined beyond financial terms to include accessibility to resources, capital, and other opportunities—in essence redefining the freedom to create.

According to Inequality.org, while ordinary people suffered economic losses during the Covid-19 pandemic, billionaires saw their fortunes expand.[30] The Credit Suisse Global Wealth Databook showed that in 2021 the richest one percent owned 46 percent of the world's wealth, and 12 percent owned 85 percent of global wealth.[31] The gap between rich and poor has widened on many levels. On January 20, 2020, Oxfam reported that in 2019 a total of 2,153 billionaires had more wealth than 4.6 billion people.[32] The widening disparities in wealth have led to immense inequalities in the distribution of resources.

Wealth inequality has been a major cause of geopolitical instability and imbalances of power between nations, resulting in conflict and threatening humanity's existence. When the world is out of sync because there is a misalignment of people's access to basic resources, disagreements easily escalate into open wars. When governments and business institutions are too absorbed in their self-interest and refuse to acknowledge the truth of what is happening in the world, they fail to make the necessary adjustments to keep peace and harmony. The rifts that separate us from one another along the lines of culture, religion, and race can only deepen.

In the aftermath of the Covid-19 pandemic, our awakening to these fractures has accelerated. This social awakening is percolating through the lines that divide communities, whether they are largely based on issues of inequality of wealth distribution or from divisions of religion, race, color, gender, and different values. Perceptible tremors can be felt as the masses everywhere around the globe seek to make their voices heard. Populations are no longer meek and submissive to their government's official top-down propaganda. This bottom-up surge of anger and resentment means many of the uppermost institutions and echelons of power are buckling and on the verge of collapse.

Voices of marginalized groups are amplified as self-organized communities emerge to fill needs unfilled by governments and business institutions. If these gaps from inequality widen, our differences are augmented, intensifying pressures and ultimately creating disruption and chaos. These are natural energetic forces seeking coherence and harmony in a chain of cause and effect—with negative results justified in some belief systems as "reaping what we sow" or having "bad karma."

The severe problems of wealth redistribution point to a problem with our capital markets. People who participate in capital markets are able to benefit from unequal access to finance, marketing platforms, media channels, and other information. Consequently, casino finance has arisen. This is at the expense of the others who are exposed to the instabilities of gambling on risky investments—the boom-and-bust cycles from speculation and manipulation.

Another source of evolutionary energy is humanity's search for freedom. In parallel with the conflicts and wars of our time, our discourses on freedom, democracy, and human rights have evolved. One basic human right, as defined by the United Nations, is the right to freedom. This is defined as the right to live a life in a way an individual sees fit without encroaching on another's rights.[33]

Freedom can be a fraught ideal. Sometimes, individual freedom can come at the expense of collective well-being. Both people and their governments know that boundaries and self-governance must be imposed. All of us have struggled with this in some way or another, particularly during the pandemic. Conflicts arise at points where policies designed to protect the well-being of the whole are perceived by individuals as repressive and limit one's freedom. Often it seems what is considered right or wrong involves a difference in worldviews and cultures.

As humans, we generally feel free to create infinite possibility. Limitations to freedom in the physical material world have been minimized by the advent of globalization. We have more mobility than ever before, and we can travel around the globe with relative ease; yet people feel stressed and constrained by the need to make choices.

Ironically, whereas animals and plants are naturally in sync with their environments, humans do not have that same automatic resonance because we have freedom of choice. It is imperative that we awaken and understand our place in the wider ecosystem and how we should interact within the holistic system.

In human communities, the natural world, and the wider cosmos, everything is pointing to wide-scale paradigm shifts of realignment in the direction of coherence, harmony, and oneness. When all systems merge into one and serve the whole, this will inaugurate an era of well-being and happiness. Human technology, that continues to develop at an exponential rate, is buttressed by the quantum paradigm. Technology will be key to the construction of a unifying common ground for humanity, empowering us to build bridges between differences of culture, religion, and race.

New technology is changing the way we live. It is determining how we accomplish tasks and where we do these things—another strand of evolutionary energy that is unfurling in response to increasing complexity of social systems. Although we have industrialization and Newtonian science to thank for our current level of affluence, the productivity and capacity of machines has now transcended earlier paradigms and increased to unprecedented levels, operating at lightning speed. The unparalleled extent of mechanization has replaced many functions human beings used to fulfil, adding tremendous pressure on our well-being. We realize that we are now competing with the machines we created.

Innovation is blurring the lines that used to separate biological and digital systems. Today, machines and new technology such as smartphones, wireless access, 3D printing products, and robotics have been integrated seamlessly into our lifestyles. Artificial intelligence is enhancing the capacity of humans to interface with machines. New inventions make possible what was previously unthinkable, including driverless cars and the remarkable printing of prosthetic body parts for the healthcare industry.[34]

As these advancements in technology continue to free us from mechanistic tasks that can be automated, what will we do with our time? What are the possibilities of having this freedom? We now truly have the power to forge a civilization beyond the pursuit of a good life so that we can create a civilization founded on a higher purpose.

When humans are no longer hampered by the laborious needs of standardization and efficiency, we regain the capacity to rebuild the relationship between the spheres of working, living, and playing that were wedged apart by the era of industrialization. These separate parts took off on their own trajectory; living, working, and playing are no longer the benign activities they seemed to be.

In their current form, they have mutated beyond their original spirit of collectivity and are now threatening the sustainability of all life. Rather than fitting into an integrated whole, our purpose was misdirected from the collective good and centered only on the individual. We narrowed our vision of ethics to focus on benefits for individual well-being to the detriment of the larger whole. During the Covid-19 pandemic, we witnessed the lethal effects of excessive self-centered individualism. Many people refused to wear masks or take precautions, thinking only of their own comfort and convenience. This type of individualism obviously cannot provide us with a sustainable way forward. This self-centeredness must shift with the advent of the new era to be superseded by a prioritization of collective care.

We are awakening to the fact that we are part of a bigger system, not isolated and decoupled from others and the environment. We are awakening to humanity's needs, and ultimately our role, responsibility, and purpose in this life we live now. It is a search for a new structure and definition that will allow us to move into a new era of oneness, well-being, and happiness. It is part of a natural evolution process to meet challenges arising from living as separate, atomized parts for too long. We can, and must, seize the opportunity.

We are privileged to be witnessing this awakening of the human species to a new reality. If we embrace it, we will be part of the change that will bring about a newfound coherence and the revival of love and freedom. We can construct a common future in which we all have a place.

The Signs of Awakening to a New System

Institutions in power, such as governments and businesses, are being increasingly challenged by bottom-up calls for change. Although the system as we know it is disintegrating and losing its form, this is hardly a sign that all hope is lost. On the contrary, precisely because the former Newtonian system that previously served humanity through industrialization can no longer retain its relevance in the face of today's reality. A transformation is urgently called for. We have reached an inflection point and must act now to begin evolving through the higher ideals of coherence, oneness, and harmony. Many signs attest to the emergence of these systemic shifts.

All life has a common purpose: to evolve and sustain itself. This has been proven time and again in the history of human evolution. Globalization, a term that has taken on different valences throughout time, originally defined the process of humans migrating from Africa to other parts of the world. Today, the Oxford Dictionary defines globalization as "the process by which businesses or other organizations develop international influence or start operating on an international scale."[35]

Globalization is an evolutionary energy, a unifying force, built primarily on international economic connections with elements of cultural and political unification. It acts as the gateway to the integration of the world's disparate systems forged out of previous eras of industrialization. In its beginnings, globalization was an economic concept to internationalize trade and boost the exchange of goods and services across regions, facilitating the melding of cultures and beliefs. Now, it represents the greatest global awakening to oneness as internationalization breaks boundaries of space in a time of heightened ease of travel and communication.

Globalization has also spurred a process of equalization where economic models naturally adjust in response to supply and demand in both production and consumption. It has the potential to be the point of integration of all the existing worldviews and systems. This movement is providing a platform for solutions to humanity's sustainability challenges. It is gradually redefining economics as a shift in worldview and culture into the era of well-being and happiness.

The process of globalization is closely related to the energy of evolution as the world constantly reconstructs itself into more complex and more integrated structures reflecting the energy at the heart of the universe. As the world is awakening to the ultimate purpose of life—to evolve into oneness—alignment and collaboration are the natural actions to establish a new globalized reality. Another complementary evolutionary energy emanates from new developments in science and economics as they continue to accelerate and add value to globalization.

Besides these shifts, an evolutionary shift is also noticeably taking place in the rise of quantum leadership across the realms of economics, politics, society, and technology. We can make the choice to be part the quantum leadership movement to act now and create our alignment to the paradigm of oneness, precipitating the world's systems toward their tipping point. Those of us who do not take the lead in this process will likely follow in the wake of transformation, adapting to the new quantum paradigm after the point of bifurcation. Whether we want to be at the forefront, forging new paths, or walking in someone else's footsteps is a matter for each of us to decide.

This transformation, then, is a seismic one, taking place on multiple levels of change across disparate social and cultural contexts. Precisely because of its scale, it might feel chaotic, but the chaos can at the same time serve as a force for connection and unity. Signs of structural awakening, broadly speaking, are observable across three different systems: humanity in general, business institutions, and political institutions.

THE AWAKENING OF HUMANITY

Our current societal paradigm dictates that we live a productive life. The education system is geared toward training us to be productive and functional citizens who have a goal to perfect our capabilities in service of industrial processes. We think about everything in terms of productivity; yet at the end of the day we still yearn for our life to have meaning. We wish to be eulogized as people who made a significant impact and contributed positively to the flourishment of society.

This system has shaped us to thrive in an era of industrialization, in which the dominant metric of value has been efficiency and productivity. Labor used to be rewarded and remunerated according to how productive it was since most humans were reduced to machines while creativity was concentrated in a small group at the top of the production chain.

The increased need for speed and accuracy in the workforce has intensified stress and mental strain. As workers are caught in these endless loops of labor, we have gradually awakened to our inability to sustain these stressors in our lives. We feel tired and unfulfilled in spite of earning more and becoming more affluent. We sense distinctly that something essential and necessary is absent, a nagging feeling that beneath our material plenitude is a profound inner emptiness.

Because of our obsession with work and wealth, we have neglected our relationships and ethics—our relationships with ourselves, our loved ones, our communities, and, perhaps more significantly, the natural world. Humans are inherently social creatures, but the environments that we have constructed ironically deny us access to our true nature. Today's escalating chaos and demands on our attention bring us further away from the possibility of relation and connection. Despite living in overcrowded areas, many of us continue to feel deeply alone and separated from others.

Work, as an increasingly specialized and autonomous field, has largely been separated from pursuing recreation and entertainment during normal, comfortable routines of our daily lives, which used to be an integrated whole in earlier stages of humanity's evolution. For most of us, it is difficult to find meaning in our work.

We no longer feel our interests and routines outside of our working day have any connection to our work. Important existential questions, like the purpose of our existence, have been obscured and forgotten by the repetitive routines in which we are mired.

An additional challenge that humanity is forced to confront today is the advanced state of technology. Artificial intelligence and robotics are so highly developed that they transform every aspect of our lives, from our work to our transportation, healthcare, and education. In recent generations increasing sophistication of robots and machines replaced many jobs humans used to perform, understandably generating widespread anxiety over the loss of jobs and livelihood.

Today our conflicts about technology often revolve more around the pressure of keeping on top of the technology and the need to constantly educate ourselves about using our computers and other advanced machines. The word, *stress* must be among the most frequently used words today, as a catch-all term to describe any state of feeling off-center. While stressed, our worst worries become reality. Yet stress is so normalized that we have all learned to accept it as an unavoidable part of life.

However, it could be said that we always rise to meet our challenges. Observing the trends and patterns of emerging businesses allow us to connect with the underlying needs behind these challenges. In recent years, one such manifestation of humanity's awakening is the proliferation of the wellness industry. In 2019, the global wellness economy was valued at $4.9 trillion. Although it fell to $4.4 trillion in 2020 during the pandemic, the Global Wellness Institute (GWI) projects that the wellness economy will soon resume its robust growth with an average annual growth rate of 9.9 percent as the wellness economy reaches nearly seven trillion dollars in 2025.[36]

We can also retain a positive viewpoint if we believe the stressors in our lives are forcing us to reflect on our anxiety and our need to search for the deeper purpose of our lives. More and more people feel the need to journey inward to connect with their inner sense of spirituality and are willing to spend freely in these endeavors. Practices like meditation, yoga, qigong, and mindfulness have become commonplace. They are commodified products in the market economy. The heightened desire and demand for wellness is a major sign that humanity is awakening to the new era of well-being. We are finding a path to well-being in ancient practices and systems of belief that we cannot find in the chaotic modern world. Consequently, Eastern and Western systems of philosophy, both ancient and modern, are being integrated into a common, unifying foundation from which everyone can build wisdom.

A new trend has emerged, especially for those who are affluent. Long retreats and sabbaticals have gained in popularity and are normalized routines. People are extending their retreats for longer periods beyond weekend getaways so that they can spend more time in stillness and deep self-connection. When journeying inward, we awaken to oneness as a part of the whole—a process which sparks in us a realization of the urgent need for collaboration, inclusivity, and collectivity. Instead of orienting ourselves mainly to the importance of individual freedoms, we realize that we must consider the greater good. We must add value to our lives by positioning the *I* within the larger *we*.

Beyond conventional well-known wellness practices, millions of people are turning to technology to help in our search of wellness. Many download apps to our mobile devices as a tool to help us to relax and be more mindful. The *New York Times Magazine* reported that mindfulness apps like Calm, Headspace, Fabulous, Roots, and Liberate all experienced a resurgence in popularity in 2020 when people were searching for a reprieve from the crushing anxiety of the pandemic.[37] Relaxation and mindfulness practices are gaining in popularity as a means of accessing this state of oneness and harmony. Although this phenomenon brings to light the intensity and desperation of people's need for connection, this alone does not appear to adequately address the roots of this generalized social alienation and loneliness.

In our age, we are discovering a natural desire to dive deeply into our souls and minds to explore intricate corners of our interior selves and transcend beyond mere bodily relaxation. When external reality seems so dissatisfying and unfulfilling, it is no wonder that we want to look deeply inward to see the world differently. We will be able to look at the world through the eyes of children, seeing it as a place brimming with joy, wonder, and mystery—evoking the curiosity and awe hidden inside us.

Beyond the wellness industry, yet another manifestation of humanity's awakening is its embrace of the new change theory. Consciousness has been one of the most frequently used buzzwords in recent years, infused into disparate fields including leadership, education, business, healing, and spirituality. New leadership and organizational models have been gradually introduced into business schools, such as those offered at Case Western Reserve University and George Washington University in the United States.

Many self-organized communities are also being formed to meet this need and desire for new change theories, including the Institute of Noetic Sciences (IONS), the emerging Global Consciousness Institute, the Laszlo Institute of New Paradigm Research, and Heartmath Institute. All of these organizations seek to break down boundaries between disciplines of knowledge to transform existing educational and leadership practices and to encourage the expansion of humanity's consciousness.

Taken together, the rise of the wellness industry and participation in the new change theories are signs of humanity's evolving consciousness. Together we are moving into a new social order of collaboration and coexistence in the interest of building a common base that unifies us all. These signs suggest to us that love and freedom can be our solutions to the threats and challenges that we all face today. We begin to consider that with coherence, harmony, and oneness humanity will be able to address these challenges in a meaningful and effective way.

Humanity's awakening will come about when we understand that each individual system serves the whole system in an evolution in search of coherence and harmony for the well-being of all and when we see that we ourselves are systems. At each moment, we are building humanity as a biosocial system that fits within the larger system of nature. Lying at the intersection of biology and society, compassion is at once a natural trait that many people possess and a skill that can be learned and refined over time.

Those of us who make the choice to start our journey inward will discover that we are able to focus on the big picture, we are at one with the universe and want to participate in leading humanity's transition to a new era. We will realize the need to collaborate to solve sustainability challenges, to take advantage of globalization as an opportunity to unite ourselves, and to leverage technology's expanding capabilities to enhance our well-being. Simply stated, the answer to all our challenges lies in our hands.

Ancient writings have bodies of wisdom and holistic practices that provide us with a learning journey to oneness. There are many routes that we can take on this life journey, but there is only one journey inward to understand ourselves. On this journey, immense possibilities will emerge. We will become aware that at this moment, humanity needs to act and shift to a new era of well-being.

Other fundamental questions exist, too. For instance, what impact will religion have on our future? How will the differences in political systems play out? What role will technology play in this evolution? These must be addressed through our new holistic insights of understanding and appreciation for the profound intertwining of economic, political, religious, and social systems and the pervasiveness of technology in all these areas. History shows us how we got here. Now we need to learn what we must relinquish, what we want to bring forward and create during this evolutionary journey to our future.

Consciousness drives the worldviews that shape our cultures and desires. Desire fuels economics, which drives social, political, and technological change in the world. It is a holistic thread of change and the ultimate driving force underlying it all is consciousness.

For us to move forward, we need to take responsibility for our choices and the impact of our roles and actions on each system. Governments and political institutions that made power and control their ultimate aims must now assume their rightful role of nurturing the flourishing of society. Businesses must take responsibility for their role in causing our sustainability challenges. Humanity must acknowledge its greed, fear, and self-centeredness in order to embody our stewardship to transcend these weaknesses. Staying at the current level of our humanity's consciousness that resulted in our misguided decisions, will only further endanger us, our environment, and the natural world—and this is no longer tenable.

The decisions we make, the actions we take, and the impact we have across these different social, political, and environmental domains have resulted in the gargantuan challenges that plague us today. We are at a crisis of our consciousness, which serves as the most important resource for wisdom and ethics. It is a change in our consciousness, above all else, that will give us the wisdom to responsibly deploy our power and resources with discernment.

Life, at the end of the day, is a continuous journey of awakening to infinite possibility. Through our inward journey, we will find that our true nature and purpose for being is to create and add value to life. What we are able to imagine beyond the limits of our current awareness will inform our desires and open possibilities that guide the actions we take. In the final analysis, we are never passive observers of the evolutionary process; every decision we make has always been borne from the larger whole.

THE AWAKENING OF BUSINESS INSTITUTIONS

The foundation of economics as we know it today was scripted by Adam Smith, author of the classic *The Wealth of Nations* published in 1776. Along with other thinkers in the eighteenth century, Smith established the concept of free trade and the imperative of growth in trading commodities. He explicated the theory of "the invisible hand," the forces that move a free market up or down within nations' private sectors and their government's commerce.

The story of capitalism since then covers a myriad of inventions and developments in finance and corporate law as well as massive industrialization. With the expansion of production capabilities and the heightening of efficiency, a new way of life was created as people moved from farms to factories and from rural to urban areas. The freedom to produce goods and services as the entrepreneurs saw fit, along with the goal of maximizing profits and the value of assets, was fundamental to the economics of the era.

Then came Karl Marx, the author of the next most influential book on economics. It was first published in German as *Das Kapital* in 1863 and translated into English as *Capital*. Unlike Adam Smith, Marx stressed collective interest over self-interest, the foundational idea underlying socialist and communist systems. Adam Smith's concept led to free market economies with individuals making their own decisions independently while Marx's generated planned economies with centralized control. From capitalism that focuses on individual freedom and communism that focuses on collectivism, economic and political systems were developed. Both are, in fact, Western-led systems practiced globally today. However, their concepts are not practiced in their pure, original form. Instead, hybrid systems arise when those in power selectively exclude elements that do not fit into their economic models. This results in sustainability challenges.

Adam Smith's and Karl Marx's concepts contributed significantly to the way the world's systems are structured today. The -isms they pioneered, namely capitalism and communism respectively, quickly gained ascendance and diluted the influence that religion wielded over the public sphere. In their own unique ways, these two systems had implications for how capital would be deployed and how economics would be performed in the future. Both planned and free market systems have their merits and is whole when it exists together as one unified system. Globally, either one or a hybrid form of these two systems are adopted in many global nations we are familiar with in our modern era. China is an example of a communist state with a planned economy that gives space for development of a robust capital market.

Singapore is another example of a democratic state with a social focus-led economy and a stable capital market.

After World War II, the world moved toward global integration after being split up along communist and capitalist lines. With intensifying consumerism, the "isms" continued to dominate. Yet these Western-led systems are increasingly being challenged by the advent of a Chinese socialist market economy adopted in China. It offers an alternative system where traditional culture and collectivity are the focus, and the dominant materialist worldview is redefined, as will be explored further in chapter 3. This is a reference point worth understanding since it appears to be working in China.

Regardless of the distinctions between Smithian and Marxist economics, the true force behind these developments is ultimately our own consciousness, both individual and collective. Consciously or unconsciously, we all have made choices about how we live, what we believe in, who we become, and how we act. The problems we experience as individuals or as groups are created by the interaction of different levels of consciousness.

There are numerous ways to analyze economics. Yet overall, in our current era, it seems apparent that economists have generally played a negative role because they have espoused the core idea that growth matters above all else. The point here is not to alienate economists; on the contrary, economists are essential to this conversation. We need concrete ideas on how to change the direction of humanity, and the functioning of the world's economic system must be seriously considered. Without changing the way we think about economics, nothing can be restructured. Economics, as the engine of human desire, drives everything else, including government policy and social change. Changing our economic worldview, conversely, will enable a new economic paradigm to be integrated into all things.

There is no correct speed of progress in the development of human beings and no correct speed for progress in our economic development.

To be faster or slower is a matter of no consequence. Rather, it boils down to the importance of our understanding of the concept of economic development. The system itself, as it currently works in this world, must be reframed. Indeed, there are signs that this restructuring is already underway. Given that business institutions have been primarily responsible for getting us to where we are today, they are also best positioned to get us out of our current dilemmas.

Yet there are promising developments that are signs of business awakening to a well-being economy. Studies have shown that businesses today do not last as long as they used to be. A 2014 study by McKinsey found that in 1958 the average lifespan of companies was sixty-one years. Today this is less than eighteen years. The study also speculates that 65 percent of companies currently listed on Standard and Poor's 500 will have disappeared by 2027.[38]

As a result, business institutions have awakened to the need to carry out some soul-searching about what exactly determines the key to a successful, long-lasting business. We have also seen the spread in recent years of "conscious capitalism," a term coined in 2008 by John Mackey and Raj Sisodia to describe socially responsible business activities that operate in the interests of all stakeholders rather than just to benefit shareholders.

This trend of self-interrogation and redefinition of business beyond a blind quest for profit was strengthened in 2019 by the Business Roundtable's groundbreaking declaration. The Roundtable, composed of major American companies, stated that commercial enterprises must serve interests wider than just those of their shareholders. In August of that year, they released a statement signed by 181 CEOs committing to lead their companies for the benefit of all stakeholders—including employees, suppliers, customers, and communities—in order to promote "an economy that serves all Americans."[39]

The Business Roundtable's statement highlighted that the economy should benefit everyone involved, giving every individual the opportunity to build successful, meaningful, and creative lives. As Darren Walker, President of the Ford Foundation and member of the Roundtable explained, "It is more critical than ever that businesses in the twenty-first century are focused on generating long-term value for all stakeholders and addressing the challenges we face, which will result in shared prosperity and sustainability for both business and society."

Riding on the wave of the Business Roundtable's definition of a successful economy are the new measurements and standards of business performance that have recently sprung up. In the financial investment sector, measurements for criteria such as Environmental, Social, and Governance (ESG) have an impact on investment, and the movement of B Corp certification for established business practices introduced an ethical dimension into the market economy. This has a powerful influence on companies and business. Itpoints to the heightened awareness among business leaders of the insufficiency of systems and organizations that do not share this mission to balance purpose and profit.

For many years, there has been a growing attempt to redefine the parameters of economic measurement.

The United Nations led the way with its call in 2012 to consider well-being and happiness as a new economic paradigm. This led to the milestone Sustainability Mandate in 2015 title "The 2030 Agenda for Sustainable Development,"[40] that set seventeen goals aimed at creating sustainable development in economic activity, society, and the environment. The goals included putting an end to poverty, ending environmental degradation, and ensuring we can have a world in which "all human beings can enjoy prosperous and fulfilling lives and that economic, social, and technological progress occurs in harmony with nature." The final goal was to "strengthen the means of implementation and revitalize the Global Partnership for Sustainable Development." This was crucial. Without the collaboration of all nations and parties, none of the other goals would be achievable. Only with a global, unified partnership could a common consciousness of the need for these goals be developed. This is where our hope lies for a flourishing future.

These measures were all targeted at the central challenge of sustainability that humanity confronts today: How do we bring about positive impacts to create a better tomorrow for all of us? Setting governance measures around money was an attempt to make money "good" by demanding ethical behavior in order to receive funding. On a practical level, these measures further reveal the growing awareness that the natural environment must be fundamental to the practice of business. Without our planet, there is no market; and without a market, no business is possible.

The ESG criteria deserves special mention. It gained prominence when entrepreneurs devised the framework of the *triple bottom line* (TBL) to measure sustainability. The TBL transcended the conventional metrics of profit to encompass environmental and social considerations. It saw the "three Ps" of people, planet, and profits are intertwined.[41] Further down the line, TBL paved the way for the ESG factors that have anchored most sustainable businesses today. In fact, ESG is only growing in strength; it has continued to gain ground, particularly in the final quarter of 2021 after the United Nations Climate Change Conference (COP26).

Today, two-thirds of dealmakers have identified ESG and sustainability considerations as key drivers of market activity because of factors such as increased pressure from the private sector and increased regulatory oversight. Moving forward, we can expect these new measurements to dominate the business mainstream.

Furthermore, another sign of the awakening of business institutions is the proliferation of nonprofit organizations all over the world. In response to social gaps, nonprofit organizations take upon themselves the goal of making an impact, driving change, and developing management skills for sustainability in what has come to be called *impact investment.*

In an ethical economy, nonprofits and philanthropy play an important role. The nonprofit economy has evolved significantly. During the past fifty years it has developed in the direction of greater efficiency. The sustainability of nonprofit organizations has been treated more seriously as an issue that demanded attention. Increasingly, nonprofit organizations are being run like businesses and adopting social enterprise models to be sustainable on their own.

But how did the nonprofit economy come to be what it is today? The word "philanthropy" comes from the Greek "philanthropia,"[42] which simply means "love of humankind." What we know as philanthropy today has its roots in many ancient belief systems. Chinese classical thought extolls the importance of benevolence. The ancient Greeks also considered philanthropy foundational to democracy.

Andrew Carnegie, the founder of US Steel, was a pivotal figure in the emergence of philanthropy in its modern form during the social and political upheavals of the nineteenth century. In 1889 he published *The Gospel of Wealth* to call upon millionaires of the epoch to distribute their wealth for the public good. In 1914, near the start of World War I, he founded the Carnegie Council to promote moral leadership and alternatives to armed conflict. When he retired from business, Carnegie used his wealth to establish numerous colleges and academic associations. He funded a system of 1,679 public libraries across the United States and many nonprofit organizations. After giving away $350 million of his fortune during his lifetime, he left $30 million directed to further the cause of world peace.[43]

Throughout the twentieth century, the establishment of nation states went hand in hand with increased government involvement in social welfare, thus redefining the meaning of private philanthropy. Increasingly, community-based philanthropic organizations supported marginalized groups and minority causes in society. This philanthropic tradition continues today.

The story of philanthropy is directly related to the story of "corporate social responsibility," which can be said to have its origins in

Andrew Carnegie's paradigm-shifting work. The term CSR was coined in 1953 by Howard Bowen in his book *Social Responsibilities of the Businessman.* Identifying the tangible impact that corporations have on society, he argued that businesses are obliged to take into consideration the common good of humanity.

In these early decades, CSR had a relatively narrow scope that encompassed human and labor rights, pollution, and waste management in their local business areas at that time. But it eventually grew with the increasing globalization in the 1990s. International frameworks and agreements like the Kyoto Protocol made businesses all around the globe more aware of how their actions influenced the planet and the environment beyond their immediate communities.

The growing importance of CSR since the 1990s prompted Business Roundtable's redefinition of the purpose of corporations in August 2019, which called for corporations "served all Americans." We should go one step further and recognize that it is humanity—our shared universe, planet, and intertwined fates—that corporations must step up to serve. Businesses now are thinking more in the long-term about trying to create social goods for humanity. At the very least, part of their business capital must be used to take account of these things. CSR entails paying attention to the relationships that a business maintains with its different stakeholders. The term "corporate citizenship" was coined to refer to the actions that a company or business takes to involve itself actively in dialogue with its stakeholders.

More and more, businesses and nonprofits are claiming responsibility for tasks and functions that should rightfully be fulfilled by the government. On an institutional level, what we need is a new configuration between the various players in businesses, nonprofits, and government. Businesses and nonprofits should not be taking on all the functions of government. Regular dialogue should be encouraged between these stakeholders so that new forms of collaboration can arise.

This new configuration represents the melting point of private, social, and public capitals. When integrated and managed in an ethical responsible manner, capital will be reallocated to produce impact when the need arises. Such an impact investing model represents a new form of wealth redistribution for a stable well-being economy. Businesses will continue to play an essential role in the new economy as they breed innovation, create jobs, provide important material services and goods, and boost overall economic growth.

Studies have shown that nearly 90 percent of consumers would purchase a product if a company supported an issue they care about.[44] An increased attentiveness to ethics will redirect capital and resources to have impact—this is the sure sign that our business institutions are awakening. A further discussion on impact investment is set out in part two of this book.

The Awakening of Political Institutions

Finally, among political institutions, a similar awakening took place that mirrored business institutions. Governments and political entities were relying more and more on matrices that measure well-being and happiness in addition to those that measure economic growth and efficiency.

This shift, of course, had its roots in the United Nations' redefinitions of economic goals. On April 2, 2012 the UN held a conference on "Happiness and Wellbeing: Defining a New Economic Paradigm." It was hosted by Bhutan, who championed the idea of replacing "Gross National Product" with "Gross National Happiness" to measure a country's national progress. More than 800 individuals representing national and international organizations in politics and government and business, and leading scholars, economists, and religious and spiritual leaders, participated in the proceedings. The participants believed this proposal of a shift toward a new paradigm of well-being and happiness as a measurement of a country's wealth would also contribute to changing the way we perceive ourselves.

On July 12, 2012, the UN declared 20 March as the International Day of Happiness, underscoring the importance of measuring well-being through determinants far more complex than that of income and wealth accumulation. Bhutan was at the very forefront of this change. The country was the first to declare the measurement of Gross National Happiness as a matrix of spiritual growth and consciousness, prioritizing the intangible over the material. New Zealand and the United Arab Emirates have also adopted "well-being" as a metric of its economic performance.

The current relationship between China and the West, in particular China's relationship with the United States, has often been equated to a "clash of civilizations."[45] This might not be unequivocally detrimental. Sometimes clash and harmonization work in tandem. One historical precedent is the world's reorganization after World War II. Many forms of integration occurred in the domains of economics, politics, and other areas and paved the way for the international system that existed for many decades following the Second World War, and much of it still exists today with all its advantages and pitfalls.

However, China today is disrupting this international system. While this could be interpreted as a clash, it is a reminder of the constancy of change—and that creation and new life originate from change and disruption. Historically, differences in beliefs are the roots of clashes. Greed, like selfish ambition, was fundamentally viewed as a problem of belief. If one believed that every game has a winner and loser, one would strive to be the winner at the expense of someone else. Such a belief system naturally includes greed in its structure. Conversely, if one's worldview is premised on the quantum paradigm notion that the outcome cannot be controlled and is unknown, and there is never a clear-cut winner and loser, a different set of responses come into being.

Most people with this worldview would experience the world today as chaotic and turbulent. They would perceive that tensions and differences are growing, and the system seems to be stuck. However, history teaches us that humanity has always found a way out; conflicts would often release tensions that brought together. Without the destructive conflicts that resulted in World War II, we would not have had the baby boomer generation and the subsequent economic prosperity that lasted for decades.

On the flip side, globalization has made the differences that have defined us more visible. The consequence of globalization was an increase in accessibility to information and an interconnectedness that pushed us to confront our differences. Globalization itself created tension, but when seen as a transition, it became evolutionary energy that evoked excitement for a new future in which today's challenges would be resolved.

New Consciousness of Life, Ethics, and Our Responsibilities

At the root of our problems today—personal, societal or global— lies a crisis of consciousness. Even as we seek well-being, any quest is doomed to failure without self-awareness and consciousness of our impact on systems. As we awaken, we will shift our consciousness and see the challenges as opportunities for a new future. By shifting our perspective, we will choose differently to achieve different results and attain the well-being and happiness we have sought. Only by shifting to the next level of consciousness will we be able to see that we are one and interconnected with everything around us and must make ethical choices about how we act.

There are three main difficulties we grapple with today: our sustainability in terms of our planet's resources, the challenges brought about by globalization, and the disruption of the status quo by technological advancements. It is important for us to remember that challenges are in reality opportunities for evolving and directing creative energy into integrated, more complex systems.

Sustainability is our ultimate challenge and is fundamentally a problem of ethics. This results from misalignments in our internal worldviews, cultures, and desires that cause systemic incoherence. When we make decisions contrary to the flow of the evolutionary energy, challenges arise. Such decisions are grounded on separation and self-indulgence rather than our natural gravitation toward unity and collectivity. In this state, we cannot be true to our purpose of life, and we move away from connection and well-being.

Everything starts with our readiness to initiate the journey inward to shift our own consciousness. This journey presents us with opportunities to connect separated parts, build holistic relationships, and create new ways to return to harmony from a state of chaos. With this mindset of our abundance, we can flourish. After all, the health of our mind as well as our body, are the most important measures of our state of well-being. Thus, the greatest point of leverage for us would be a transformation of our consciousness. We must change what we are, to inform how we act; our *being* must inform our *doing*.

We are living in an era of affluence and abundance; humans are producing more than enough to support every person on the planet. But we lack a common worldview built on the change theory of holism. This Polaris of well-being would unify us all, compelling us to have a sense of ethical responsibility to add value to evolutionary energy that seeks alignment with coherence and harmony. Accordingly, with the transformation of our needs and desires, our economic, political, social, and technological structures will adapt and adjust to fit the new goals of evolution, sustainability, and oneness.

Conversely, when our relationships are not healthy, we lose the possibility of good connections to others. Left unchecked, such a state of relational malaise can easily spiral into destructive chaos. To recuperate our well-being, we must rebuild and work on our relationships. As the evolutionary energy is natural and unstoppable, the choice for us is how we will participate in this flow.

The search for meaning, purpose, and self-understanding has always been the central question of human existence. However, our humanly constructed identities have been shaped and conditioned to fit the exigencies of the modern world. Our original elves have taken a back seat and sometimes have even been extinguished, suppressing the original motivation of life. In our relentless attachment to our identities, we forget our true selves.

The sages advised us to "Know thyself," because change cannot happen in vacuum. Ancient wisdom has taught us to approach this discovery systematically, getting closer to the core of the self and observing the noise and narratives that our minds project. Regardless of the specific traditions that have oriented and guided each of us, the essence of self-understanding remains consistent. We seek stillness of our inner world and harmony of our bodies and mind.

Today's global challenges can be healed and resolved from an elevated state of consciousness that prioritizes relationships, manifesting our ethics. How ethical we are reflects how consciously aware we are. Unsurprisingly, an increasing number of wellness centers, retreats, and institutes—many concentrated in the West—have focused on practices of connectedness as the pathway to accessing wisdom and intuition. The practices that are taught are mostly ancient Eastern and indigenous practices, often from yogic and Zen traditions. These centers are less prominent in the East where communal traditions are already naturally embodied within its cultures and expressed in rituals and festivals celebrated by the family and community. These are all signs that the cultures of East and West are approaching unification.

The most useful practical tool for us might be mindfulness practices, sometimes called "practices of connectedness." These encompass different forms in Eastern and Western traditions. All aim to quiet the mind and shift our consciousness to heighten our awareness of our experiences. Meditation, which is a form of mindfulness, has been practiced for thousands of years for the purpose of connecting to "true awareness," a transformative experience that gives a glimpse of reality without the filter of our beliefs and self. Unlike the way meditation is widely marketed today, it is not a technique for greater productivity but a movement toward a state of consciousness; a state of deep stillness, openness, silence, and balance which transcends words alone. In that mentally-cleared and emotionally-calmed state, meditation represents the exploration and dissolution of self, which is achieved through unification and letting go.

Through such practices, we connect to the origin of consciousness itself and slowly awaken to holism. From that collective space of "we" and "us," we grow in personal power. We clean up our traumas and trapped emotions from the past and discover our gifts and purpose in life. This approach has offered people everywhere a pathway to a world in which we can all prosper and flourish with one another and with nature.

It is not only a matter of changing what we do; we must also discover who we are. This is traditionally where a shift in consciousness enters the picture. Without such deep-rooted change, we cannot address the challenges of the new era effectively. Having a consciousness of connectedness will change how we think and act, enabling us to become more empathetic and compassionate. When we see ourselves as an integral part of the natural world, we become more attuned to how our actions affect not only people but all life on Earth. With this mindset, we can understand how we relate to each other and rebuild our relationships with all living beings on our planet.

As I have said, the awakening of humanity is a movement, a source of evolutionary energy, that is evolving us toward coherence so that every system can be in harmony within itself and with each other. Holism and well-being will be the solution to our sustainability challenges.

Reaching the Tipping Point

Many have risen and responded to challenges of sustainability from different sectors, including various institutions, businesses, and technology. They have all attempted to develop a range of solutions to address the problem. Indeed, humanity's social systems have already awakened to the challenges of sustainability. As conflicts intensified and heightened social pressures, the status quo no longer remained acceptable for most of the world. Seeing the collapse of institutions and the failure of many businesses to solve our problems, a bottom-up force of social change was catalyzed and reached the tipping point of creating new possibilities for collaboration.

It is surely a welcome sign that awakening has occurred in so many places. However, these movements appear to remain in insular pockets, separated from one another without traction. They are awakening separately, in different time and different places. Instead of coherence, what has emerged is a state of confused chaos. Humanity must evolve into a higher state of consciousness to turn this confused disorder into a creative chaos, from which solutions to these challenges might then emerge. The different enablers, although coming into being as uncoordinated, isolated initiatives, are amplifying in frequency and intensity, potentially evolving into a great awakening that will permeate the entire global system and move humanity to a tipping point. This turning point may appear chaotic on the surface; however it is calibrating to coherency in a deeper level—as it forms the transition to a new era.

In his book, *The Upshift*, Ervin Laszlo describes this state of crisis as a point of "bifurcation," a forking in the trajectory of the system's evolution that can be the passport to the system's continued evolution.[46] This process of bifurcation is irreversible, but it makes room for choice. For the choice to happen, a critical mass of people is required along with a shift and elevation in consciousness.

The fact that bifurcation has not been predetermined places it as a matter of choice. All states of crisis and chaos, then, could be regarded as humanity's opportunities for growth and evolution as this allows us to make a choice. Every challenge could be an opportunity, and every opportunity can be directed in an evolutionary manner. Herein lies the difference between bifurcations that take place in human systems in contrast to any other system: Human beings have an evolved consciousness with the potential to continue evolving. Each time we evolve in the direction of our challenges and rise to meet them, a new state of consciousness will be required. This time, humanity's bifurcation will be centered around ethics and sustainability.

At the same time, bifurcation contains the possibility of destruction and further ruin. Given humanity's monumental challenges—such as social inequality and climate change—bifurcation can exacerbate the crises we currently have to confront. We must decide at this key juncture whether we want to participate consciously and create the future we want. We must keep in mind that we have only one planet and that we exist only in relation to the collective natural world. This task of participating in the elevation of our consciousness is a responsibility that we must all share.

To help facilitate this bifurcation and find the tipping point for evolutionary change to project, we need quantum leaders. Laszlo has written that given sufficient instability in our systems, "even a small group of dedicated people can influence, even critically influence, the way the system evolves."[47] Fundamental change seldom comes from the top; it usually originates at the bottom. Even a small group of people responding to the calling and inner awakening activated by the cosmos to become quantum leaders can provide our world with the necessary potent kick for our misaligned systems to be calibrated into a new harmony. Once this kick is set in place by a dedicated group of quantum leaders, the paradigm is changed, and the whole path of human evolution will shift. Only then will everyone awaken to the reality of the new era.

The observable signs show that systemic shifts have begun, and the world is awakening to a new worldview built on the following principles:

∞ We live in a systemic interconnected world.

∞ We are separate and whole at the same time.

∞ The chaos we are experiencing is part of the evolutionary process.

∞ The purpose of our lives is to add value to this evolutionary process.

∞ We are aligning toward an overall state of coherence and harmony.

∞ At this threshold of bifurcation, we have the power to choose the path forward and create a future we want.

The quantum paradigm is what will give us hope that humanity can survive the endless challenges of sustainability and separation that plague us today. This development has propelled the emergence of a new era of well-being and happiness, and the new science of consciousness has begun to reshape the way people see the world.

The similarities between the seemingly opposing fields of wisdom and science, tradition and modernity, and East and West are no coincidence. Although ancient Eastern wisdom is not limited to Chinese culture, China has made the biggest waves in the world today on economic, social, political, and technological fronts. Its economic development and unconventional social structures and governance system have remained largely misunderstood, inviting both curiosity and caution. In our search for a common worldview and culture, it is imperative that we understand China's history and culture for us to grasp the developments that have brought it to its current state of social and economic pre-eminence.

CHAPTER 2

The Particular Example of China's Growth

Why is there a need to understand China? What is the imperative—and case—for allocating a significant portion of this book to China? A core reason is that the example of Chinese history is both unique and generalizable. It is unique in that a series of non-contingent and distinctive factors that paved the way for its success. And it can be generalized in the sense that much in the story of China's exponential growth trajectory can be learned by other states, peoples, and individuals.

What the Rise of China Tells Us About the Relationship Between Well-Being and Governance

Over the past sixty to seventy years, the two opposing systems of the democratic West and communist China developed in tandem within the market economy, differing only in terms of the degree of planning and regulation of their respective economies. China's economy moved from being entirely planned to one driven by the market and eventually gave rise to a flourishing private sector beginning in the 1990s. Today, 80 percent of jobs are created by the private sector in what had been called a "socialist market economy."[48] China has emerged as an efficient performer, and its policies have always accommodated the social demands and needs of the times. For instance, Beijing made improving the environment a priority in the Fourteenth Five-Year

Plan, including policies that included cutting carbon emissions and promoting clean energy.

In parallel with this shift to an economic model of well-being and happiness, we cannot ignore the far-reaching spread of human rights discourses across the globe as an important sign of the awakening of political institutions. Since the exponential growth of the global population after World War II, the West has been at the forefront of the capitalist system and has promulgated its core values of freedom, human rights, and liberal democracy. As we know, the notion of democracy has had a long history in Western political thought, a genealogy that includes philosophers Thomas Hobbes, John Locke, and Jean-Jacques Rousseau.

In 1948, the Universal Declaration of Human Rights was adopted by the United Nations, inspiring and paving the way for the adoption of more than seventy human rights treaties applied globally and regionally. Subsequent treaties, for example, covered the rights of refugees, civil and political rights, and women's rights.

A world accustomed to these notions of human rights now finds it is being challenged and destabilized by the advent of China's thriving economy. Because most of the world has perceived such rights to be nonexistent in China, many cannot reconcile explanations for why China, who is operating on the other end of the socially accepted spectrum, has enjoyed such tremendous growth. After more than four decades of isolation, China's re-entry into the global system felt like nothing short of a tsunami that would displace and rearrange everything we once knew. Long thought to be autocratic and dictatorial, China's political institutions are nonetheless demonstrating a miraculous level of economic performance that many thought was not possible.

Many people ask if the democratic empire helmed by the United States is now ending, soon to be superseded by the Chinese empire. This mode of thinking is quite traditional; it asks about the decline and fall of empires, the passing of the historical baton from one empire to another. Yet, in place of the either-or separatist mindset, let us embrace the possibility of integration as one. After all, this is consistent with the quantum paradigm in which everything in the world is interconnected in one unified system.

We are past the point of defining the world only in terms of separate states or systems. Our global reality follows the nature of evolution, as a constant reconstruction into more complex, sophisticated, and integrated systems.

China's presence as a formidable force cannot be overlooked or ignored. The level of unity of its one and a half billion population is clearly observable by the extent to which the country has succeeded in eradicating its poverty and the impressively high levels of approval among the population for their government. A survey by the Harvard Kennedy School, Ash Center about Democratic governance and innovation in July 2020 found that compared to public opinion patterns in the U.S., in China there was very high satisfaction with the central government. In 2016, the last year the survey was conducted, more than 90 percent of respondents were either "relatively satisfied" or "highly satisfied" with Beijing.[49]

According to the Edelman Global Trust Barometer of 2020,[50] the Chinese government continued to enjoy the trust of 90 percent of its citizens—the highest level in the world. In contrast, the governments of Germany, the United States, and the United Kingdom received only 45 percent, 39 percent, and 36 percent, respectively, in the barometer of citizens' trust in their government. This trend was corroborated by Gallup's report in February 2021: Polling of United States citizen satisfaction with the broad aspects of the way the way the country functioned revealed only 39-percent of respondents were satisfied compared to 53 percent the year before.[51]

According to recent studies, the Chinese government has evidently built a strong level of trust with its people that is now a habitual part of its culture. It can be surmised that people feel they can trust the government to care about their best interests, as reflected in how government policies and actions are developed from an established consultative system from the bottom up coupled by a responsive policy from the top down. What has China's system done right, that the rest of the world can (and must) learn from?

Understandably, China's top-down model of power induces discomfort in the hearts of many, especially in populations that are accustomed to prioritizing the rights and entitlements of individuals in liberal democratic systems. In capitalist systems, awakening originated in the marketplace rather than the government. The opposite occurred in the Chinese context where awakening emanated in a top-down direction led by the government.

Evolutionary energy naturally brings these two seemingly opposing systems to a meeting point. From the democratic system comes a bottom-up freedom movement bearing a common theme of equal rights for all; and from the communist system of a top-down planned economy springs central coordination as its thrust. Both systems move to the same oneness and harmony. China's top-down system does not contradict the Western democratic model of bottom-up power, and neither has all the answers. Instead, oneness is only possible through the integration of both systems into one common global governing system so that they function as complementary rather than opposing systems.

China's government can only garner such high ratings because its people feel they are heard. It systematically collects feedback from the masses and develops its policies in response to that. The five-year plans so characteristic of China's recent economic history are now more tailored toward setting a direction for economic development rather than dictating a detailed plan for how to get there. This is a transition from a planned economy to a socialist market economy, and can come about only after rounds of consultations with experts and practitioners. Starting from the eleventh Five Year Plan, these plans (and *jihua* 計劃 in Chinese) have been known as "guidelines" (and *guihua* 規劃 in Chinese).

In contrast to the West, which sees prosperity as a means to achieve stability, China reversed that dynamic and viewed stability as crucial to achieving prosperity. China taught us that leadership must be strong and reliable for anything to prosper; stability and growth are necessary conditions for prosperity. China's model of leadership has shown us that strong leadership must be ethical leadership, as ethics are an expression of consciousness. For the Chinese government, nothing was negotiable about life. In its current affluence, it cares about life more than any other country on the planet, as crystallized in the phrase "people-oriented" (*yiminweiben* 以民為本 in Chinese).

Despite the influence of the Western-led *isms* and their dilution of the religious sector, the presence of traditional culture continued to endure in China. It was deeply rooted not only in the way the country was managed, but also in the people's psyches and values. The concept of *jia* (家) or family manifests in the extent to which family has been prioritized: It is common in China for the whole family to work together to raise a child. When this occurs, two grandparents on the paternal and maternal sides all pitch in, so there were effectively six people collaborating to nurture and care for a child. Such a phenomenon, conversely, is practically unheard of in the Western world. China's rise attested to the existence of an alternative worldview that was not grounded in Western-led *isms* but instead revolved around a cosmology that placed ultimate value on life and family.

In essence, China's system was and is a collectivist one built upon a foundation of social stability and prioritizing social needs. It was within a stable environment that capitalism could thrive, and the government was responsible for building, nurturing, and sustaining a stable environment accessible to everyone. As the global system awakened, it became increasingly clear to many that China's evolutionary direction was one that showed results and was worth understanding on its own terms because China's alternative worldview would certainly give rise to a different set of human desires that would also shape the functioning of economics in the new era.

We needed to collectively build a political system that is capable of governing in a sustainable way. The dominant Western-led systems, founded on a material worldview, have served us positively. However, a new system is needed to serve us as we transition into the age of well-being. The Chinese system has not been without its difficulties and faults, but it has evolved steadily over millennia, bound by one culture of ethics and collective good. In understanding China, we can integrate the best of both systems into one that will serve the new era of well-being, bringing happiness and prosperity to mankind.

The Chinese Cultural Paradigm

As we look back at ancient China's millennia of thought and culture, we might find its remarkably high degree of congruence with the quantum paradigm both surprising and intriguing in equal measure. Beyond the concepts of time and space, there is a shared core of the tenets of a quantum paradigm worldview and ancient Chinese wisdom: In the holographic web that is the universe, an evolutionary force emerges that drives all things toward coherence.

According to ancient Chinese wisdom, the universe arises from a field of "ultimate nothingness" called the *Wuji* (無極), in which the energy of the universe, the *Dao* (道), creates all things, known as *Taiji* (太極). All forms of matter, or *taiji*, have a basic binary code, a dynamic *Yin-yang* (陰陽) counterpoint, like a sine wave constantly oscillating back and forth. It is within these cycles that humans evolve. All humans need to do to live in accordance with the Dao is to listen to the impetus of the universe.[52] This fundamental principle echoes perfectly the new understanding of the world within the quantum paradigm.

In the I Ching (易經), it is written that everything originated in nothing; the word *wuji* means "without a center, boundless, and endless." Daoists use *wuji* to refer to the concept of the ultimate nature of the Dao, supporting their belief that the universe was originally an unbroken whole. *"Wuji generates taiji,"* a Daoist may add, meaning that chaos defines the living process of everything in the universe as it moves from nothing to something. Everything in the universe is engaged in a constant movement of yin-yang. Although this appears to be a pair of differentiating forces, yin-yang refers to a relationship or dance between the two inseparable and interdependent elements. Yin-yang generates templates for different opposing concepts or objects in binary, such as gender (man and woman), direction (up and down), space (heaven and earth), time (the four seasons), orientation (north, south, east, west).

The heritage of Confucian, Buddhist, and Daoist cultural norms and practices constitutes the most fundamental bases for Chinese culture. Among them, the Daoist doctrine, as a school of ancient Eastern philosophy, has stood the test of time and embedded unforgettable wisdom. In the Daoist cosmology, questions of where everything comes from and why it is there and the relationship between humanity and nature form the primary concerns of many Daoist thinkers, including Laozi and Zhuangzi.[53] Daoists traditionally believe that all natural things in the universe are born from the Dao, creating the basis for their existence and development. In essence, the Dao is the origin of all natural things. In *"Daodejing, Chapter 42,"* Laozi put forth his belief that the Dao generated all things and they are the supreme force. *"Zhuangzi - Qiwulun"* (庄子·齊物論)[54] clearly states that all things in heaven and earth—including the "I"—are subsumed in the Dao. Unlike quantum science that was conceived relatively recently, only a century ago, Daoist practices founded on a holistic cosmology have been the bedrock of Chinese culture and wisdom for more than 2,500 years.[55] It is from this immense cultural inheritance that the concepts of *"Dao regulates nature"* (道法自然)[56] and *"the unity of cosmos and humanity"* (天人合一) were derived.

The traditions of following the Chinese wisdom of life has changed over thousands of years as they passed between generations and gradually evolved to respond to the ever-changing needs of various time periods. In our contemporary era, these ancient Chinese concepts can be compared to the new emergent science of consciousness. Structured and logical, these systems that have provided the foundation of Chinese culture for the past fifty years or so have proliferated throughout the rest of the world, at the same time partaking of global prosperity and disrupting the dominance of an existing Western-led global order.

It is conventional for Western media and news outlets today to refer to China as leader of "The New World Order."[57] They emphasize China's rapid economic growth, advancements in scientific and technological development, and the speed of infrastructure construction and urbanization since the reform and opening-up in 1978 launched under the leadership of Deng Xiaoping. On the other hand, over the last decade—especially during the Trump administration—China has been regarded as a threat to the global order. The Covid-19 pandemic situation has further aggravated international aggression and skepticism about China. It has been increasingly seen as a force that the rest of the world must work together to contain. In this worldview, China is perceived as an opposing force that seeks to divide the world along national and geopolitical lines rather than a country that wants to contribute to the inclusive, collaborative efforts that define the new quantum paradigm of oneness.

Although the Western system has long been dominant, the Chinese system presents an alternative model that is worthy and warrants our understanding. Over the past few decades, the ascent of China's powerful economy has been impossible to overlook as it became an indispensable player in globalization, and its influence—along with the disruptions it brings—is destined to go hand in hand with this evolutionary process.

China, an ancient and mysterious country, witnessed nearly miraculous economic growth as it gradually developed into the world's second largest economy.[58] It is incumbent upon us to appreciate the full depth of China's historical development and civilizational roots.

While understanding Chinese society, two questions are often invoked: (1) How has Chinese civilization survived so long in human history compared to other ancient civilizations? (2) After its glory receded into generations of stagnation, why has Chinese society suddenly gained in vigor and might in recent decades?

In the past one hundred years, China experienced the decay and decline of the feudal system with the fall of the Qing Dynasty and lagged behind the rapid development of Western modernity. The monarchy that had ruled China for thousands of years descended into total crisis, and all its attempts to emulate capitalism ended in failure. In the face of unprecedented threatening changes and social instability, tension brewed on Chinese soil until the eruption of the October Revolution when Marxism-Leninism was introduced and Mao Zedong announced the establishment of the Central People's Government of the People's Republic of China in 1949.

The theoretical framework that transformed modern Chinese society began in the mid-1960s with the "Four Modernizations" proposed by Zhou Enlai.[59] However, in the process of attempting to define a new identity for Chinese society and its economy, China also experienced a Cultural Revolution initiated by its leaders and exploited by counter-revolutionary groups to prevent the restoration of capitalism. The aftermath of this was a decade of civil unrest.

After the end of the Cultural Revolution, Deng Xiaoping proposed a comprehensive economic overhaul and initiated the reforms of 1978. Deng's vision facilitated the rise of China's economy in the mid-20th century as he instituted policies that modernized agriculture, industry, national defense, science, and technology.

By the mid-1980s, Deng elaborated a "three-step development strategy" quantifying the goals of political and economic development. The next leader, Jiang Zemin, rode on this wave to develop the concept of modernization and prosperity with "Chinese characteristics." In 2004, the fourth generation of leaders (Hu Jintao and Wen Jiabao) introduced the concepts of the "Scientific Outlook on Development" and the "Harmonious Socialist Society," thus providing the government with a more comprehensive and integrated view of China's path to modernization.

On February 25, 2021, the centennial of the founding of the Communist Party of China, the current leader Xi Jinping gave a speech in Beijing to announce that China had officially eradicated poverty. China had solved the problem of poverty for nearly 100 million people. Soon after this, the Chinese government focused its efforts on establishing a new pattern of seeking happiness, not only for the sake of the Chinese people and the rejuvenation of the Chinese nation but for the evolution of mankind and the benefit of the world.

Through all these political shifts, it can be easy to overlook what has remained constant and immutable about China despite the sweeping changes China has undergone in the last hundred years. What has remained constant is the country's thousand years of their culture built on the Dao. Although the practices of Eastern culture appear to be somewhat at odds with Western ideas derived from the industrial revolution and the era of modernization, the latest cutting-edge developments in quantum science seem to be finally giving Eastern traditions their proper recognition and respect.

As the American historian of China Philip Alden Kuhn expressed it, "China's unique destiny is that its civilization has persisted long after other ancient civilizations have died out; this persistence entails not rigidity, but a series of regenerations."[60]

China is now undergoing a comprehensive revival of its cultural traditions. The concept of harmony, which has been passed down for thousands of years as a traditional wisdom, is seen in the 21st century as a way to serve a global community and forge a shared future for humanity.

Evolutionary Force in the Course of Chinese History

For thousands of years, Daoist, Buddhist and Confucian practices have remained foundations of Chinese culture—evolving, expanding, and growing over time. This is closely related to a well-functioning and effective system of state and a national government that since ancient times gradually formed in China out of numerous branches of knowledge. The study of heaven and humanity led to the clarification of ways of self-cultivation; the implementation of ancient strategies of governing the country led to the expectation that the world is equally shared by all who inhabit it; the ruling of the wise leaders evolved to people-oriented governing; the unity of righteousness and profit led to peace.

The study of history broadens our perspective, stretching the time line of human development beyond our customary frames. Thus, we can observe and analyze the features of the developmental process from a global perspective. Our understanding becomes more profound and meaningful when the organizing principles of a theme, such as governance, constitutes an evolutionary journey over a long period of time. In China, the governance system has withstood vastly different dynasties and been refined into one that is tried and tested, flexible and relevant, even today.

Just as individuals often ask themselves existential questions, every nation is also constantly searching for its roots. China, too, has undergone a difficult and protracted process of civilizational development. To adopt a view of the historical cycle of China's rise and fall from the quantum paradigm would allow us to glimpse a spiraling evolutionary force fueling every tangible historical event.

From Primitive Chaos to the Heyday of Ideas: Laying the Foundation for a Worldview

In ancient times, society was underdeveloped. People's knowledge of nature was extremely limited, and there was constant strife among the various tribes. The Xia (2070–1600 BCE), Shang (1600–1046 BCE), and Zhou (1046–256 BCE) dynasties were eventually formed amidst bloody conflicts. During this period, people believed in the connection between humanity and god in the spiritual world. Everyone from the rulers to the masses prayed for the blessings of heaven.

In their reverence and worship of nature, people followed their faith based on the ways of heaven and the natural laws on Earth. They created the I Ching, one of the oldest classical texts in China. This set of divination books, with sixty-four hexagrams that foretold future fortunes and misfortunes, carried traces of ancient Chinese cosmology in which agricultural activities were conducted in accordance with the laws of nature. It was also at this time that concepts such as *yin-yang*, *"the favorable timing of geographical and human conditions"* (天時地利人和), and *"the unity of heaven and humanity"* (天人合一) were developed.

The Zhou dynasty was subsequently divided into two parts, the Western Zhou and the Eastern Zhou. After more than 270 years of the Western Zhou's reign, various feudal conflicts erupted and led to widespread societal turmoil. By the time Emperor Ping of Zhou founded Eastern Zhou, China had left behind a long phase of both chaos and enlightenment and entered the Spring and Autumn Period (770–476 BCE) and the Warring States Period (475–221 BCE). Amid great precarity and transition, the vassal states successively carried out changes and reforms to establish a new social order that stimulated economic development and technological progress. Thus, they laid the foundation for a thriving civilization, supporting a vibrant cultural atmosphere in which many thinkers established competing ideological claims.

The most famous of these is the Daoist classic *Daodejing*, an important and influential text that is thought to have been written between the 6th and 4th centuries BCE by Laozi. In this sacred work, he not only expounds on the idea of a holistic view of the universe and the concept of the Dao but also derives the management principle of *"governance by doing nothing that goes against nature"* (無為而治) and the strategy of *"overcoming the strong with the weak"* (以弱胜强). This is in line with the quantum worldview of listening, attuning oneself to the harmony of the world, and finally answering the impetus of the universe. In a similar vein, the "weak" does not pertain to literal weakness, but rather the ability to flow like water and become invisible in service of the goal, through a moment-to-moment, natural calibration toward the coherence of the whole system.

During the same period, his seminal work, The Analects of Confucius, also emerged. A compilation of the wise words of his students, the ancient book is composed of a unique system sayings and ideas of governance that emphasizes the Chinese principles of propriety, self-restraint, and benevolence in ruling.

The Analects' distinctive approach to ethics and politics has ensured its longevity. Even today, Confucius is studied and mined for his wisdom. In addition, thinkers such as Mencius and Xunzi (on Confucian teachings), Zhuangzi (on the Dao), Han Feizi (on legal systems), and Mozi (represented by Mohism) are among those who laid the essential ideological foundations for the development of Chinese culture over thousands of years.

From the birth of the I Ching to the formation of the doctrines of the "hundred schools of thought," this period saw China move from a state of unrestrained chaos to an era of culture and philosophy in which people attempted to grasp and represent, as insightfully as they could, the relationships between the individual, nature, society, and one's own self. Thus, a unique worldview with "Chinese characteristics" emerged.

QIN AND HAN UNIFICATION LAID THE FOUNDATION FOR CENTRALIZED POWER

At the end of the Warring States period, Qin, the most powerful of the seven vassal states, fought a war to destroy the six other vassal states and complete the unification of China with the establishment of the Qin Dynasty (221–206 BCE)—the first unified, multi-ethnic, centralized authoritarian feudal state in Chinese history. In the extreme centralization of this feudal regime, Emperor Qin Shi Huang unified writing, currency, weights and measures, and languages. His core ideology of governance was expressed in multiple dimensions of political, economic, ideological, and cultural centralization. However, Qin Shi Huang and his successors' unprecedented brutal oppression and exploitation of peasants led to widespread revolts and the eventual overthrow of the Qin Dynasty after only 15 years of their rule.

Later, Liu Bang, the founder and first emperor of the Han Dynasty (202 BCE–220 CE), established the Western Han Dynasty, combining lessons learned from the fall of the Qin Dynasty and adopting the use of civil and military power. From this foundation the rule of Wen and Jing emerged. The reigns of Emperor Wen of Han and his son Emperor Jing of Han was a period known for the benevolence, thrift, and pacifism of the two emperors. This time of general stability was marked by reductions in taxes and the lessening of other burdens on the people. This period is often viewed as one of the golden ages in Chinese history and paved the way for a long and stable reign. It also enabled Emperor Wu to maintain a powerful army and employ an aggressive foreign policy that greatly expanded the empire and ultimately pushed the Han dynasty to its zenith. With the further strengthening of the state, Emperor Wu's policies established the orthodox dominance of Confucian teachings and practices.

Ideologically and culturally, The Three Cardinal Guides and The Five Constant Virtues were implemented. From then on, valuing the practices of the laws of Confucian morality and ethics became more important than an individual's judgment about what is right or wrong. Confucianism, in a nutshell, is a value system that emphasized the dutiful fulfilment of one's roles in a network of relationships. Between father and son there must be filial piety (孝); between lord and official, loyalty (忠); between friends, ethics (義). At the heart of all virtues is benevolence (仁), from which ethics (義), propriety (禮), wisdom (智) and trust (信) become visible. Relationships built on a Confucian system of ethics continue to dominate Chinese culture today, where every relationship is always in service of a system bigger than itself. In other words, if there is no country, there is no family; where there is no family, no self can exist.

The stability of the Western Han Dynasty did not last forever. After its collapse, social conflicts once again intensified to an unparalleled degree. Wang Mang established the Xin Dynasty in place of the Han Dynasty and implemented a series of reforms that offended the vested interests of the most powerful bureaucrats and eventually led to uprisings. In the wake of all this chaos, Liu Xiu destroyed the Xin Dynasty and established the Eastern Han Dynasty under the name Emperor Guangwu. During his reign, he vigorously promoted economic development, strengthened centralized power, and eased ethnic conflicts with peaceful measures, creating a situation in which the government flourished and people lived in harmony with one another.

The two Han dynasties spanned more than four centuries, and many of their achievements have far-reaching historical implications to this day. The dominant Han nationality, the characters of the Chinese language, and Han culture can all be traced back to the Han Dynasty. During the period of great unification in the Qin and Han dynasties, production was rapidly accelerated, and the economy flourished. National defense was consolidated, science and culture reached new heights, and outstanding feats were achieved in the fields of medicine, astronomy, and geology. In particular, the invention and refinement of the art of papermaking forever changed the course of world history.

During this period, from the Mediterranean and West Asia to the east coast of the Pacific Ocean, the world was majestically dominated by four empires.[61] Among them, the Han Dynasty and Rome were particularly important. With Zhang Qian's mission of opening the Silk Road to the West during the Western Han Dynasty, China's glorious culture began spreading to the rest of the world. In turn, the outstanding contemporary civilizational and cultural achievements from other parts of the globe were absorbed and integrated into traditional Chinese culture. With these symbiotic movements of trade and exchange, the expansion of Chinese culture beyond national borders commenced.

THE ECONOMIC PROSPERITY OF THE SUI AND TANG DYNASTIES

After the fall of the Eastern Han Dynasty, political uncertainty and class tensions coincided with the Yellow Turban Rebellion, a civil uprising that precipitated the Great Schism of the early feudal period among the Three Kingdoms and Jin Dynasties (220–420). This era saw the decline of political, cultural, and technological development from extended periods of chaos and instability. It was not until the conclusion of the war and return of reunification that China was able to regain its former prosperity in the Wei, Sui, and Tang dynasties.

Yang Jian, the founding emperor of the Sui Dynasty (581–618), unified China amidst all the pandemonium and restored its prosperity. Unfortunately, his successor Yang Guang was a tyrant with no regard for people's livelihoods. A peasant uprising initiated by Chen Sheng and Wu Guang toppled the Sui Dynasty after a short-lived thirty-eight years of rule. As in the Qin Dynasty and numerous other instances in history, the failures of the Sui Dynasty proved that ruling with hostility and brutality and focusing purely on amassing power for self-gain were profoundly unsustainable.

The Tang Dynasty (618–907) inherited and extended the great unification of China, ushering in the heyday of feudal economic development based on the foundations built by the Sui Dynasty. The Tang Dynasty was politically enlightened, ideologically emancipated, rich in talents, and vast. It consolidated national defense, brought harmony among ethnic groups, and established effective forms of wealth accumulation.

In Chang'an (present-day Xi'an), then capital of the country, the prosperity was astonishing. The Tang rulers maintained extraordinary peace and stability, barely impacting the daily life of the people even as they conquered neighboring countries. Their foreign policy relied more on soft power than on violence and war. Reviving the abandoned Silk Road to its former importance in global networks of trade and commerce, China in the time of the Tang Dynasty attracted many diplomatic missions from Europe and Africa, who arrived to trade and to pay tribute to China. To this day, diasporic Chinese communities are still known as "Tang people" (唐人), and the Chinatowns where they live abroad are literally called "the street of Tang people" in Chinese (唐人街).

During the Sui Dynasty, the imperial examination system was developed under the Confucian doctrine "He who excels in study can follow an official career" (學而優則仕). Subsequently, this system was institutionalized during the reign of Wu Zetian—the only female emperor of China—in the Tang Dynasty, and thereafter continued for 1,300 years. As a standardized process by which talent is filtered and selected, this system has also contributed to the modern Chinese educational landscape structured around the college entrance examination and the Communist Party's selection and appointment of cadres.

THE ROAD OF NATIONAL INTEGRATION IN THE SONG, YUAN, MING, AND QING DYNASTIES

In the late Tang Dynasty, decadent political rule led to peasant uprisings and a period of great division in China. But when the emperors of the Song Dynasty, (960–1279) reunified most of the land, this period became a prosperous era for the commodity economy, culture, education, and scientific innovation. Woodblock printing techniques, one of the four major inventions for which China is known, originated in the Song Dynasty. In addition, the invention of the compass, shipbuilding techniques, and canal transportation facilitated advancements in maritime culture. In addition, the widespread use of gunpowder gave birth to the world's first primitive cannon tubes and cannon projectiles in the Song Dynasty.

In the year 1000 CE, it was estimated that China's GDP was $26.55 billion in US currency, accounting for 22.7 percent of the world's economy, and the per capita GDP was US$450, exceeding the US$400 of Western Europe at that time.[62]

Looking back at the changes in governance throughout the Song Dynasty, many of its lessons and insights continue to be relevant today. These include the courage to innovate in response to the changing needs of the times. The dynasty established the strong administrative foundations necessary for constructing a stable economy, the promotion of institutional reforms, the optimization of resource deployment, the strengthening of rule of law, and the full mobilization of the masses to promote social progress with the "theory of enriching the people."

The dynasties of Song (960–1279), Yuan (1271–1368), Ming (1368–1644) and Qing (1644–1911) collectively made great leaps and strides under the helm of a unified multi-ethnic state. The Mongolians and Manchurians entered the Central Plains and indirectly promoted the integration of cultural systems between the Han and the ethnic minorities. Since the Ming and Qing Dynasties, rulers have continued to strengthen centralized control while promoting the goal of "grand unification" in the governance of ethnic groups and frontiers. This new wave of prosperity allowed China to surpass all other countries in Asia or Europe in terms of economic output in the 19th century.

In the era of nation-states, cultural identity became the cornerstone of national identity. China's governance in this period further deepened the concept of great unity that characterized Chinese civilization and defined the basic territory of the present-day People's Republic of China.

In retrospect, Chinese feudal society spiraled forward in cycles of history, shuttling from stability and chaos back to stability. The lessons and insights we can derive from these vacillations are of great significance to humanity's evolutionary process in our contemporary era. Observing the patterns associated with the emergence of prosperity in China's history, we might conclude that it always occurred under the following conditions:

1. Social divisions were addressed, and national unity was achieved.

2. The ruling class focused on adjusting its policies to meet the specific needs of social development within a certain period of time.

3. The system of governance was people-oriented and meritocratic.

4. A stable social environment existed alongside a foreign policy of harmony and communion.

Conversely, the fall of dynasties is usually precipitated by deviations from the central goal of serving the collective good and is replaced instead by power, greed, and self-interest. This led to:

1. decadence, mediocrity, and tyranny of the rulers

2. weakening of centralized power, which facilitated the expansion of local factionalism

3. internal contradictions fragmenting the ruling class

The stories of the rise and fall of every dynasty are those of power being misaligned to values, creating gaps and divisions where the collective social good is not served. From the perspective of the quantum paradigm, the fragmentation and differentiation of these dynasties meant that their rulers had strayed from their people-centered roots and ultimately devolved into chaos and self-destruction. After all, when we forget history, we see history repeat itself in cycles of evolution along a continuum. Extreme wealth accumulation stirs ego and internal misalignment and unmet needs foment uprisings for the justification of the collective. Each cycle brings forth new insights; in the 21st century, the new generation of Chinese leaders are learning from the lessons of the past and bringing the true essence of wisdom from Chinese culture to their governance of the present.

The Inheritance of Worldview and Modern Development

Despite the numerous junctures of fragmentation and reunification, and the evolution of different ways of governance throughout history, the holistic people-oriented worldview of Chinese culture—including the rule of the wise, the unity of righteousness and profit, and the value of peace and stability—has been wholly inherited and preserved through the interplay of decadence and innovation, conservatism and openness, and combining the old and the new.

When we look at the more than seventy years of contemporary China's political history, we find these concepts from start to end and see how they have been innovatively adapted to suit the new era:

1. The salient feature of Chinese governance is a top-down system of governance with democratic centralism as its fundamental principle, and the flexibility of grassroots governance is sought in a constant, dynamic process of adjustment.

2. The adoption of the governing philosophy of being people-oriented and people-centered is in line with the traditional culture of people-based thinking.

3. The five-year plan helmed by scientific advancement provides the ground for forward-looking and flexible goals and directions for national economic and social development.

4. The general keynote of governance is "seeking progress while maintaining stability," which ensures long-term development and prosperity amid stability.

After seventy years of development, the Communist Party of China has become the world's largest party, with more than ninety-five million members. This is undoubtedly one of the most noteworthy political phenomena of the twenty-first century. Mere coincidence or luck cannot adequately account for it. Western academic theoretical frameworks might flounder when explaining the achievements of Chinese society in the last half-century; it is necessary for us to seek answers to explain these "Chinese characteristics" from the perspective of a new paradigm—a quantum paradigm built on holistic thinking.

Democratic Centralism, the Fundamental Principle of Contemporary China

The head of China's new generation of leaders, Xi Jinping, has pointed out that "democratic centralism is the fundamental organizational principle and leadership system of our party." Democratic centralism was pioneered by Lenin in 1906. In Lenin's view, a proletarian party must have strong unity and collective power to achieve revolutionary victory in other countries.

After the practice of various political systems such as feudal imperialism, constitutional monarchy, the parliamentary and presidential systems, the wheel of Chinese history finally landed on the Chinese Communist Party, which adhered to Marxism and democratic centralism to extend the concept of Chinese civilization's great unity.

In an interview with the British journalist James Bertrand in 1937, Mao Zedong systematically stated the following principle for the first time:

> There is no deep ditch between democracy and centralization that cannot be crossed; for China, both are necessary. On the one hand, the government we require must be one that is truly representative of public opinion; it must have the support of the masses of the Chinese people, and the people must be free to support the government and to have every opportunity to influence its policies. This is the meaning of democracy. On the other hand, the centralization of the executive power is necessary; when the policies demanded by the people are delivered to the government elected by the people through the organs of public opinion, they are carried out by the government, and as long as they are carried out in a way that does not contradict the policy once adopted by public opinion, their implementation will be smooth and unhindered. This is the meaning of centralism.[63]

Under democratic centralism, all state organs constitute a unified whole, with a rational division of labor, close collaboration between its ranks, full exercise of democracy and effective centralization. It is also in the long-term enactment of this holistic principle that the enthusiasm, initiative, and creativity of the whole nation have been fully on display.

People-Centered Values in Chinese Culture

The tradition of people-centered thinking can be traced back four-thousand years to the Xia, Shang, and Zhou periods. The core foundation of the Chinese focus on the well-being of its people is reflected in the following three aspects.

First, the core meaning of this stems from the maxim that "The people are bigger than the sky." Such thinking necessitates that a ruler practice moral and benevolent governance at the level of ideological construction to establish goals for the heart on heaven and Earth, goals for the life of living people, and a dedication to follow the teachings of the past sages to establish peace for all generations. This indicated an important pathway for sages in Chinese culture to realize the value of their own lives.

Secondly, it affirms the importance of being master of the people. *Shang Shu* states: "The people are the foundation of the state, and the foundation is solid." Confucius also advocated for "valuing the people" and "loving the people" along with "benefiting the people" and "teaching the people" as the key to capturing the peoples' hearts and minds.

Thirdly, the people make the decisions and affirm their fundamental political status.

In modern society, the birth of the Chinese Communist Party was also based on the people's choice. According to the American scholar John King Fairbank, the Chinese Revolution of 1911 that brought down the Qing dynasty, ending 268 years of imperial Manchu rule over China, failed to establish a new Westernized China because of the lack of popular participation.[64] Although the new government established the Republic of China in Nanchang, it could not unify the country under its control. This proved that social change that does not draw approval of the masses was destined to fail when the people are not willing to mobilize themselves to support the change.

On July 1, 2021, at the celebration of the 100th anniversary of the founding of the Communist Party of China, President Xi Jinping said: "The people are the foundation, the bloodline, and the strength of the

Party." [65] This also reflects the people-centered ideology of development and the necessity of adhering to the wishes and needs of the people.

Since the founding of New China, the system of the National People's Congress—with its important role in the fields of legislation, supervision, and decision-making—has become the best form of democratic practice in which the people are granted the power to contribute to the decision-making process. The materialistic view of history, which the Chinese Communist Party firmly believes in, holds that the people are the creators of both material and spiritual wealth, as well as being the decisive force of social change and the creators of history.

If we use a big picture portrayal to describe changes in New China over the past 100 years, women living in 1921 would likely have been characterized as illiterate, frequently crippled with bound feet, and had few opportunities to speak of. Because of the war and the paucity of medical resources, their life expectancy would probably be forty years at most. [66] In stark contrast, Chinese women in the year 2021 resided in a country with the highest number of university students in the world. They had the freedom to obtain higher education through hard work. They were likely to have a stable job, to have the right to be elected as a member of the National People's Congress, and many could expect to live until the ripe old age of seventy-nine. These two versions of China are worlds apart from each other, representing a microcosm of a century of the country's dramatic evolution.

Kishore Mahbubani, a veteran Singaporean diplomat, noted: "It is also a fact that relative to its peers around the world, the Chinese governing class generates more good governance (in terms of improving the well-being of its citizens) than virtually any other government today." [67] His opinion further illustrates the solid foundation of the Chinese government's "people-centered" approach to governance.

The Guiding Theory of Family, State, and World

The unique spiritual character of Chinese people originates in the prioritization of family and country as one in ancient Chinese society.

Traditional Chinese culture has always advocated for the relationship between family and country as a whole, considering the family as the basic unit of the country, and country as the ethical combination and common interests of millions of families. This Chinese concept of "family" or *jia* (家) is expansive and paves the foundation for constructing the individual and the family, the family and the society, and the society and the state together, in inseparable interlocking systems that define the unique attitudes and value systems of Chinese people.

"The foundation of the world is the state, and the foundation of the state is the family."[68] In the ancient Chinese family, there has always existed "family discipline, family rules, and family style." In the Chinese value system, the family is the basis for national development, national progress, and social harmony.

The homogeneity of family and state is also intrinsically inflected by Confucian teachings. The love inherent in kinship and blood ties germane to family ethics serves as the starting point for the love of others, and becomes the basis for a sense of social and ethical responsibility and the spirit in which one is initiated into the world. People traditionally adopt the title of "parental official" (父母官) as high praise for ruling officials, likening them to their own flesh and blood.

In these times, social forms, family structures, and values have been greatly altered, and people live in a modern society where instrumental rationality is paramount. However, the family concept of the ancient Chinese farming civilization, based on the idea of settling down and relying on the land, has persisted to the present day. Furthermore, the meaning of family continues to transcend economic cost-benefit analysis. While religious pilgrimages take place in Mecca and the Vatican, the annual Spring Festival in China is the "largest cyclical human migration in human history,"[69] known as the *Chunyun* (春運), when more than three billion passenger journeys are made over a forty-day period. Overcoming all odds to return to their homeland where they were raised and nurtured to reunite with their family and pay homage to their ancestors is an important cultural tradition of the Chinese people.

At the National Commendation Ceremony to Combat the New Pneumonia Epidemic in September 2020, Xi Jinping noted that "Chinese people have always held a sense of family and country, believing that the rise and fall of the world is the responsibility of each man." To understand the essence of how the Chinese regard *family*, we must grasp the synchronicity of the *small family* and the *big country*. In this worldview, every person's future resonates with the fate of the country.

Five-Year Plans Show the Way

For most of its seventy-plus years in power, the Communist Party of China) has laid out a blueprint for development through a series of five-year guidelines (originally called the Five-Year Plans). By 2020, China had successfully completed thirteen cycles of Five-Year Plans.

The first of these was drawn up in 1953 by the just-established New China, based on the Soviet Union's economic development framework. From the First Five-Year Plan to the Ninth Five-Year Plan, China continually promoted industrial construction and surpassed the primary stage of industrialization.

From the Eighth Five-Year Plan to the Thirteenth Five-Year Plan, a new type of industrialization was established, and China improved its socialist market economy system. This included manufacturing the nation's first cars and fighter jets, improving the quality of life of the rural population, and developing China's soft power on the global stage.

The Five-Year Plan is considered China's essential macroeconomic and social management tool, and it importantly encodes China's governance. However, not all of them were approved by the national legislature and strictly implemented. For example, the purpose of the Eleventh Five-Year Plan was to set the direction of the national, economic, and social goals and provide macroscopic, strategic, and forward-looking guidelines for the next phase, rather than specifying a detailed development route.

With the accumulation and integration of lessons learned, this system has been dynamically adjusted in accordance with China's internal and external environments and market developments and has achieved remarkable results in recent decades. China's latest Fourteenth Five-Year Plan lists the following as priorities: the construction of a modernized economic system, a "dual circulation" development pattern, balanced social development, scientific and technological innovation, and green and sustainable growth.

The Culture of Harmony and Stability as Prosperity

Unlike maritime and nomadic civilizations, Chinese civilization originated in inland farming, and is a moderate and self-protective civilization. It took self-sufficiency and self-reliance as its mode of survival and way of thinking, forming a close-knit sense of unity and family on the land. For the sake of preserving their farm lands, Chinese civilization has sought stability and peace for generations, abhorring the variability and instability that war brings.

Underlying the desire for stability and peace is a broad cultural philosophy: "By gaining the people, the kingdom is gained, and, by losing the people, the kingdom is lost." On this account, the ruler will first take pains to uphold his own virtue. Possessing virtue will give him the faith of the people. Possessing the good will of the people will give him the territory. Possessing the territory will give him wealth. Possessing the wealth, he will have resources for expenditure. Virtue is the root; wealth is the result.[70] Popular Chinese thought holds that morality transcends wealth and is the root of being human, and at its core is the goal to achieve "centrality" and "harmony" *zhizhonghe* (致中和),[71] a state in which heaven and earth are in their places, and all things live in harmony.

This spirit of harmony is not only the unity of heaven and humanity but also the harmony in diversity and a regard of harmony as a fundamental value. Harmony encompasses society, personal cultivation, and neighborly relationships. In ancient Chinese wisdom and cultural awareness, when all people are aligned, society will follow the Dao and develop in a stable, harmonious, and long-lasting way. In this sense, harmony, or *he* (和),[72] in the language of the new era is synonymous with coherence, the oneness of a connected living system. Coherence, in other words, is central to the Chinese cultural worldview.

Harmony creates stability; stability brings development, and development leads to prosperity. At present, China is ushering in unprecedented changes. Confronting severe complexities, such as diminishing demand, supply chain disruption, and epidemic prevention and control, the Chinese government insists on prioritizing stability while pursuing progress and proposes to keep macro policies steady and strong while reassuring people and stabilizing the overall situation. During China's two sessions of the National People's Congress and the Chinese People's Political Consultative Conference (NPC and CPPCC), General Secretary Xi Jinping pointed out that "With a long-term stable social environment, people's sense of gain, sense of happiness, and sense of security are significantly enhanced, and the level of social governance is continuously improved, renewing the miracle of long-term social stability."

For 1,500 years from the Han Dynasty until the early Qing Dynasty, China was a world leader in economy and technology. Yet China did not rely on power to expand. The opening of the Grand Canal in the Sui and Tang Dynasties achieved the first north-south interconnection and became an important political, economic, and cultural link for more than five hundred years. More than two-thousand years ago, Emperor Wu of the Han Dynasty sent Zhang Qian to the Western Regions to open up a large corridor spanning Egyptian, Babylonian, Indian, and Chinese civilizations. This established an extensive grid of world transportation routes for the first time and replaced aggressive expansionism with commodity interchange, cultural convergence, and different civilizations seeking common ground while preserving differences and fostering an idyllic picture of human civilization and prosperity.

Today, two-thousand years later, China is the world's second largest economy. The Belt and Road Initiative draws on the success of the Grand Canal and the corridors opened during previous dynasties. The intention is to construct a road of peace, prosperity, openness, innovation, and civilization—seeking to build a win-win cooperative platform through soft power. It may also provide a model of peaceful development for the global economy.

There are, of course, always two sides of a coin. China's initiatives such as the Belt and Road project and the expansion of Chinese businesses outside China, such as Huawei, have been perceived by much of the outside world as a desire to conquer and control. However, China's long history shows that the fundamental elements holding this culture together are inclusiveness, harmony, and shared prosperity. Indeed, China has always been more interested in expanding by trade and cultural diplomacy than by aggressively exerting brute power over other parts of the world.

As Martin Albrow, one of the people who defined globalization said in 2021, "China has integrated its deep cultural traditions into the process of governing, creating a unique model of governance that is different from Western representative democracy and is people-centered. China has proven that it can prosper without following the Western path by its firsthand experience."[73]

From a Characteristic Chinese Socialist Market Economy to a Community of a Shared Future for Mankind

Adam Smith and Karl Marx were the fathers of capitalism and Marxism. After World War II, the world split up into the communist world and the capitalist world. Since then, these Western-led systems have been dominant, creating a full-fledged materialist era where economics influence social, political, and technological development. Thus, the "ism" becomes the driving force.

China, when undergoing this process of refining its economy, called it a socialist market economy with Chinese characteristics. As early as the Song Dynasty, China experienced a period of extreme affluence. According to statistics, the production of iron exceeded the sum of the regions of Europe, excluding Russia, seven-hundred years later. In addition, the traditional Chinese culture of the Dao— including the people-oriented style of governance, the unity of family, state, and world, and the spirit of harmony—has been transmitted and preserved to the present day. In this light, the Western-led *isms* are effecting a complete reversal in China. The Chinese have always focused on how to live in harmony with everything around them, and Chinese cosmology acknowledges that the ultimate aspiration in life is to be one with the universe.

Since Deng Xiaoping proposed reform and opening-up in 1978, the Chinese Communist Party has gone through a long and complicated process of adjusting, refining, and implementing the economic system. In October 1976, China ended a decade of civil strife caused by the Cultural Revolution. For Chinese society, which found itself at an inflection point, it was necessary to reform the rigidly planned economic system of the past, establish a new orientation to the market, and forge a new path.

The traditional socialist economic theory not only does not account for the concept of the "socialist market economy," but also believes that socialism and the market economy are fundamentally opposed to each other. The theory of the socialist market economy with Chinese characteristics must be regarded as a pioneering innovation of Marxist theory.

When the top leaders of the Communist Party of China began to explore the future path of China's economic development, they pointed out that failure to regulate the market had brought about many negative economic consequences. In these initial explorations, three things arose:

First, the evaluation of the market changed from a total rejection in the past to a relatively positive affirmation.

Second, the market economy was no longer regarded as the monopoly of capitalism but more as a form of economic regulation that did not carry the exclusive attributes of the social system.

Third, the value of the market in meeting the diversified needs of the people was recognized, and it was suggested that market regulation was an indispensable part of the socialist economy.

After that, China went through two transitional periods: planned economy with market regulation, and planned commodity economy based on public ownership. The socialist market economy system with Chinese characteristics was formally established at the Fourteenth Communist Party Congress held in 1992. From then on, the market played a fundamental role in resource allocation under the macro-control of the socialist state.

China has gradually transformed from a highly centralized, planned economy to a more dynamic socialist market economy, improving the livelihoods of more than a billion people. In 2020, China's GDP exceeded the one hundred trillion-yuan mark for the first time. Geoffrey Garrett, dean of the Wharton School at the University of Pennsylvania, has said that China's accelerated economic development since 1978 may be "the greatest economic miracle" in the history of the world.

Our worldview determines our desires and wishes; on a national and cultural level, this has implications for how an economy is developed. According to American economist Douglas North, "Without a clear ideological theory, we are left with innumerable dilemmas in our ability to account for either the modern allocation of resources or historical change."[74] This suggests that an understanding of the Chinese government's management of its worldview is essential to understanding its economic development. In understanding China's economic miracle, it can be seen that China was moving from a revolutionary paradigm to a reform paradigm, i.e., focusing on economic construction. It can also be seen that the age-old Confucian culture, which espouses diligence and frugality while opposing wastefulness and extravagance, was directly conducive to economic development. [75]

During the last fifty years, China has enjoyed peace and gradually moved from being closed to having an openness and has gone from rigidity to prosperity. But at the same time, we cannot ignore that rapid economic growth has brought with it many ethical and moral problems. While prioritizing economic construction does help to bring innovation and vitality to the market, the confusion in value systems and the tendency to focus on money at the expense of all else also affects the sound governance of the investment and economic environment. At its worst, development takes a toll on the environment. In practice, in an economy without morality, unheeded growth and unethical management are frequently seen.

Ethical problems associated with incidents of enterprises not taking social responsibility for their actions are too many to count. Is a market economy inherently ethical or unethical? Do enterprises need to comply with ethical constraints beyond the law in their operation? In this context, the Chinese government and many scholars have devoted themselves to the study of economic ethics, suggesting that the prerequisite for the establishment of a market economy is a rational and peaceful social mentality and sufficient supply of cultural soft power. They have begun to dig deeper into philosophies of economic ethics in traditional Chinese culture.

In 2001, China officially joined the World Trade Organization (WTO). With the further opening-up of China and the influence of the globalization, the problems of integrity, fairness, justice, and ecological economic ethics in the development of China's market economy were highlighted. The one-sided pursuit of GDP growth along with the excessive pursuit of economic development and corporate profits induced numerous social problems. At the Sixth Plenary Session of the Seventeenth Communist Party of China Central Committee, a proposal was made for the first time to "carry out concentrative

education and treatment of outstanding problems in the field of morality, resolutely oppose money-worship, hedonism and extreme individualism, and resolutely correct the perverse wind of using power for
personal gain, price fraud, forgetfulness of righteousness and self-interest." Since then, the issue of moral governance has begun to receive
widespread attention.

Transitioning into a new era, China embarked on a new path from
a rich country to a strong one, and new leaders have successively put
forward new directions and concepts for development. Unlike traditional Western ideals of freedom, democracy and equality, the Chinese
are exploring the feasibility of an alternative model with unique regulatory mechanisms. At the Eighteenth National Congress of the Communist Party of China, socialist core values were proposed. Xi Jinping
summarized them as follows: prosperity, democracy, civilization, and
harmony are value requirements at the national level; freedom, equality, justice, and rule of law are value requirements at the social level;
patriotism, dedication, integrity, and friendship are value requirements
at the citizen level. In a large country with a population of nearly 1.5
billion and fifty-six ethnic groups—where great diversity and pluralism
are realities to contend with—the cultivation and practice of unifying
core values provides an important ideological foundation for enhancing national cohesion.

In 2021, China victoriously completed its fight against poverty
and declared that it had built a moderately prosperous society in all
respects. Achieving common prosperity for all people through a just
and reasonable system of wealth and resource redistribution is a fundamental element of Marxist political economy and China's modernization. Under the leadership of the socialist market economy system with
Chinese characteristics, the Communist Party of China has proposed
to build a basic institutional arrangement that coordinates the primary
distribution, redistribution, and third distribution of resources. The
latter has been a hot topic during the past two years.

Unlike the first distribution based on market mechanisms and the second distribution based on administrative mechanisms, the third distribution focuses on the spontaneous transfer of income, wealth, and other resources to others. This is made possible under the influence of moral and spiritual forces arising from cultural customs that promulgate these values—thus promoting a more just flow of resources in society.

Both East and West must grapple with the issues of global collaboration in economic and social development, poverty eradication and social inequality, but the paths they decide to take are different. In many countries, shared development for all is often the missing link. But with the outline of the Fourteenth Five-Year Plan (2021–2025) for National Economic and Social Development and Vision 2035 of the People's Republic of China, we may find a novel solution to this problem of global shared development. China's future offers us a way forward.

At the same time, as economic globalization becomes unavoidable for accelerated development and closer ties in the world economy, the Communist Party of China has begun to lead its people on a firm path of cultural confidence. In the past, because of the strong position of a Western economy globally, Western culture had a strong material basis that strongly influenced Chinese culture. Standing at the crossroad of multiple civilizations, China's rise will have to continue promoting the revival of Chinese culture and demonstrating the place of Chinese subjectivity in the pluralism and unification of the global cultural stage.

Indubitably, the Chinese nation has formed a unique tradition of thought and culture during its lengthy development. Thinkers such as Laozi, Confucius, and Mozi explored astronomy and geography and extensively discussed the true meaning of the relationship between man and man, man and society, and man and nature. The profound sum of their philosophies encompasses ideas in politics, economics, ethics, culture, and the military that continue to have widespread application today. The unique spiritual world of Chinese people today is built on their ancestors' wisdom and rational thinking. The high degree of consistency between traditional Chinese wisdom and today's quantum worldview is of great value in addressing the problems and challenges facing humanity in general.

At present, changes continue to accelerate, global challenges emerge, the epidemic of the century repeatedly appears. Our world history has found itself at a new crossroad. Human society is facing a major choice between cooperation and unity or isolation and division. All countries must inevitably explore pathways to cope with these dilemmas. Back in 2017, Xi Jinping delivered a keynote speech at the United Nations Headquarters in Geneva, systematically elaborating on the important concept of "building a community with a shared future for mankind."

Xi's speech called on all countries to "adhere to dialogue and consultation to build a world of lasting peace; adhere to common construction and sharing to build a world of universal security; adhere to mutually beneficial cooperation to build a world of common prosperity; adhere to exchange and understanding to build an open and inclusive world; adhere to green and low-carbon to build a clean and beautiful world." This provided clear guidelines for action in terms of partnership, patterns of security, economic development, civilizational exchange, and ecological construction. Indeed, "building a community with a shared future for mankind" has been written into several UN resolutions, a clear indication of the intention to turn this concept into a global consensus.

Klaus Schwab, founder of the World Economic Forum, was present in person to witness Xi Jinping's speech. In a book reflecting on where the world is headed in the post-epidemic era, he writes that the experience of the epidemic has fostered a deeper understanding that "We are a community of human destiny on the same planet, and that we have and should work together to create a common future."[76]

One thousand years ago, Zhang Zia, a famous thinker of the Northern Song Dynasty, offered writing on various subjects, including: "To ordain conscience for Heaven and Earth. To secure life and fortune for the people. To continue lost teachings for past sages. To establish peace for all future generations." Today, we see that China, a rising Eastern power, remains faithful to the wisdom of its ancestors in the Dao and has grappled with the challenges of each historical stage through a holistic, coherent view of the universe and the world.

The future has arrived, and the inheritance of the culture of harmony has allowed the Chinese to open their doors to the rest of the world, choosing a win-win path from division to unity, from isolation to cooperation. With the advent of an era of happiness and well-being led by the quantum paradigm, we would do well to understand the wisdom of the Chinese model.

It is likely that, in the near future, China will be a key source of inspiration to humanity on this road of awakening, alignment, collaboration, and creation that we must jointly embark upon and lead into the well-being and happiness era. The future may well bring to life the ancient Chinese concept described in the I Ching (Book of Changes) of *qunlongwushou* (群龍無首),[77] referring to an ancient belief that dragons, while being the strongest and most powerful mystical creatures, strangely never fight for dominance. Only the most magnanimous and humble, ones who are able to manifest and represent the will of heaven, would be selected to rule. Similarly, leadership in the quantum paradigm is an internal authority, naturally arising when we listen to the impetus of the universe.

CHAPTER 3

A Vision of
Quantum Leadership

The Emergence of Quantum Leadership

When there is an awakening, change happens. Reaching a critical threshold, it precipitates a global shift that will demand a new form of leadership built on a foundation of ethics and responsibility. Such leaders are stewards of entrusted resources, capable of tuning into the impetus of the universe as it permeates their being, creating a passion that can reach the fever pitch of obsession.

Geniuses like Einstein and Picasso were possessed by such a spirit. To many, the unwavering commitment to their purpose seemed crazy, as if they were bewitched. Yet it is precisely from such passion that they manifested the creativity, vision, and leadership essential to usher in the new era. They—and people like them—reflect and exemplify the underlying trends of the emerging consciousness of society. The world today is not well, and a new normal must emerge to confront the challenges that plague us. Here at the crossroad of our metamorphosis, such individuals see this as an opportunity to take ownership and define a new reality. In the quantum paradigm, this is the rise of *quantum leadership*.

In the era of well-being, the rise of quantum leadership is a natural awakening of an evolutionary energy. Originating in this evolutionary energy of creation, quantum leadership indicates a systemic awakening when changes in energy within the material world permeate the system and are transmitted to us, consequently influencing humanity's course of action. As active participants in the evolutionary process, humanity will necessarily respond to these broad, powerful, energetic shifts.

Understanding humanity's response in the well-being era will likely invoke Adam Smith's *Theory of Moral Sentiments* on the nature of ethics written in 1759. He argues that human morality is natural and inherent to our being. In his view, morality makes visible our true nature and draw us towards holism. As social beings, we are naturally drawn to social engagement and will develop a set of shared behavioral rules that shape what we have come to know as *conscience*. This morality guides the way we live our lives, providing the consistency necessary for social cohesion and harmony. Holism, as a form of connectedness, is intricately linked to our instincts as social beings. Love is the expression of holism and compassion is love in action. We are now experiencing these moral sentiments, in a more integrated way, pointing and guiding us toward the challenges that we must confront.

According to Smith, members of society are virtuous to the extent that they contribute to the creation and maintenance of a harmonious society. However, most of the world's population today cannot live up to this ideal. Instead, our moral compasses are broken—rather than being oriented by the interests and harmony of the collective, our morality is governed by selfish individual desires. Conditioned to care only for ourselves in a dog-eat-dog world, many of us have developed a tendency to look out for our own interests at the expense of others. This is clearly a world away from our natural, original calling, and it is threatening the land, biodiversity, and ecosystems of our shared planet with extinction. We must awaken to the truth and remain mindful of our securing a sustainable future for humankind. Because this awakening is systemic, and all parts are connected to one another, with this awareness we can be collectively stronger and wiser in this current era.

The proliferation and spread of the mindfulness movement in our time is a sign of a collective awakening. To deal with the stresses of modern life and the relational challenges they bring, many of us feel the need to search for solutions. Fortunately, when we cannot find it in the external world, we can choose to begin an internal journey, travelling deep within ourselves to discover an awakening at the quantum level. When we understand that our true nature is holistic, we can express that holism as love and compassion. Such is the awakening of our moral sentiments to the essential oneness of being and to the awareness of the common ground that connects us all. From this shift and elevation in our consciousness, a desire for social engagement, connection, and love will arise.

From this space, there comes about a natural motivation and need to align to holism and oneness. Understanding the nature of this challenge, and the distance that can separate each of us from holism, individuals will experience visions full of possibilities that show them the way forward. They will naturally follow this inner calling, which only becomes stronger and more resolute with time and deepens their awakening and awareness. When the path forward is clear, they will act. Since aligning to holism is the ultimate purpose, quantum leaders, who collaborate with one another and draw on their internal authority to act, will pool together a collective resource of wisdom that can create the future.

The arrival of the new era calls for a radically new kind of leadership. Of course, the quality of leadership is essential in any process of transition. Quantum leadership is built on value systems grounded in humility, such as a heightened awareness of the necessity of lifelong learning and a consciousness of the transformation toward holistic oneness with the cosmos—this oneness entails flowing with the evolutionary energy of the Dao. With the right kind of leaders, a transformation of this scale is possible. These quantum leaders will intuitively guide humankind onto the path of fulfilling the purpose of life, which is none other than to create and to evolve, to add value to life by living authentically and naturally.

As we awaken to our true purpose in life, we will be fully prepared to listen to the impetus of the universe, ready to participate in adding value to the evolutionary process and actively contribute to the creation of a new future. From the paradigm of quantum leadership, a new system of relational ethics will emerge, which has long been the practice of the Dao, the sustaining principle of Chinese culture for more than two thousand five hundred years. Relational ethics also constitutes the core of the Confucian classic, *The Great Learning*, that seeks to account for life in a systemic and relational way.

There are numerous ways to describe quantum leadership. But the reason we use the word "quantum" is that a quantum leader's reality is grounded in the quantum paradigm, which places metaphysics at the heart of physics. Both creativity and management are needed in the context of our era, and quantum leadership is embodied in both individual and collective realms. Not only is quantum leadership about alignments in personal management and creativity in the context of one's own life; it is also about expressing and broadening those alignments to the collective whole—whether it is our family, our company, or government. This is the pulsing soul of quantum leadership.

Quantum leadership describes this mindset of leadership in the well-being era that is urgently necessary to confront and resolve the challenges we face today on both individual and global scales. It is through this leadership that new possibilities, new paths forward, will be forged for humanity. Proactive in their quest for solutions, quantum leaders are also stewarding the work to create sustainable prosperity rather than short-term advantage and profit. They have the foresight to prioritize holistic well-being over immediate material needs that will not benefit the future.

Quantum leadership represents the rise of a new consciousness in the business world. More fundamentally, it represents a new consciousness of life. It is about letting our inner light shine through freely, expressing our authentic, natural selves. After all, quantum physics teaches us that we are essentially a form of consciousness itself, made of nothing more than bio-photons at the quantum level.

Quantum Leadership and a Shift in Consciousness

We are reminded of the saying that we cannot solve a problem from the same level of consciousness that created it. This sentiment is pertinent to discussions on creativity and innovation. If we persist on using the same worldview to frame new challenges, the course of action we choose will also be the same—or, at best, an attempt to reduce undesired impact. Remaining stuck in a less advanced state of consciousness, we will not be able to make the best choices for the future. This condition, often referred to as a *scarcity mindset*, is the opposite of what quantum leadership builds on, which requires a shift to an elevation in consciousness, a heightened awareness to develop a mindset of abundance that allows us to see new possibilities in everything we do.

A shift in collective consciousness can be likened to boiling water. When heat is applied and water reaches its boiling point, it will boil and change its form completely, evaporating into gas. This is not a gradual process. Similarly, *yin-yang* is not separable; they move in tandem, just like in the *taiji* symbol, the black and white "fish" chasing each other in an eternal circle. These visualizations are representative of the interlinking of opposites and how every extreme contains within it an element of the opposite extreme, constantly oscillating in the shape of a sine curve, moving in alignment to rhythms of the universe, the energy to form everything that comes into being. Where a shift in consciousness happens, quantum leadership can emerge.

This shift happens when people awaken to the quantum paradigm, and it becomes seamlessly integrated into their sense of identity, cognition, and intuition. For a new worldview to truly be part of us, having solely an intellectual knowing will not suffice. Instead, we must move from a kind of intellectual knowing to a deeper intuitive and embodied knowing. Only then can we respond to stimuli organically.

Upon internalizing the quantum worldview, these leaders accept it as an irresistible natural force that calls for alignment—the precursor to survival and forward movement. It is this alignment with one another while evolving into a common worldview to enable collaboration that will ensure challenges are overcome. Given the systemic nature of our challenges, creativity will be needed to solve them.

To awaken to our calling, we need to be willing to receive the message of the reality that this material world—along with our misguided desires—are ultimately illusory. Only then will we have a chance to shift our consciousness to make choices aligned to holism and create well-being for all. The way we live our lives and create our worlds will then be guided and directed by evolutionary energy that always naturally seeks coherence and well-being.

Traditionally, the Chinese believe in three forms of evolutionary energy—the energy of the universe, the energy of Earth, and the energy of humanity. When they are aligned, the systems within them will flourish. Of the three, humanity can harness its own energy and possess the freedom to make conscious choices. These choices branch out in two possible directions: either they bring humanity's actions into alignment with the power of the universe and of the Earth leading to holism or they travel in the opposite direction, focusing narcissistically on the self and creating a state of separation. Those who are capable of moving in the first direction will awaken to their true purpose in life and commence their quantum leadership journey.

This journey for the cultivation of quantum leadership must start with self-leadership. The well-being of business and political leadership in larger systems can be measured by this factor of leadership. Self-leadership is a choice for us to make, an action we must decide to take individually for the good of the collective systems we inhabit, such as our societies and nations. When we change ourselves, the world will change around us. Then we will discover a meaning to life that motivates us to take further action that contributes to overall joy and harmony. Only with a shift in consciousness can we move from an intellectual understanding to a fully internalized worldview filled with a deep sense of awareness and the courage to act in the new era of quantum leadership.

Quantum leaders are also integrators who bring together seemingly disparate forces and harness collective energy to drive the transformation that begins with a shift in consciousness to a new mode of being based on oneness and wholeness, explained thousands of years ago by Chinese sages. This mode of being founded on the belief in the oneness of everything will serve as a force for correcting our contemporary tendencies to foment nationalism and tribalism. This key to quantum leadership enables leaders to avoid the "us versus them" cleavages along political, ethnic, cultural, and national lines that are so deleterious to human affairs.

A shift in consciousness is needed for change to happen in large systems of businesses. The business world, as the most efficient institution to meet human desires, will have an important role to play in this transition to a new paradigm. Ideas like social entrepreneurship and "conscious capitalism" are useful steps that address the outer transformation of markets and the world. But because these measures require a shift in consciousness, which can only happen inside us, we must work on our inner transformation to awaken to the deep connections that bind every person to one another, to the system, and to nature. These inner transformations will activate the authentic, natural tendencies—present within each one of us—to create prosperity and flourish together.

Quantum Leadership and the Quantum Paradigm

According to the quantum paradigm, everything continually rebuilds itself in the direction of coherence with greater complexity, constantly calibrating itself to a state of balance at every single moment. The purpose of life is to connect with the impulse of the cosmos and the universe. When we connect with the cosmos and listen to the universe, we can understand that we are holistic, that reality and life are holistic, and that life is everything and everything is life. At the same time, evolution, and creation in this field of energy can only happen with movement. The natural calibration of these movements toward coherence is dependent on the conscious actions of humanity and also the wisdom and value that quantum leadership can add to the process.

How can we fulfill our purpose in life and add value to life through the evolutionary process? What does connection and listening to the impulse of the universe look like in daily life? How does it allow us to live in coherence with the larger systems that enfold us? How do we make decisions that lead to greater alignment with the natural process of calibration from moment to moment? What does balance and holism feel like and how do we know when we have attained alignment? Given that we are holistic beings with material form, how do our minds, bodies, and spirits work?

In most mythological traditions, nature is imagined as an active communicator, sharing a secret language with trees and forests, conveying a need to naturally exist in harmony. Just as natural ecosystems can continuously communicate and listen to one another, so too should humans listen to the universe for the sustainability of our future. The concept of the morphic field might offer us some insight on how this process can unfold.

Research on the morphic field, an idea originally introduced by Rupert Sheldrake[78] in the early 1980s, describes patterns that govern the development of forms, structures, and arrangements. Sheldrake proposed that there is a field within and around a morphic unit which organizes its characteristic structure and pattern of activity. According to this concept, the morphic field underlies the formation and behavior of morphic units and can be set up by the repetition of similar acts and thoughts.

This hypothesis implies that a particular form belonging to a certain group will tune into the group's morphic field and read the collective information through a process called "morphic resonance," using it to guide its own development. Within this field, communication and connections inform its structure, its arrangement, and the development of its form. Since the field transcends constraints of space and geography, the natural resonance emanating from it—constantly calibrating itself and searching for harmony—will be perceptible by quantum leaders all over the globe, as long as they are ready to tune into the energy of the cosmos and the universe.

Morphic resonance is a feedback mechanism that receives and relays information between the field and the corresponding forms of morphic units. The greater the degree of similarity, the greater the resonance, leading to the persistence of particular forms. In other words, the existence of a morphic field facilitates the existence of a new similar form that is coherent and continually expanding with the addition of more morphic units into the field. When we shift our consciousness and connect to the field in oneness, we develop a sensitivity to how the information in the field seeks to build new networks and expand the form. As part of the quantum field, quantum leaders can tap into the morphic field's intricate web of connections and information to ultimately add value to the universe's evolutionary direction.

When the level of intensity peaks, the system tips over and initiates the bifurcation process. In an organic body, bifurcation happens when a small group of cells discover a novel way of detoxifying and receiving nutrients and soon communicates that information across all networks that constitute the cell.

Bifurcation is a concept used in systems theory that implicates the modeling of complex systems with constant inputs and outputs. In a system with such dynamic flows of energy and information, it is possible to drive it into different states. Governed by chaotic attractors, an unstable system will be full of new and unpredictable behaviors. Bifurcation, then, describes the tipping point—or the point of no return—where these chaotic attractors make their appearance.

It has been believed for a long time that a critical mass is needed to achieve movement in social systems. However, this is unsustainable as it focuses on what needs to stop rather than what needs to be built.

Although such movements can increase awareness, they seldom ignite sustainable change by themselves. Instead, change results from the actions that follow awareness. Action, motivated by and transcending awareness, is what will make the difference. The bifurcation principle similarly draws from the importance of action. Similarly, the bifurcation principle draws from the importance of action. The tipping point is reached when a small group of leaders who have attained awareness can act accordingly in response to a common challenge, building a locus for change and eventual resolution.

In other words, change pivots on action that is inspired by the desire to create a different future. Large numbers of people with awareness are necessary but are not sufficient to bring about a condition for change. According to a quote attributed to sociologist William Bruce Cameron, "Not everything that can be counted counts, and not everything that counts can be counted." [79] This maxim is often evoked in relation to metrics of cultural evaluation. Another framework titled the "theory of the critical yeast" argues that the construction of social change requires a different strategy from the concept of critical mass that is commonly applied to generate shared social energy. [80] What does such a strategy look like?

In the current era, the holism of systems underpins the direction of our evolution. Multiple connections must happen concurrently through all systems across the globe, moving in coherence to harness the energy of change. In his book, *The Tipping Point*, Malcolm Gladwell presents three characteristics of the tipping point: first, that the idea is contagious; second, that something seemingly small will produce a significant impact; and finally, that when change happens, it will happen suddenly, changing everything all at once. The relevance of these concepts to the study of pandemics is clear, especially in the Covid-19 pandemic as we still deal with its consequences.

Thus, the important takeaway is that it is not the numbers or the masses that will activate a paradigm shift. Even though the awareness of the masses is necessary for the impact to ultimately be significant, it is fundamentally the ideation behind action that will precipitate the shift, creating a desired future by transforming the core of the system. Given the systemic nature of the shift, the results will be sudden, and possibly earth-shattering, when amplified by the speed at which quantum technology has enabled scientific developments.

Synthesizing these concepts, we can derive the beginnings of a new change theory. In the quantum theory realm of evolution and holism, quantum leadership arises when we listen, receive, and accept information from the universe, naturally embodying our inner calling that guides us toward movement and change. As we choose our course of action in the direction of coherence and harmony, this change will impact others. When these courses of action are shown to contribute to collective harmony, they will attract others to the core and create bigger ripples in the world around us. The evolutionary process of change will then also affect other systems.

This transformation has an ontological threshold, depending on the position of the system within the whole. A *system* can be the individual person, any larger organization in which they are a part, or perhaps humanity in its entirety. When a system finds its point of connection with one another, the change reaches the threshold and the ontological divide is crossed to attain unity with the next complex system, thus shifting it to the next state of consciousness.

Similar to the theory of the critical yeast, which is more invested in the *who* rather than the *how many*, we must also ask the following question. Who, even if not like-minded or situated in proximity to one another, would have the capacity to make other things grow exponentially beyond their numbers? Whatever the threshold, when we find our ability to connect with one another, we will naturally begin collaborating with and integrating in conjunction with one another. Beginning in smaller communities, transformation will slowly but surely reverberate throughout the species, leading to massive paradigm shifts.

Another powerful, well-researched mechanism is the *Maharishi Effect*, an informal social experiment aimed at increasing a population's consciousness. A review of 15 published studies conducted on city, state, national, and global levels found strong evidence that crime rates fell and the quality of life improved when even one percent of a population practiced meditation.[81] This phenomenon is a small reflection of how individual consciousness can reverberate into collective consciousness, reshaping it on a systemic level.

Although we do not know how many quantum leaders humanity will need to reach the point of bifurcation, it seems certain that the new quantum paradigm will spread with great speed when quantum leadership reaches this threshold, precipitating us over the ontological divide. Whether the exact proportion of leaders is 1 percent, 2 percent, 20 percent, or any other number is less consequential. Rather, it is the *who* as well as the intensity of the energy that will make all the difference.

The Ontological Divide

Quantum leadership is an emergence, an evolutionary energy that arises as a response to the fractures that separate the world today. Self-interest and unethical actions reign in the marketing economy, and the Earth itself is threatened by sustainability challenges. However, humans are inherently good social beings at heart, naturally seeking engagement and connection. In fact, in a time like this, our innate moral sentiments—as theorized by Adam Smith back in the eighteenth century—will awaken, drawn from the holism and love of the universe to generate a quantum awakening that will spread to every sector.

Quantum leaders are the ones who kickstart this process by pursuing their inner calling, collaborating with one another, and elevating themselves to the next level of consciousness. They are precisely the people who have made themselves available to information and who are willing to make the change within themselves before influencing others. The conditions of the Covid-19 pandemic that facilitated deep existential reflection have induced an increasing number of people to awaken to the quantum paradigm. Their homes become their whole universes, in which they live, work, and essentially spend their free time for recreation and entertainment. Their family is their community, reinforcing the importance of relationships.

This is not a process that will unfold as a linear sequence on an individual level; instead, it is systemic and contagious. Quantum leadership emerges as individual units within the system start to shift, affecting the field that connects and holds everything within its net. As quantum leaders awaken, the common purpose that unites them will start to influence others. Individual units will become institutions, which will then coalesce into networks of institutions. The process spreads and repeats until the attractors reach a tipping point, cross the ontological divide, and integrate into the next larger system.

According to the concept of ontological divide, the tipping point is reached when the traditional fragmented, mechanistic, and utilitarian conception of being is subjected to interrogation and challenge.[83] Typically applied to businesses and companies, the ontological divide is crossed when a company realizes that their habitual way of seeing and acting is not connected to the true holistic and interconnected nature of being, often expressed as a "sustainability challenge." Systemically, it naturally moves to seek new connections by reframing business practices from the next level of consciousness [84] that is evolving in order to sustain itself in the future.

The Chinese traditionally believe that success results from a confluence of space, time, and human collaboration, which is a harmonious state of all the core elements. We are already at the stage where we have a more holistic and less conflicted approach to science. Scientific discoveries are more capable than ever of integrating our purpose and well-being into the frame of life. We are, in other words, very close to success.

Seeking a unification between intellectual and intuitive knowing, quantum leaders move into an expansive mindset of abundance, leaving behind the mindsets of scarcity that constrain the leaders' potential. This mindset of abundance is a growth mindset, catalyzing actions to

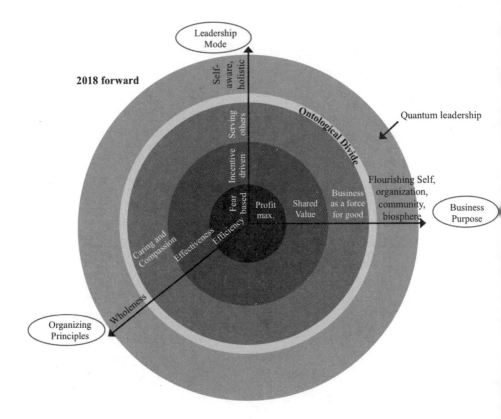

THE ONTOLOGICAL DIVIDE [82]

Used with permission from Stanford Business Books.
Originally published in *Quantum Leadership: New Consciousness in Business*
by Frederick C. Tsao and Chris Laszlo, 2019

build a collective future. Beyond snuffing out the flames of what is not wanted, this mindset is proactive, creative, and integrative rather than reactive or defensive. In a state of abundance of growth, quantum leaders will transcend survival and indulgence to finally live with purpose and meaning, an evolution that corresponds to the Chinese concepts of survival (*shengcun* 生存), living (*shenghuo* 生活), and life (*shengming* 生命).

The process of elevating our awareness will be supported by the revival of ancient systems of wisdom and philosophy from different cultural and spiritual traditions, enabling totally different ways of relating to ourselves and our natural environments. Nature is a dynamic process in which everything is constantly aligning with the whole, reflecting collaboration in diversity. We are awakening to the deep truth of this natural movement. Without knowing they are collaborating, all things work in flux with flourishment. It is a worldview that acknowledges the inherent value of non-human life in recognition that all living beings are members of ecological communities bound together in a network of interdependencies.[85]

In our era, this ontological way of being is related to the evolving nature of humanity and the role that businesses play in expressing a set of values, expectations, and cultural norms. Economics is the foundation of political, social, technological, and environmental progress. It is not reducible to any ism—but if there was one that was relevant to our contemporary reality, we ought to call it *life-ism* and *well-being-ism*: an era of life, in which we are all united by a common outlook and our common mission to add value to well-being of life.

Bifurcation, therefore, is supported and urged on by this life-ism and by shifts in humanity's evolutionary energy. All we need is a small number of the world's population to awaken to the common purpose of life that is present, although latent, in every one of us. This will help to initiate the change as quantum leaders begin to lead their lives differently. They will reorganize the way they operate and begin an inner journey, helping humanity to reach the tipping point. Soon, the rest of the people will come together and cross the ontological divide.

Another enabler is technological advancement, which will facilitate this leap. Each moment we are seeing new innovations emerge, creating previously unimagined possibilities for connection and communication across disparate geographies.

The so-called metaverse, in which any kind of virtual experience can be constructed, is one such example. It furnishes a platform of oneness that breaks down physical and spatial boundaries. Everything can be found in one virtual place, opening up totally new possibilities for human beings to connect, collaborate, and create together. It will provide people with new kinds of shared experiences enabling quantum leaders to be able to unite people in service of their common vision. As we surpass the spatial boundaries that divide us from one another, the metaverse will embody us within its virtual universe in unprecedented ways. When physical separation is eradicated, it will become far easier to shift mindsets and facilitate a general awakening to the quantum era. The metaverse carries deep implications for how we express creativity and how we influence others. Instead of creating products, we now create reality and experiences in the metaverse before the physical creation that rewire our neural circuits in profound ways—creating the possibilities of impossibilities.

Additionally, the metaverse will enable new forms of creativity and utterly transform the distribution and accessibility of almost everything. Industrialization and material creation will be redefined and look completely different from what it used to. All our processes, from building infrastructure to food production, will be reinvented. It is another resource available for deployment in the quantum leadership era—and when ethically deployed—this will transform the ecosystem we live in.

Individual people, families, businesses, countries, nature, and the environment are all instrumental components of our ecosystem. Businesses, in particular, must take individual and societal well-being into account.[86] They are one of the most important stewards of our shared resources along with the institutions that have the potential to serve humanity in the most efficient way possible. Because business has the role of creative integrator, it is best positioned to lead humanity into the new well-being era, in which "human beings and other life forms will flourish on the Earth forever."[87] Only by creating life and adding value to life can businesses interface with the market to drive economic activities that serve well-being and happiness. Business is positioned to direct the market by promoting a culture of love, unity, and harmony and displacing the current capitalist model that profits from human greed, vanity, and ignorance.

In oneness and holism, no ontological divide can exist. An awakening to this worldview will happen when quantum leadership emerges, reaches the tipping point, and crosses the ontological divide.

An Inner Life Journey

If humans are inherently good and loving, what went wrong? We understand that today we are often unequipped to express love or offer compassion to one another; nor are we frequently able to embrace the interests of the collective. Instead, we are obsessed with ourselves, full of fear for the future and burdened by the past. The norm seems to be a selfish, destructive "I win, you lose" philosophy guiding morality and actions. But we need not be alarmed. Even this situation is nothing more than a normal evolutionary process moving to create new life—like yin-yang. Without these struggles nothing can evolve, and no new creation can emerge.

Social behaviors are developed for the purpose of maintaining some consistency and social order in the community. In reality, we have been conditioned by our environment to behave in ways that are distant from our inherently kind and loving nature. Such conditioning has in fact taken control of our actions, to the extent that many of us make choices dictated by unconscious indoctrination rather than conscious will.

Neuroscience has theorized that more than 95 percent of our decisions are not made by the conscious mind in our left brains but by the subconscious and unconscious mind. Given that so much happens that is unknown to our conscious selves, it is all the more imperative that our process of awakening must include journeying inward to discern with clarity the deepest parts of ourselves. This is a highly spiritual process from which we emerge with a very different way of seeing the world and interacting with it —a world where the systemic right-brain that determines our being will drive the "doing" processed through the left-brain.

It is crucial that we understand how the mind works if we are to understand quantum leadership. It is not easy to recognize the effects of neural rewiring and to fully internalize those changes. Even as our brains are being rewired, traces of the old configuration still remain. We must achieve coherence by journeying inside the self, discovering our conditioning, and changing our behaviors and the way we think. Quantum leaders' bodies can heal and open up their receptivity to new information; the very energies of their bodies become lighter. Miraculously, our whole worldview will shift because of a conscious change in neural wiring.

Deep inside all of us goodness can be found, from our natural need for connection and an instinctive attraction to positive social engagement. We spontaneously wish everyone well, because deep down we know that we can only be well if everyone else is well. There is an innate wisdom within us, so that when we are well-endowed with consciousness, we gravitate toward behaving in a way that serves and contributes to the greater good.

But many events and schools of thought have intervened between the time of our birth and the present day, resulting in our development of a set of conditioned tendencies or unconscious behaviors utterly misaligned to the goals of goodness, love, and compassion for which we were originally designed.

Developments in contemplative science have offered us a clearer understanding of our brain and its responses. Dr. Gabor Mate, who works extensively in the fields of addiction and trauma, explains that a child has two basic needs: attachment and authenticity. [88] As social and relational creatures, human beings naturally seek social connection. This is visible in how children hunger for social connection and bonding with their parents and extended family. The environment that children inhabit, and the signals they receive, will shape their being and behavior. This is carried into adulthood as the identity they use to interact with the world.

Human's first basic need of attachment, differing from reptiles, is the natural desire of closeness and intimacy with other human beings. Beyond attachment, authenticity—being true to our deepest intentions—is also a great need. Authenticity is as important as attachment to allow us to be in touch with our intuition and the gut feelings that protect us from harm.

How do the two basic needs relate to our conditioned tendencies? When we are born, we see the material world with new eyes; reality is immediate and visceral. The problem arises in the process of socialization when we begin to construct our world based on a set of experiences. While growing up we learn the importance of being accepted, first by our parents and then by our extended family. This is followed by our communities in school, the workplace, and society.

Often we are made to compromise our authenticity for the sake of attachment. A primal example, and likely one relatable to many, is when parents inflict punishment on their child by forcing them to sit in a corner until they stop crying. Through this experience, the child learns that they do not have permission to cry, as crying will come at the cost of attachment to their parents. We learn that to be loveable and acceptable, we must suppress our true selves. We might construct a carapace for the sake of social acceptance, an identity that eventually hardens and determines how we view the world. Over time, we can lose touch with our authentic selves, coming to believe that the conditioned selves we have constructed are who we are. These forms of conditioning color the way we see the world and have immense impacts on ourselves and society. Having built up a personality influenced by society, the individual in turn polices and controls others in a vicious loop.

But social conditioning is not eternal or irrevocable; we have the autonomy to reverse and undo it if we choose to do so. Thus, to be prepared for the challenges of the new era, we should not wait until society and its institutions change. We must begin our inner work within ourselves at the part of the cycle that is under our control. We must quiet ourselves so we can observe the noise from a distance and reconnect with our authentic selves.

We are created beautifully and have natural defense mechanisms that constantly scan our environment for danger. But these mechanisms are, in a sense, overworked and burdened by our past experiences that form a massive databank locked in our bodies and minds. When we have a negative experience, our bodies associate the smells, touches, and other sensory stimuli with trauma. Absorbed into our bodies, the experience forms associations that can trigger visceral responses in us when reactivated. We might instantly despise someone whom we have never spoken to in our lives; we might judge them by their looks or their demeanor simply because it triggers something within us we are not aware of. These automatic, unconscious responses are a form of trauma. Trauma is not what happens to us, but what happens inside of us because of what happened to us.

These habits and behaviors are automatic responses take a front seat in our unconscious being, creating a disconnect between our inner and outer world. Our unconscious can react at lightning speed to external stimulus as if it is reacting to a past experience. To the unconscious, conditioned by trauma, the past appears to be replicated in the present, and the mind wishes to avoid the harm done when it was previously unprepared. These traumas give rise to chaos and noise in our inner world, becoming increasingly unbearable the more this is amplified. It is no surprise that many of us feel a sharp sense of disconnection from the core of ourselves—we have lost the ability to connect with the meaning of our lives and the authenticity of ourselves, our thoughts, our ethics, and our intentions.

Our alienation from authenticity has led to an unprecedented existential crisis. Millions of us feel useless and struggle to locate new directions and purpose. But the answer is inside us; we only need to journey inward to find it. Having explored the external world for centuries, our focus must now turn inward.

How Do We Get There?

This is a journey of unlearning and relearning, rebuilding connections with our inner world, increasing awareness of mind, body, and spirit and the connections among them. Reconnecting with the authentic self is an essential part of this journey and these practices are present in most ancient traditions. However, the Eastern consciousness-based cultivation practices are aligned to the science of consciousness. The Chinese tradition is explored in more depth because it is a relational model based on journey between self and the collective—this is "self-cultivation."

Everything begins in the individual with a shift in our own consciousness. The Daoist classic work, *The Daodejing*, offers a hier-archical chain of human states of mind. Human beings should strive to embrace the highest level, the Dao. While the universe constantly calibrates itself from moment to moment, opportunities keep opening up to find new avenues and connections for shifting our consciousness. Humanity always evolves in the direction of its challenges; the more chaotic the challenge, the bigger the shift in consciousness.

When our relationships—with ourselves, others, and the environ-ment—are unwell, connections are lost, and chaos reigns. Rebuild-ing relationships is our only way to achieve well-being. The Dao (or *the energy of the source* in the quantum worldview) constantly expands to create new and more complex systems. How we as human beings participate and how much pain we need to endure to achieve align-ment is within our control—we must make the right choices.

Although the quantum worldview resonates with the core concepts of the Dao in Chinese culture, it does not provide practical rules about how to live our lives. In contrast to this, traditional Chinese culture contains a deep resource of wisdom and practical advice, providing a tried-and-tested framework that has proven efficacious for thousands of years. A synthesis of the quantum worldview and the wisdom of ancient Chinese culture could furnish us with a point of reference to practice ethical modern mindful living in our modern age.

All spiritual practice involves listening. To hear the Dao, we must still and quiet ourselves. As we listen to it and journey further inward, we will recognize the calling and the impetus of the universe. Even-tually, we will be able to tap into that impulse and fulfill our gift of creation while exploring the connections between our internal and external relationships, as well as the delicate dance between them. This is the essence of evolutionary alignment to the energy of the universe as we shift and elevate ourselves to a higher state of consciousness. We get there by embarking on a journey of life.

Venturing inward into the deepest recesses of the self, we move from the physical body to the mental and emotional body and finally to the life body. We become more and more unified with ourselves, immersed in a state of oneness, learning that life is everything and everything is life.

One school of Buddhism teaches that there are eight levels of consciousness. For true access to our innermost selves, the seventh consciousness is key. Known as *manas-vijnana*, it describes the intuitive consciousness that simultaneously localizes and universalizes experience through both intellectual and intuitive knowing. While this seventh level is akin to what modern psychology calls the subconscious, to penetrate even deeper into the eighth level means reaching the unconscious.

In contemplative science, the mind in meditation heals itself. Trying to explain how people emerge from meditation feeling like they have had a spiritual experience, scientists have observed changes in gray matter concentration in brain regions involved in learning and memory processes, emotion regulation, self-referential processing, and perspective taking.[89] The experience of spiritual revelation in scientific and biological terms translates to a shift in our neural wiring, a connection between the left and right brain.

As quantum leaders change their values, they spend a substantial amount of time in quiet and stillness, consciously choosing a meditative state over a life of indulgence and pleasure. Spiritual growth happens in that stillness from which creativity springs. New kinds of urges and motivations arise, driven not by desire but by purpose. They bring the quantum leaders back to the source, to the wholeness of reality.

In truth, what blocks real learning is the "ego." Our ego is the source of self-centeredness and individuality. An over-inflated ego blocks out humility and the possibility of learning, resulting in a tightly closed system. Although we tell ourselves our ego is a story, a definition of ourselves that we impose on our lives, it's difficult to eliminate once it roots itself in the mind. We must constantly open our system to greater receptivity and come to terms with the fact that the ego is not real. The ego must serve us, rather than the other way around.

People typically allow themselves to be guided by their desires and preferences. Receiving stimuli from the external world, which shape our emotions, we make decisions by thinking, "I want . . ." and ponder what steps we must take to acquire and possess the things we want to have.

However, quantum leaders transcend the "I want" to reach "I wish" and "I dream." Rather than being dictated by their desires, they make their decisions based on the wishes and visions they hold. While transient emotions and desires can be likened to small waves in a sea, wishes and dreams are more like the boundless ocean itself: holistic, collective, and infinitely creative in nature.

Aside from wishes and dreams, quantum leaders also learn the value of "I care." While the caring emanates from them as a separate, individual part, it is directed through the evolution of the collective. The way caring manifests in quantum leaders' relationships with others reflects their value system. The care they exhibit firmly establishes a link between the individual and the collective, placing the "I" in "we."

Creativity is essential to quantum leadership and occurs when we are connected to the Dao, the source of our evolutionary energy. It is a construct of our consciousness—necessary to find new, innovative solutions for creating capital and resources. When quantum leaders are creative, their bodies are mere vessels for delivering and enacting that creativity.

It is from a place of creativity that quantum leaders gain the ability to see the source, to understand the meaning of the transition to a new quantum era from a different context, and to grasp their calling. Understanding the system as a holistic structure, they see how they and others fit within the larger whole. They see the journey they must travel and know what it takes to get *there*. There are different levels of "there" with different destinations. It takes the strategic mindset of a quantum leader to decide which is best.

Thus, quantum leaders align their actions with the direction of evolution to get where they need to be. Once they are internally aligned, they must commence an outward-facing process of alignment. That means engaging and collaborating with others, as no progress toward a common goal is possible without collaboration. They must engage with the bigger picture and adopt a bird's eye view, from which they can see everything and understand what needs to be done. Whether through inspiration, negotiation, or aspiration, quantum leaders forge a common language to bring the new world into being. Leadership is nothing but the impulse of the creative universe.

The quantum leaders' awakening shifts their awareness and that of the people around them. Their alignment always moves in the direction of eventual coherence. Concretely, as we have seen, this also means that they rewire their neural pathways and circuits through these experiences to accommodate their awakening. Rewiring, all in all, requires a practice of self-cultivation—a connection to the Dao, the evolutionary energy of creation where our calling resides.

A Practice of Self-Cultivation

The process of internal exploration entails stillness; the practice involves descending into a state of meditation. Regardless of whether a person has a spiritual or physiological connection to meditation, it is important to understand the significant physiological and energetic changes that take place in a meditative state. For the experienced practitioner, meditation has the potential to carry oneself to states beyond the levels of body and mind in ways that cannot be measured or quantified by empirical devices. Contemplative science thus lays the foundation for a new paradigm of science—the scientific exploration of the subjective, unquantifiable realm of consciousness.

Whether we are mentally active, at rest, or asleep, the brain always maintains a level of electrical activity. The changes in electrical brain-wave activity that meditation creates are associated more with wakeful attention than with resting on a couch. Although some of us occasionally experience gamma waves—the highest frequency of brainwaves—when we have an epiphany or moment of insight, the brainwave signature looks profoundly different for advanced meditators. We can conclude that this special state of consciousness is a new state of being different from our ordinary state, an unprecedented phenomenon in science that we have yet to fully understand.

The science that deals with the effects of meditation on the human body is often referred to as "contemplative science." Yet, there is no consensus around the definition of contemplative science. In a paper published in *Frontiers in Psychology* in 2016, Dorjee Dusana proposed that "contemplative science is an interdisciplinary study of the meta-cognitive self-regulatory capacity of the mind and associated modes of existential awareness. [90] It is a natural propensity of the mind enabling introspective awareness of mental processes and behavior and is necessary for effective self-regulation and well-being."

However, the current field of contemplative science research rarely involves the participation of masters of meditation. A rare exception occurred in 1970 at the famous Menninger Foundation's laboratories. Swāmī Rāma, a master from the Himalayas, demonstrated the capacity to control his autonomous nervous system, his heart, and his brain-waves. In addition, he also evinced an ability to concurrently focus on his inward state while remaining aware of his external environment.[91]

In subsequent experiments carried out at the Institute of Noetic Sciences in California in 2006 under the experimental leadership of Dean Radin, Swāmī Veda Bhāratī (a close disciple of Swāmī Rāma) was observed to be in an almost perpetual state of yogic sleep, in which his brain was producing theta and delta waves even as he was talking and moving around with his eyes open (Bhāratī, 2006, p. 69). Unfortunately, no scientific consensus yet exists on how such feats are possible, and not many peer-reviewed scientific publications have dealt with the topic, perhaps partly because spiritual masters did not see the need for scientific validation.

Despite the paucity of scientific findings, the truth of meditation cannot be denied. The process of meditation rests on two strong pillars: the stillness of the body and the serenity of breathing. How we prepare our body and breathing greatly affects the depth of meditation. Balancing these two aspects allows our mind to quiet down and turn inward. We can then step back and observe at a distance instead of engaging external stimuli with our five senses. As the mind turns inward, it converges gradually into one single point, becoming simultaneously steadier and more relaxed. Sharpness and softness of the mind are experienced at once in this stage of concentration. When we remain in this state of concentration, the observer and the observed eventually merge and the state of meditation is achieved.

The ability to observe the senses through our minds is very important in the path of meditation. Since the information that passes through our systems of sensory perception covers or masks our inner world, it is exhausting for the mind to be constantly pulled outward by the senses and the stimuli it receives. When we step back and observe the senses from a distance, we are able to enter a natural resting state at the threshold between our external and internal worlds.

The most significant, and perhaps least understood sense, is that of the *self in space*, otherwise known as *proprioception*. When this proprioceptive sense is under control, the other senses retreat into the background, creating a state of clean relaxation that can be described as *witnessing*.

Sensory information dissipates and disperses the mind. But when the senses are withdrawn, the inner journey begins. Internally, the mind and body connect, and our choices and actions will naturally flow from the clarity we feel from this connection. Springing from a place of deep relaxation, this process recharges rather than exhausts the mind.

In ancient times, archery was taught alongside meditation. Indeed, there are numerous points of similarity between the two practices. The process of meditation can be likened to the process of aiming an arrow at a target. If the concentration is forceful, the body remains tense, the breath is shallow, the arms tremble, and the target will inevitably be missed. Conversely, involving the whole body through deep diaphragmatic breathing and unwavering concentration will lead to success. When the fingers release the string, the process is irreversible—the target will be struck. The arrow and the bullseye become one; the observer and the observed merge.

When the state of effortless concentration is maintained and intensified, we enter a state of meditation. Since words and labels exist only when there is a separation from the core of things, it is nearly impossible to describe the state of meditation when oneness and unity are achieved.

It is easier to define meditation by what it is not. Meditation is not the act of thinking of different inspiring concepts or visualizing images and objects. It is not about trying to catch your thoughts or stop their flow. It is not a state of hypnosis or autosuggestion. No programming or manipulation of the mind's contents is involved. On the contrary, sages say that meditation is the opposite of hypnosis; it is a state of clarity and freedom from suggestion or outside influence. While meditating, one simply observes the mind and its thoughts and emotions, letting everything quiet down into stillness and calm.

Meditation is not a religion. It is a practice of journeying inward, a process of self-discovery on all levels to help us to receive answers to our existential questions about the purpose of life can be derived. Meditation is highly reactive to individual capacities and tolerance levels. If one struggles to sit still or to stay awake while meditating, it might be more effective to keep the meditation sessions short. It would be counterproductive if we associated meditation with bodily struggle and pain. Instead, we can choose to return to earlier steps in the process of improving our awareness of our body and our breathing before re-attempting meditation.

Meditation is not a tool for stress management. It is much more than that; it helps us to remain undisturbed and still in the midst of life's chaos. When we are in a state of stillness and tranquility, meditation gives us access to the wisdom and insight inherent in our life journey. Seeing the world through the lens of an observer, we can glimpse new possibilities, enabling creativity within ourselves. Though these are qualities that we all long for, they in fact belong to every one of us by virtue of the gift of being human. Mediation opens a gateway that transcends the self, offering a vision of something far more elemental: unity, oneness, and the very nature of consciousness.

To reap all the possible benefits of meditation, we must turn it into a regular practice and incorporate it into one's life. Accessing our inner world and the state of meditation can also be achieved with other practices of connectedness. Traditional Chinese society had seven activities and pursuits illustrating the ancient origins of many of today's practices of self-cultivation. These were, respectively, playing the zither (a plucked stringed instrument), the game of Go, calligraphy, painting, poetry, wine, and tea (琴棋書畫詩酒茶). All were regarded as essential for the pursuit of a meaningful and refined life.[92] Every individual has their own preferences and inclinations, and the key is to find a comfortable practice that works for themselves. This might take time, but time should not be taken as an indication of failure. We can only discover ourselves by experimenting with different practices and building a habit and relationship with the practices we choose. When we find the right one, we are closer to locating the true purpose of our lives.

For the Chinese, another life journey for systemic relationships exists, one framed by the Confucian ethical structure. This structure constitutes a basis for elements that are integrated Daoist traditions of longevity, freedom, and health and Buddhist elements of arriving at eternal happiness and ending all suffering. In collective terms, the goal of the journey is the creation of a harmonious community of humanity which in traditional Chinese thought is known as "The Great Unity (大同)," [93]—ultimate commonality and freedom in humanity. For individuals, the life journey makes room for the full expression of creativity, empowering us to achieve our full potential while maintaining good health in a holistic manner.

The purpose of the journey of life is to be in "oneness with the universe"—to follow the Dao, which is the most basic Chinese aspiration of life. To achieve this is to find harmony, inside ourselves, with others, and with our natural environments.

As more and more quantum leaders practice these forms of engagement and collaboration and recruit others to participate in the same journey toward a common goal, the quantum awakening will spread throughout the system. It will draw more connections to itself and incorporating them into one harmonious whole until it reaches the threshold and crosses the ontological divide. At that moment, the awakening will reverberate throughout humanity, expanding in sudden exponential ripples.

PART TWO

The Era of a Well-Being and Happiness Economy

In the rising era of well-being and happiness, I am on a life-long journey of learning about life and effecting changes from the inside. Instinctively, like many others, I am protective of the way I live. However, when I open my mind, I see new possibilities. When I began to make efforts to widen my mind, everything shifted—from my worldview and perspectives to my actions and habits, and I discovered a new way of living that is flourishing and joyful. Grasping the power of a purposeful life, mindfully lived, I claim the freedom to create and constantly add value to the collective whole. Ultimately, I realized our power is derived from within us, and it is in the deepest recesses of our soul that we discover our life's purpose and our creativity and authority to act.

From the Cosmos, the Universe, and Us to a New Theory of Well-Being

How are we to make sense of well-being? To understand well-being, we must look toward the fundamentals of life— the cosmos, the universe, and our relationship with the both of them. Through clarifying these structural questions, we can then come to understand what an ideal, new approach to life can look like.

Revisiting Humanity's Existential Questions

As modern science meets human consciousness, we are forced to confront the meaning of our own existence. Humanity remains the most conscious and self-aware beings on the planet, with the capacity to observe, analyze, and form assessments about our lives and our purpose. We ask questions because we have free will and the power of choice. This power renders it more necessary that we address the most pressing existential questions that define us as human.

WHAT ARE WE? WHAT IS LIFE?

We are nothing more than consciousness. We can take any form, since all forms and life are created from consciousness. When life is all we have, everything that human beings do is to sustain and flourish life.

In traditional Chinese culture, life is created from the meeting of the energies of Heaven and Earth. The aspiration of all life is directional; we seek growth and creation. Humanity is simply one unit of consciousness spun off from the universe and aligned with its movement centered on well-being. Humans are at the very forefront of evolution; they represent the most valuable life form on Earth. As we participate in the creation of life, we create a dance with the Dao. In the language of science, to align ourselves with the Dao is to respond to the impetus of the universe and answer the call of the cosmos.

Humans are expressions of different levels of consciousness, an idea which resonates across Chinese, Indian, Buddhist, and Vedantic systems of belief in such Chinese concepts of the five eyes of the mind and the Vedantic concept of the five sheaths of the body. In exploring these traditions, we will arrive at an awareness of what we are from the perspectives of our minds and bodies. Such a union of two major ancient Eastern traditions represents a holistic way of approaching the self, building a common language that supports the new science of consciousness.

The Buddhist concept of the five eyes[94] makes clear to us that there exists a multiplicity of worlds and forms of consciousness concealed beneath our visible reality. The emphasis on sight evokes the Chinese phrase *mingxinjianxing* (明心見性), which means "with a clear heart one sees the Self." By understanding these five eyes, we can better travel through the five levels of stages to harness our various states of consciousness.

The number five appears in Vedantic philosophy as well. According to ancient Vedantic philosophy—which informed much of Hindu and Yogic philosophy—each person has a physical, a subtle, and a causal body. These three bodies are supplemented by five interconnected and interdependent sheaths (or *koshas*),[95] which layer onto one another like nesting dolls, covering the Self (*Atman*). The Vedantic belief has it that for us to live a blissful life, one must take care of all these five *koshas*.

What helps restore us to that initial state of bliss is meditation, the ability to identify what exists in each *kosha* of our being. In so doing, we understand that our Self is irreducible to a single layer, enabling us to penetrate further and further into pure consciousness. Similarly, moving deeper into ourselves and journeying through the five eyes allows us to see much more, and thus to align ourselves more closely with the hidden realities of the universe.

Passing through these different eyes, koshas, and states of consciousness is also a journey through different worldviews to reach the ultimate worldview latent in all of us. This is met by the science of consciousness that seamlessly bridges physics and metaphysics into a complete, coherent whole. In this state we recognize the reality that we are spiritual rather than material beings, and we capitalize on the power to create our reality; when we know we can create this—if we believe we can—we will create it.

The journey through the eyes and koshas is also a journey of coming to realize the power of choice and belief. If we have faith in a vision, no difficulty is unsurpassable. We will harness infinite possibility and creativity to bring the new reality into being. These Eastern traditions corroborate the findings of the quantum paradigm about the concept of consciousness. From Daoist and Buddhist teachings, Chinese Traditional practices, Indian Yogic practices, and quantum science, the key is to note that humanity has the ability to choose.

The time is now, and we must make the right choice. We are at a crossroad, and we need a common language and a common belief system. Every moment is unknown because our choices affect the totality of the system; the system must constantly recalibrate itself to return to coherence. It is up to us, then, to choose to move into awakening and alignment of our mind and body; to integrate ourselves into the whole as we discover that all we are is consciousness, and that with our belief comes the power to create.

WHAT IS LIFE'S PURPOSE?

If we accept that we are consciousness, our purpose in life is to evolve—to propagate life and strive for alignment with the universe[96] in sync with its evolutionary energy and creation of life. We have followed our true nature and are in a state of well-being.

Because life is consciousness, we participate in creation. Given that the quantum worldview is one of oneness, coherence, and harmony, we are part of that evolution as well. Humanity's purpose is to evolve through ever higher states of consciousness to refine our systems into greater complexity and to expand into the next level of integration and oneness. We are here to actively participate in evolution, to transmute energy cycles from lower frequencies of energy into higher ones. This expressed in material form as a continuous process of separation and integration into a more wholistic, more complex structure of life.

An essential phrase from the *Daodejing* is 無為而無不為, which means "Do nothing and nothing will be left undone." This does not literally mean "do nothing," as some common misinterpretations have it. Instead, the Dao calls upon us to listen to and follow the flow of the universe so that all can be well. Everything is possible and achievable if it flows with the Dao. The message for us here is to be one with the world around us to understand that what is good for the whole is good for all its parts. Life's purpose, then, is indissociably linked to the impetus of the universe. Rather than enforcing our desires and will, we should strive to arrive at a place where our minds are at one with the universe. We do this because the universe invites us to the next level of integration. All creation stems from that foundation.

Our life purpose at present is to participate in the evolution and unification of a complex system of eight billion people, a new living system called humanity. This is the expression of oneness—the true unchangeable essence of reality—in honor of the well-being of the greater whole, and love and compassion is the guide for us to make that choice. Love enables us to purify our intentions so that we can harmonize and align with evolutionary processes larger than us and ultimately evolve on our journey to oneness. Love helps us to hear the calling of the cosmos and respond to the impetus of the universe, so we can be at one with the whole.

At the individual level, we can work at this greater purpose by cultivating an awareness of what we are, performing our role in evolution and expressing love to align ourselves with the oneness of the whole. For us to be able to fulfill our purpose, we must first be well individually for the next larger system to be well. In the quantum era, this exceeds mere wellness. It refers to a state of well-being.

WHAT ARE WE HERE TO DO?

As we see, humanity plays an active role in adding value to the evolution of life. In nature, everything has a role—the trees, the birds, and the bees all perform essential functions that contribute to the ecosystems to which they belong. The movements of humans, too, are imbricated and interconnected with all other organisms. Being able to understand and position ourselves in relation to our roles is a capacity unique to humankind because we are the most creative beings on Earth and have the greatest potential for self-awareness.

Worldviews can go in two directions; they can either divide or unite us. Without a doubt, every country and nation-state fear different worldviews because they appear to present a threat to their own integrity. Different worldviews lie at the heart of all the conflicts and wars that plague humanity today.

In the new quantum worldview, the common conviction that has the potential to unite us all is that life evolves toward oneness and we can add value to evolution. If we all believe this is the purpose of our existence, we can move from *I* to *we*—from the individual to the collective. After all, our beliefs form our worldviews inform our thoughts, frame our intentions, and determine our choice of action.

Believing in this principle means that individuals will not only create value for themselves but will try to add value to others' lives as well. Since no part can be well unless the whole system is healthy, we must find a way of reorganizing human society so that we can all evolve together in equitable ways. If we respond to our calling in the right spirit, the bigger picture of humanity will contextualize and ground all our actions and decisions, allowing us to understand our position within a system that goes beyond us. An era of shared abundance awaits us.

The ability to add something worthy to our own lives and to the lives of others might be the quality that distinguishes human beings from all other existing forms of life. However, we must first evolve our consciousness and evolve our awareness of the overall system of humanity.

The creation of our future hinges upon the conscious choices of each one of us. To be aligned with the universe and with the energy of the Dao, we must make the conscious choice to do so by collaborating with others to create the new system that will serve us in our evolved state of awakening. We must elevate our consciousness to shape our new future.

Moving Toward a Renewed Model of Well-Being

In Chinese systems of morality and ethics, well-being is when every system inherently calibrates and reconstitutes itself naturally—this is a journey into coherence and the full spectrum of flourishment. In the well-being state, every part evolves because the whole system is functioning. The term *ziyouzizai* (自由自在) captures the Chinese conception of well-being, referring to a state of being "free and present in the moment," open and without resistance to the natural forces of evolution.

Thus life is an expression of evolution and is inseparable from it. The purpose of life can be considered as striving for alignment with the Dao and the impetus of the universe—the evolutionary energy—to collaborate with all other living things for the flowering of even more life. This is known in Chinese as *tianrenheyi* (天人合一), a state of inner unity and oneness with the cosmos. In that state of unification, humanity returns to the source of its true nature of coherence that creates harmony and collaboration.

In the context of oneness with the cosmos, this is a state of continuous calibration of all systems to be coherent, a state in which everything is well. It means being carefree and living in the moment without resistance, as open to the rhythms of the universe as a newborn baby. In the same way that the trees, birds, and bees are aligned and collaborate with one another, we create life through collaboration as we naturally adjust to one another's movements and foster harmony. Unified with the cosmos in a condition of oneness and well-being, we forge a "blessed," *xingfu* (幸福) life, achieve unification with the universe, and reach a state of joy and bliss.

Human beings are perpetually engaged in a delicate dance with the external environment. However, only when we are in a state of inner unity can we live according to our true nature and purpose of being by listening to the impetus of the universe and making choices that are at one with the universe. Our physical, energetic, mental, and emotional bodies have self-regulating systems so that our mind, body, and spirit can be coherent and in harmony with our world.

Both science and ancient traditions share the same core tenet that well-being is never exclusively individual. It contributes equally to the whole and is influenced by the whole. We are a part of the larger system; therefore, no individual can be well until the whole system is well. Conversely, when the whole system is well, all parts within it, including human beings, will also be well.

Well-being is a state of coherence and harmony, and we need practices, measures, and strategies to ensure that our inner world responds in tandem with the outer world—in alignment with the cosmos. Based on their observation-based astronomy, the Mayan people have practices that align their living habits to the cycles of the sun and other celestial objects. In their cosmology these rituals and ceremonies guide the agricultural cycle of corn.[97] Similarly, *The Yellow Emperor's Inner Canon, Huangdineijing* (黃帝內經),[98] the Chinese foundation of life and medicine is a fundamental doctrinal source of modern traditional Chinese medicine. It documents a holistic approach to practices for well-being and can be thought of as the medicine for good living.

Our individual well-being should also not be equated with "wellness." The former is an aspirational state of life, while the latter is defined by the Global Wellness Institute (GWI) as the active pursuit of activities, choices, and lifestyles that lead to a state of holistic health.[99] According to the GWI, such wellness encompasses physical, mental, emotional, spiritual, social, and environmental health. Wellness is proactive in taking preventive measures regarding illness and is driven by self-responsibility. All of us need to take charge of our own wellness.

Therefore, wellness is only one part of well-being; it is a response to external stimuli. Well-being takes place on a far more profound level. It comes about when we can access our deep inner worlds to form a new worldview in unity with the greater whole. This intention, which characterizes a journey to well-being, is driven not by the external environment but by an internal expression of pure love, which is our nature.

The opposite of wellness is sickness, defined by both ancient Chinese thought and Buddhist teachings as being ignorant. The Daodejing addresses the difference between well-being and sickness in this way:

> To know what you don't know, is best.
> To not know, but believe yourself to know, is to have sickness.
> Sages do not become sick because they know what sickness is and so avoid it.
> Treating sickness as sickness is the only way to avoid sickness.[100]

The medicine of life keeps human beings on the path of alignment to our true nature of being, preserving our authenticity. Awakening into a new awareness, we collaborate and create. These are practices or interventions that we cultivate that redirects our decisions and actions to be in alignment with natural forces of evolution—the Dao or in scientific thought is known as the energy of the universe. It increases our awareness that shifts our consciousness of life, so that we can transcend ignorance. From this space, we are empowered to move toward alignment to oneness and whole system flourishment.

Daoist and Buddhist teachings point to ignorance[101] as the source of all sickness, the root cause of all *Dukkha* (suffering and pain). In a state of ignorance, we are unconscious of our true purpose of life—thus unable to access the inner unity or wisdom to make the right choices for ourselves. We can only avoid sickness by increasing our awareness and elevating our consciousness of life. This is a journey of life learning, beyond an intellectual understanding of life and well-being, that can translate into an ability to make judicious and informed choices about how we live.

Human desire is at the core of ignorance and sickness. It interferes with our true nature and circumscribes our horizons of possibility, imposing limits on our beliefs, worldviews, intentions, and thoughts. When we are misaligned with nature and the Dao, we make decisions that are incongruent with the rhythms of the universe, resulting in deep imbalance and pain.

The Four Noble Truths of Buddhist teaching is that the origin of all pain and suffering in this lifetime is human desire. We can stop this suffering only by eliminating and detaching ourselves from that desire. It is our ignorance that has distorted our ability to discern between wants and needs, leading to misguided choices. Because of our ignorance caused by foolish desires, we want things that we do not need and overlook the things that we *do* need. Ignorance is a poison that produces mindsets of greed, avarice, and acquisitiveness. Only by eliminating ignorance can we learn to choose with wisdom to configure our own lives to meet our real needs.

In this modern affluent world, we are driven by our self-focused, endless material desires to want more and more accumulation of wealth. We remain trapped in our material consciousness and neglect our true needs and desires. What holds us back from making the right choices is our level of consciousness.

Ignorance and consciousness exist on a continuum. The more conscious we are, the less ignorant we become. To move closer to consciousness means to move away from ignorance.

There is perhaps no graver error than hubris and the pretense of knowledge—to make a show of knowing what one does not know. Conversely, those regarded as sages are those with the wisdom, vigilance, and self-awareness to treat their own symptoms of sickness and make the right choices for their own well-being. Humanity's true medicine is self-cultivation to elevate our consciousness so that our choices are in sync with the forces of evolution.

Human beings are driven by the aspiration to flourish and to create, but we are also the greatest agents of destruction. Our thinking has been so dominated by the need to accumulate wealth and power that we have exploited Earth's resources and rendered extinct much of our planet's wildlife and biodiversity. This is evidence that we do not yet understand the systemic nature of life, that our state of consciousness is not evolved enough for us to act for the greater good. The heart of humanity's problems is our focus on what we want at the expense of what we need. We mistakenly believe that nature belongs to us and forget that we can only be well when everything around us is also well.

But all is not doom and gloom. Thankfully, there are signs that we are awakening and gradually becoming aware of the truth that we are spiritual beings in a material form. Consciousness is the foundation of our creativity, the means by which we can come into alignment with the rhythms of the universe. Shifting consciousness is our way forward.

As we awaken to this new quantum understanding, and as we become aware of and embrace our role in the process of evolution, how do we align ourselves to the movements of the whole? In the quantum field, truth is coherent, and the nature of coherence is to return to its source.

Since we have the ability to make choices, and we must seize the opportunities presented to us to evolve our consciousness of life. Because each future moment is unknown, humanity can either spiral our consciousness upward or downward—seeking coherence or conversely flailing into destruction. We have the power of this choice in our hands.

Moving from an era of material separation into one driven by the energy of unification and oneness, our era of awakening echoes the United Nations' call for a new well-being and happiness economic paradigm. Now, indeed, is the time to unite all our disparate worldviews.

What we need is one common worldview, one common ground, for us to have common sense, so we put together common effort to resolve our common challenges. In the absence of a unified worldview, there would be no commonality among us.

Living Well to Achieve Mindful Living

Well-being is a state of coherence and harmony between our inner world and outer worlds. Conversely, ignorance of who we are is the source of our suffering. If stress is the origin of our illness, awakening and alignment with our true nature is the medicine. The success of our lives depends on how we live it. When we live in alignment with our true nature, we will add value to life, connect with the holistic system, and evolve. Joy and happiness will come from healthy relationships with ourselves, people, and nature.

In the new era, a new concept of living and culture will be forged, centered around well-being and happiness. Through a process of awakening, aligning, collaborating, and creating, we will learn life from inside out, journeying inward to discover that the true calling of our lives is a state of connection and oneness with the cosmos. This process is one of lifelong learning, as life is everything. Our love for life and living will surpass our desire for indulgence and heighten our sensitivity to sustainability challenges, thus catalyzing the evolutionary energy for the flourishing of all.

Consequently, our living habits will change as we move from mere survival and wasteful indulgence to living lives flourishing with meaning and purpose. As this well-being and happiness economy arises, a whole new infrastructure will come into being. This economy, systemic and holistic, will integrate humanism, socialism, and capitalism into one whole life-ism—where Gross Domestic Product will give way to Gross National Happiness. In place of the wasteful indulgence and depletions that characterized the era of consumerism, we will learn to live in harmony with nature and the environment, respecting Mother Earth and collaborating to add value to life.

Our education and healthcare systems will evolve. Education—the foundation of knowledge, skills, and competencies—will be reoriented to prioritize learning about life. Character building will be its emphasis, inculcating responsibility in every individual as a member of civil society and as a human being. Healthcare will be integrated into a new wellness system where self-care and communal care constitute the foundation of holistic well-being. Self-care will play a pivotal role in physical, emotional, and spiritual wellness centered around a change in living habits that cultivate and nourish one's own well-being.

A new way of interacting and relating will facilitate the convergence of communities' living, working, and recreation activities. The emergence of community centers designed like extended family living rooms will facilitate this form of interaction that integrates learning, care, and entertainment. It will house activities that celebrate life, such as music, arts, reading, outdoor activities for connection with nature that will transform the way we connect with ourselves, others, and nature—ultimately discovering the joy, grace, and gratitude of life. Such infrastructures will support communal, intergenerational cohabitation.

Our relationship with food will also change because plant-based diets will predominate. Food will be cultivated in closer proximity to the community, making it accessible at low costs to all members of the community. At the same time, responsible cultivation will contribute toward restoring the environment and its biodiversity.

City and urban living will be redesigned. In place of present-day models will arise city infrastructures that facilitate dispersed living arrangements in urban nodes with lower population densities that are closer to each other. High-speed trains and other efficient modes of transportation will connect these urban nodes into a collective urban system of living, a design that resembles a spiderweb and a honeycomb. Such a design will free up arable land in between the urban nodes that can be used for community farming and nature reserves. Travel patterns will change to longer-stay, shorter-distance, which will reduce carbon footprint.

Employment patterns will consequently shift as a result, enabling individuals and communal systems to assume larger roles in this new economic model. New forms of employment and income-generating activities will arise, giving everyone flexibility and autonomy in how they add value to the world around them. Self-employment and entrepreneurs will present themselves to serve community needs.

As a result of this, individuals and communities will feel empowered to take responsibility for their own needs, rather than relying on traditional institutions for platforms and resources. Indeed, this new economic structure will thrive precisely because of its people-centered nature. Supply and demand will become more localized, as people live in closer proximity to the markets that produce the food they consume and the resources they use.

Systems of governance will serve as a guardian of social stability, functioning as a check-and-balance system instead of being a watchdog. Public systems will be designed to be responsible for the building and maintenance and safeguarding the critical areas against potential disruptions to the thriving and flourishing of all systems. A central umbrella will be needed to manage research and development in new technologies, business ethics and wealth distribution, education and healthcare, currency and finance, as well as environmental management systems.

Governments will co-invest with businesses in a symbiotic manner as they collaborate to inform policy and social needs. Businesses will be the integrator for profit, nonprofit, and impact investment institutions as one holistic business model. With individuals and communal systems taking greater ownership, checks and balances on business ethics will come from within the system as Environment, Social and Governance (ESG) and impact investments will gain ascendance in measuring business performance.

New technologies will play an essential role in enabling the redesign and construction of this well-being and happiness economy. From social media to new computing power increasing the speed and complexity of computing to virtual and augmented reality and the metaverse, as well as new technologies in healthcare and energy generation. These will truly be a game changer in this transformation.

This is the new way of living, replete with new habits, a new mindset, a new culture, and a new worldview driving a new well-being and happiness economy. Most importantly, we must make that one choice to take the journey inward into our inner world.

Consciousness—A Journey into Our Inner World

We will write a new narrative of life that encapsulates the new mode of living we desire and imagine. This is the basis for everything we will build, and we can consciously choose how we live. In an era of well-being and happiness our lives will be journeys that promote unification and oneness with everything. Actions will be collaborative in nature, adding value to whole systems. Actions fomenting separation and fragmentation will naturally cease to exist when we discover the true purpose of our lives.

It is inherent in human nature to seek well-being, which is a state of oneness through connection and harmony within ourselves, our environment, and all the systems within it. Internal harmony is needed so that we can live in coherence with ourselves and with our environments. This inner peace will be expressed as love for family, company, society, and environment.

This inner peace can be found when we take the journey inward. Embarking on a journey to our inner world is self-cultivation; it transforms the way we see the world and our purpose in life. We will discover that the power and authority to act comes from within, and we exist so we can create and add value to the system—this is the new quantum paradigm manifested as well-being and happiness. This is the new consciousness in life, in which nothing stays as the status quo, and life as a whole will be well when we actively participate in this dance of continuous evolution.

Creativity will emerge from these new states of consciousness, and it is the hallmark of the quantum leadership journey. When rewriting our narratives of life and rethinking how we live to add value to life and all systems, we will reclaim consciousness as the mother of all capital, the solution to all our challenges. Living in this new well-being state where higher consciousness prevails, we will find our intentions aligned with our natures as we participate actively in adding value to life. We will be happier and healthier beings leading purposeful lives in the era of mindful living.

ON LEADERSHIP AND MANAGEMENT

Leaders in the well-being and happiness era will be naturally selected by their consciousness and calling. Their role is to build the leadership and to bring about the journey of awakening aligning collaborating and creating. This requires an internal authority to act authentically when they make the choice to journey inward, renew their consciousness, and bring out latent qualities of creativity from within.

Leaders have been shaping the organization of systems for centuries and managing the evolution of bigger and more complex systems. Leadership is an energy like an attractor. When in its natural flow of creation, it attracts others onto its "ship" to sail in the same direction, seeking coherence and harmony. As different forms of leadership become connected in an intricate network, the power of self-management will arise.

In the era of well-being and happiness, management is stewardship. It is an ethical and responsible way to effectively develop and deploy entrusted resources and to achieve an agreed set of objectives under the guidance of the bigger mission and vision. The new consciousness of life will inform how management adds value to the evolving system of life.

As needs evolve and worldviews shift, systems will become more complex and organizations will expand. The movement toward connecting bigger and more complex systems will integrate them into networks, which are conglomeration of agile, interconnected structures constantly co-creating and collaborating with one another. A network system is akin to a web of roles and relationships that overlays and supersedes conventional systems of hierarchy. In this network, management will take a different shape because it is relational, no longer linear or driven by a particular process.

Network systems are self-organizing, like a dance into which everyone naturally fits, forming a living system in which all parts organically align with one another to create coherence. Guided by the larger evolving purpose that seeks harmony and coherence, self-organizing systems testify to the fact that leadership is an energy, and management is self-driven.

The self-organization of network systems finds a parallel in nature in the example of bees that naturally reorganize themselves despite disturbances. The human body, with its extraordinarily complex network of fifty trillion cells, also represents a microcosm of such a system, with all its individual parts healthily collaborating and creating in alignment with the direction of evolution. Every unique part contributes in its own way toward a common goal. The well-being and happiness era, then, is merely the self-organization of humankind, a shift into a living system that connects all life on Earth into a cohesive and harmonious whole called humanity.

ADDING VALUE TO LIFE AND A NEW MEASUREMENT OF SUCCESS AND HAPPINESS

To live harmoniously in the unified system of humanity, composed of nearly eight billion people, is to live mindfully—with ourselves, our families, and others within the natural environment. In such a world, where collective needs and well-being are guided by decision-making patterns, our ingrained behaviors of overconsumption need to be addressed and reshaped. The emphasis on the prosperity and flourishing of all life will compel a total rethinking of the materialistic desires and the hierarchies of status and worth generated by a market economy.

This new vision of the future is nothing short of a systemic transformation, a redefinition of all systems—from the concepts of economics itself to all types of infrastructure. Imagine a world where happiness fostered through education and learning, healthcare and wellness, and community involvement become the goals we collectively seek to attain. The outdated and conventional matrices of success and value will fall to the wayside. All these interconnected systems working in tandem with one another will create a lifestyle of a harmonious relationship between humanity and the earth, between different communities, and within ourselves.

This new life revolving around internal exploration, creativity, and harmony will empower us all with an inner authority to choose the lives we want to live rather than seeking external approval and validation for intensely personal choices. New belief and value systems grounded in unification, integration, and collectivity will inform our intentions, shape the decisions we make and the actions we take. We will trust that the results will be as they should be—and we will greet the unfolding of events with peaceful acceptance and equanimity.

Consequently, measurements of success and happiness can no longer be exemplified in the symbols of earlier times. In place of the outmoded definitions of productivity and results-focused metrics so prominent in the era of industrialization, a desire for alignment and coherence will guide our actions and serve as the matrix by which happiness can be evaluated.

In a nutshell, rather than being assessed for what we are *doing*, we will learn to concentrate our energies on our *being*, choosing an inward spiritual journey to accumulate non-material wealth over outward markers of wealth and success. With these reorientations, we will nurture an inner world and impact the world outside of us.

A Design for the Economy of Well-Being and Happiness

As we build a new worldview and a new culture, a wholly new design will be needed. This is a systemic reconstruction rather than a cosmetic renovation as we are building a new system with new software and new infrastructures that support the well-being and happiness economy.

On Education and Learning

The concept of education in an age of well-being will focus on our inner journey to learn life. The responsibility for shaping the next generation will be collectively borne by parents, communities, government, and the teaching community—this is also the community's own learning journey. When we engage in the self-cultivation that attends an inward journey, we will learn to be ethical, responsible, and creative in adding value to the living system of happiness and well-being. Shifting our thinking to growth and abundance, we will flourish and invent new possibilities, away from fixed and scarcity mindsets.

The bedrock for education in the new era is the inculcation of healthy relationships, moral character, and what it means to be human. Its goal is the cultivation of stewards who are invested in adding value to build a harmonious civil society. Skills and knowledge from the liberal arts, such as the creativity needed for self-actualization, will displace the former emphasis on training technicians with the specialization and technical know-how to operate mechanistic systems—much of which will be taken over by machines. When we invest in building civil society, our being will inform our doing.

The system will nurture stewards who are concerned with building a healthier community with longer life expectancies and higher quality of life. Stewardship is an attitude, a sense of responsibility that permeates beyond the social system to integrate the environment as one living system. A steward is someone who can demonstrate in his actions the ethics and responsibility that comes with being a global citizen capable of directing all the entrusted resources into serving the common good.

Learning and education in the age of well-being will primarily be aimed at nurturing healthy relationships to build one global village with a common language and worldview. Lifelong learning is a journey where education starts from a young age to embed knowledge, expose children to important experiences, and nurture the development of global citizens. This is a journey to new consciousness—the wisdom to create solutions for sustaining a better, more equal, and integrated world. Learning is the solution to challenges arising from separating and fragmenting humanity along ethnic, religious, and political lines in the old paradigm.

Character development, will be the cornerstone of this paradigm of learning. This system reorientates education and learning to focus on liberal arts and teaching self-actualization skills—how to choose awakening, relationship, and creativity, as well as how to nurture the qualities of grace, gratitude, and joy. Learning activities around arts and music, along with myriad spiritual practices such as mindfulness, will gain ascendancy because of this new pedagogical focus. By planting the seed at an early age, education allows this trajectory of character development to gain the force of habit.

Responsibility for learning will be assumed by families as well. Parents, in particular, play a primary role in cultivating the new belief and value systems. Cultivating an inward journey from a young age will solidify into habits, patterns, and will eventually form personalities. Such a system would cultivate personalities for whom stewardship and responsibility are second nature. Alongside practices of mindfulness and stillness, the education and learning system will instill social skills of collaboration, cooperation, and co-creating wisdom. With developments in neuroscience and research in neuroplasticity, new pedagogies will focus on embedding awareness as a core learning output needed for the growth of the creative mind.

The concept of home, *jia* (家), will be redefined, expanding beyond our immediate biological family to include our community and wider social relationships—truly bearing out the truth of the maxim that "I can only be well when everything around me is well, and everything around me can only be well when I am well."

Learning will also be a communal responsibility in this new era. Group learning will provide support and encourage accountability for commitments to growth. Integrated as an indispensable part of living, learning will be integrated into group and community living. This form of learning will develop relationships, and inform the way we connect, relate, and create at home, at work, in the community and with the larger environment.

Because learning is continuous throughout life, it will expand beyond the physical space of home, school, or community. Instead, it will happen everywhere, anywhere, and anytime—blurring the boundaries that are used to define learning. Community centers will serve as our extended living space like living rooms for communal engagement in recreation, our work, and socialization while our homes remain refuges of safety, security, and intimacy.

These community centers will provide numerous opportunities for learning while also including entertainment and social activities, living out a system where needs are provided by the community and for the community. Neighbors will spend time with one another, sharing wisdom and co-creating activities that fit specific needs in their lives. It is the essence of communal learning to be supported by an extended family, a community beyond blood ties, and the integration of social, economic, and cultural activities into its midst.

The integrated facilities for living, working, and playing centered around the community center will encourage cohesion and harmony in each community. Common values and habits will be collectively developed and refined, paving the way for a common worldview cultivated from a lifelong journey of inner exploration.

In the well-being and happiness era, we will prize our commonalities and embrace our differences, naturally resolving conflict. The emergence of a culture of stewardship and responsibility seeded by the new education and learning system will naturally bring out the latent creativity deep within us—our key asset in this new quantum age.

On Healthcare, Life Science, and Integrated Medicine

In parallel to changes in education, paradigm shifts in healthcare will take place. Integrated and holistic medicines will dominate healthcare in the well-being economy with medical care performed by an extended group of health professionals that includes doctors, nutritionists, molecular biologists, and holistic doctors.

Shifts in education and learning will promulgate the knowledge needed for self-care. Self-care, indeed, will become the responsibility of every individual; everyone must take ownership of their own health. Learning and healthcare are indissociably intertwined as the cultivation of one's own well-being translates into the good health and happiness that enable us to work and live in harmony with others. In fact, life will be oriented around the community centers with integrated healthcare centers that can be readily accessed as needed. Healing, learning, and self-care are different facets of the same crystal.

The true meaning of wellness transcends mere physical health; wellness encompasses much more than having a body without illness. Instead, it is a complete integration of mind, body, and spirit, and includes the ethics and relationships we form with people and systems. Only with a holistic sense of health can we understand the essential maxim: Life is everything and everything is life.

The Daodejing teaches that the origin of all illness—which can be physical, mental, or psychological—begins with ignorance.[102] Such ignorance is more than not knowing. If one knows that one does not know, this creates a condition that can be remedied by learning. The worst situation is when one does not know this and believes otherwise. In such a state, sickness will arise. The new healthcare system will be an ecosystem of knowledge, learning, practice, and support for holistic self-care of the mind, body, and spirit that provides us with the conditions to thrive and flourish in life.

Our bodies are mysterious, complex, and powerful self-healing machines; they are uniquely efficient pharmaceutical factories that sustain and regulate themselves. Learning how to activate our internal healing system through self-care is our best gift to our health, endowing us with the ability to listen and respond to the complex needs of our whole system. While we would, of course, still need medicine to stimulate our body's self-healing, medicine alone will not heal us.

As we awaken to the reality that well-being is feeling a state of balance and harmony we see that healing is the process in which mind, body, and spirit strive for coherence. Indeed, the support we receive from this new ecosystem of healing that threads through healthcare education and wellness practices presents us with the solution to the current crisis in healthcare posed by an aging global population.

Healthcare starts with self-care. Staying true to the well-being era, self-care is based on holism and oneness of the mind, body, and spirit. For more than two thousand five hundred years, traditional Chinese medicine has evolved based on exactly this principle of viewing human beings as integrated mind-body-spirit entities. In contrast, the epistemological assumption of Western medicine relies in part on the germ theory of disease, which states that many diseases are caused by invisible microorganisms resulting in different modes of healing human bodies. Other forms of traditional medicine[103] besides traditional Chinese medicine have also offered us this integrated wisdom. It is noteworthy that traditional medicine is gaining popularity and widespread acceptance in the modern world.

The application of integrative medicine will also expand to include different modalities of healing and care in the science of consciousness. Of course, medicine is a crucial part of science and will remain relevant in healing our physical bodies and will continue to play an important role in the well-being economy. However, medicine will be integrated with medical care as one holistic wellness ecosystem for healthy living. This broadened definition of healing will be the solution to our present healthcare challenges.

The United States spends around 17 percent of its total GDP on medical care.[104] In most countries, medical spending in the last twelve months of life accounts for approximately 8–11 percent of aggregate medical spending.[105] Without any changes in lifestyle, this cost will continue to rise. According to World Population Prospects 2019,[106] one in six people in the world will be over the age of 65 by 2050, up from one in eleven in 2019.

Self-care will herald healthy lifestyles and an improved quality of life. This will reduce healthcare costs and the strain that these pose to society. Healthcare is a big-ticket item, a system that needs to be revamped everywhere and reoriented with the concept of self-care as a priority. Rather than resolving health problems when they arise, self-care is an act of nourishment, focusing on the way we live in the world and seeing all aspects of our integrated lives as connected to our health and wellness.

In this system of self-care based on holism, everything impacts everything else. We cannot detach ourselves from this holistic system; when we act for the greater good of the collective, it also benefits us.

Traditional practices of wisdom will form the core of self-care, while medical care will play a supporting role to provide solutions for acute conditions in the well-being era.

Governments will continue to be responsible for providing care and ensuring that it is accessible to the community. Larger, more complex, and specialized medical facilities can be built to be connected to an emergency medical transport system. Communities will be able to access and rely on larger systems of medical care as the need arises. However, the extent of this need will be substantially reduced with the advent and proliferation of self-care. The pharmaceutical industry, too, can be centrally controlled and managed through a transparent system of governance to provide medicine as needed at a cost accessible to everyone.

This new form of healthcare revolving around self-care and the integration of the human body with its environment will be grounded in the belief that everything is holistic and part of life. At the same time, the future of healthcare and medicine will not sacrifice efficiency or efficacy because self-care will free up huge amounts of money for reallocation to other needs in the emerging well-being and happiness economy.

SELF-ACTUALIZATION IS SELF-CULTIVATION

All these changes in our conceptualization of education and healthcare will stimulate a holistic integration of life into communal systems, strengthening and reaffirming relationships and consequently building healthier communities. Activities that celebrate life—such as music, arts, reading and outdoor activities for connection with nature—will transform the way we connect with ourselves, others, and nature, allowing us to ultimately discover the joy, grace, and gratitude of life. Forms of entertainment will also align with these activities of self-actualization.

Families will start living together again and treasuring one another's physical presence. Relationships will be at the center of our lives.

Multiple generations living under one roof will foster a nurturing environment for the younger generations to mature while providing the older generations with a space to age gracefully, happily, and with dignity.

Stemming from the consciousness of our inner being, we will develop different practices for our well-being. On top of the community centers that support communal interactions across generations and social classes, the culture of well-being will be invested in activities of self-actualization such as music, chess, literature, art, and poetry. These pursuits will gain prominence as conduits by which we can celebrate and express the beauty and meaning of our lives. In doing so, we will solidify bonds within communities, creating a sense of common cultural identity and fulfilling our inherent need for social engagement.

Ancient Chinese practices of refinement and cultivation offer the *Scholar's Eight Arts of Living.* These practices are music, chess, calligraphy, painting, poetry, wine education, flower arrangement, and tea ceremonies (琴棋書畫, 詩酒花茶). We will revive these ancient and traditional practices that impart stillness and peace in the hearts of those who practice them. These practices manifest inner creativity and alter human desires, thus creating the conditions for a redefinition of economic activities that prioritizes well-being and happiness.

With our worldview of holism, we will access new possibilities and choices for actions and behaviors, forming one axis around which a communal identity can be built. Activities that connect us to one another and to our environments will gain in popularity. These include group activities of yoga, tai chi, martial arts that facilitate connections between mind and body.

We will also have a greater interest in engaging in activities that bring us into closer proximity with nature, such as food cultivation, hiking, camping, and other outdoor activities. We will see our multiple talents put to work as we channel our energies into a multitude of value-adding activities in different professions, interests, and projects.

As the concept of well-being becomes global, there will be simply one human community. However, this is far from a homogenized, standardized unit of life. Instead, the gifts and talents individuals offer and unique cultural novelties of local customs and rituals will continue to be cherished as essential for the whole system to flourish. Creativity springing from the stewardship of our separate parts in service of the collective whole, will allow all of the systems within communities to thrive and prosper.

Rituals, expressions of culture, and celebrations of life will remain rooted in the communities in which they originate. The recognition of this profoundly beautiful diversity and the experience of cross-cultural travel through many geographical boundaries will allow us to share and celebrate the diversity that makes us all human, unique, and yet connected to the inseparability of the part from the whole.

On Food

The new age of well-being will also see the extension of self-care to self-sufficiency in the provision of food and in our relationship with food. Food supply chains and production processes will revolve around communal markets and local communities. Communal farming will return, and the logistics of food production will change.

As we learn to live in attunement with the rhythms of the holistic universe, we will change the way we eat and sleep. For a long time, we have been consuming food that is far from natural, when it is heavily processed, genetically modified, and tainted with chemicals and fertilizers. In the frenetic pace of our modern lives, eating food from fast-food chains and convenience stores is frequently the most convenient and viable option. We often do not consciously seek out healthier, more nutritious meals for ourselves.

In addition to these habits, we are rarely mindful of how food is produced or how it ends up on our plates; nor do we pay attention to the invisible cruelty that characterizes the unethical processes by which animals are slaughtered to produce meat. The industrialized food system[107] is inefficient and necessitates an extravagant amount of waste, increasing real cost to consumers and exacerbating environmental destruction. Our diets are no longer a means of connection to nature; instead, chemical, and industrial processes are invading our bodies.

Over time, these changes have impacted everything from our life expectancy to our average height and weight. Among diverse factors that contribute to human aging and mortality, mitochondrial dysfunction[108] has emerged as one of the key hallmarks of the aging process and is linked to the development of numerous age-related pathologies. Mitochondria[109] are vital for life since these organelles serve as the powerhouse or energy currency of cells. Mitochondria generate energy in the form of adenosine triphosphate by breaking down food. The role of this in aging was first proposed more than 40 years ago by Denham Harman.[110]

With all this in mind, a sustainable way of cultivating, planting, harvesting, cooking and eating that is more connected to our natural diets must be the way forward in the well-being and happiness economy. Food will be cultivated in closer proximity to the markets of people that consume them—on arable land in between urban nodes in the spiderweb-honeycomb infrastructure (described below), in and around homes, including rooftop farms. The food we eat can be organic, fresh, and nutritious without us having to worry about the prohibitive costs of production.

What we eat directly affects our lives. Our brains are always switched on, taking care of all our thoughts and movements and dictating each breath and heartbeat 24/7, even while we are asleep. This means that our brain requires a constant supply of fuel that comes from the foods we eat. What is in that fuel makes all the difference. Put simply, what we eat directly affects the structure and function of our brain and, ultimately, our mood.

It is important for all energies in a system to be aligned, and food is energy in digestible form. The closer we are to the origins of life, the better off we are in terms of integration with nature. When we produce and consume food that is aligned with nature and our natural diets, our bodies will naturally absorb and incorporate the food with greater effectiveness.

As Thích Nhất Hạnh,[111] the Zen Buddhist master says, "When practiced to its fullest, mindful eating turns a simple meal into a spiritual experience giving us a deep appreciation of all that went into the meal's creation as well a deep understanding of the relationship between the food on our table, our own health, and our planet's health."[112]

We achieve this when we become mindful of the processes and relationships entailed in the creation of food. In the well-being and happiness economy, the responsibility for feeding the entirety of humanity is borne by communities. As we live mindfully, we gradually amend our dietary need. Soon enough we find ourselves consuming more plant-based foods that supply our bodies with better and cleaner energy, ensuring environmental sustainability. An increasing number of people are transitioning to organic plant-based diets with compassionately produced meat.[113]

We have the choice of our diets, and they will necessarily vary according to our body types and natural preferences. While meat will probably remain a part of some people's diets, the point is that we ought to be more mindful and aware of how the food we eat ends up on our plates. Our diets, in fact, are probably the clearest illustration of how interconnected we are to nature, for it is through our diets that connections are forged, inextricably binding together our lives, our bodies, and the natural environments that we inhabit.

In the well-being era, because of the integrations effected between different systems, we will have access to a much wider range of choices to calibrate our diets with our wellness and the planet's wellness. Communal, urban, and rooftop farms, and alternative collective approaches to growing, preparing, and consuming food will be the norm in this era.

We are built and sustained by food; food is the fuel that lies at the heart of life. To eat mindfully is a form of self-care; it allows our bodies to absorb necessary nutrients for the nourishment of our brains and different parts of the body. These nutrients we get from food serve as the building blocks for more complex proteins that construct healthy tissues, regulate our sleep, and ensure our well-being.

As we align our eating patterns with our circadian rhythms—the innate 24-hour cycles that signal to our bodies when to wake up—our bodies will be able to attain optimal functioning. We will have freedom to choose for ourselves what and when we want to eat, so we will build and sustain healthy bodies and brains for mindful living in the new era of well-being and happiness.

Infrastructure Design and Planning for Living in a New Era

As we shift to living in communities closer to nature, new infrastructures, logistics, and forms of transportation must be designed and built. Urban planning will see a spread of urban nodes with high-speed train connections in a hub-and-spoke design that can be multiplied and expanded, to resemble an intricate spiderweb and a honeycomb. This design efficiently integrates different systems for living in an age of well-being, sustaining a low carbon footprint while improving accessibility for everyone. We will be able to live in nature while having access to different urban nodes for work, play, and social connection.

Urban Nodes Design for a Relational Lifestyle

We are inherently relational beings,[114] naturally gravitating to social engagement and communal living. The new era of well-being and happiness will be built around this principle of viewing life as an ongoing process of self-cultivation and shifting in consciousness for the ultimate purpose of union with everything around us. This union, in concrete terms, is living in harmony with the self, family, others, and nature. A more efficient infrastructural design, then, is necessary to support community engagement, an efficient system where production and the servicing of needs are closer to the market.

Currently, the urban-rural designs that have emerged from previous eras of industrialization with high infrastructure and population density in urban areas is unsustainable. The set-up is complicated and expensive, characterized by high-rise housing, inefficient transport systems, high levels of energy consumption, expensive environmental management, and unequal access to social services such as healthcare and education.

Things have not always been this way. Urbanization[115] is a relatively new development in human history. For a long time, communities lived in low-density centers. In a 2014 report, the UN Department of Economic and Social Affairs mentioned that 54 percent of the world's population lived in urban areas, a proportion that is expected to increase to 66 percent by 2050.[116] In the 1960s, only one in every three people lived in urban areas, while in the 1800s this number was a mere 10 percent. Urbanization was set up to sustain industrialization and transformed the way people lived and worked, as infrastructure and networks were designed to support those needs.

While the urban-rural system of the present era served its function well, it is no longer sustainable. The well-being and happiness economy needs a new design structure that enables a generative, self-servicing, responsible community with intimate ties to nature. The structure must be cost-effective, accessible to the community, and supportive of well-being. A tightly connected system will reduce waste as it integrates activities of our daily lives. Collectively, this urban hub design will form smaller communities near each other.

These smaller self-sustaining communities are bound together by a common purpose and will be self-governing as they safeguard their collective needs. They jointly contribute to the community's economic, social, and environmental development and are functionally and socially bound by cooperative living. In the stability of such a community, we can relax in the comfort of home, where familiarity and safety reign; within such an environment we nurture our closest and most endearing relationships with our families and members of our communities.

The very relationship between urban and rural areas will be redefined, as sustainability becomes the key priority of urban planning and infrastructural design. The size of each urban node will be context-dependent, influenced by the extent to which services can be distributed. Urban nodes with smaller populations and more decentralized arrangements can benefit from a higher quality of life, enjoying lower land and property costs than those living in larger urban nodes. Each urban node would be manicured and vibrant. Orderliness, with spacious, sustainable installations of both parks and recreational areas will quite literally break up the concrete and asphalt density that pervades most modern cities.

These urban nodes will be connected to larger hubs, forming an extensive and intricate web, allowing lower-density clusters of urban living to become the new norm. Major cities, home to tens of millions of people, will be redesigned and distributed across a myriad of communities, while the land between urban nodes can be used efficiently for communal economic activities, such as food cultivation, and family-friendly, biodiverse parks and nature reserves. Urban spaces will primarily serve as meet-and-greet hubs, avenues for social interaction and recreational activities. Travel patterns will change as social and business travel needs will reduce. Any travel will be for more extended periods and shorter distances.

Through these efforts, the cost-of-living will be significantly reduced, while the quality of life will be heightened. Accommodation, so heavy a burden in the industrial era, will become much more affordable along with other basic needs, such as healthy food for healthy minds and bodies. Electrosmog and other polluting electromagnetic fields will be reduced in urban nodes with lower population densities, contributing to better health and wellness.

This is the new way of life; cities will gradually adopt and shift to these dispersed living patterns in the well-being and happiness economy. Indeed, the speed of such transformations has unquestionably been accelerated by the pandemic. Only a small critical mass is required to push the system over the tipping point. Once that happens, many aspects of our lives will change. Ultimately, we will live more serenely and be happier, healthier, and more productive.

A Spiderweb-Honeycomb Design

Infrastructure in the new era will be redesigned as a hub-and-spoke system to meet the physical, social, and communicative needs of urban nodes as one living system. This design will create an environment in which our new narratives of life and well-being can be fully and creatively expressed. The infrastructure for this living system must work in concert to promote harmony throughout different concentric circles of existence with oneself, others, and the environment for overall well-being. This replaces the design from past eras of industrialization of high-density urban cities, a soulless and dehumanizing design for efficiency and productivity.

The future lifestyle will require community-centered dispersed living arrangements where environment and humanity are inseparable parts of a larger whole. Infrastructure, design, and urban planning will all reflect a central worldview founded upon the integration of humanity and the natural world. At the same time, the system should remain flexible to allow for continual adjustments to contextual, cultural, and social specificities.

The new setup contains an infrastructure that favors the dispersal of populations. Rather than suburban sprawl, the central principle is a well-planned spiderweb network of urban nodes, connected by an efficient, well-managed inter-city transportation systems of rail

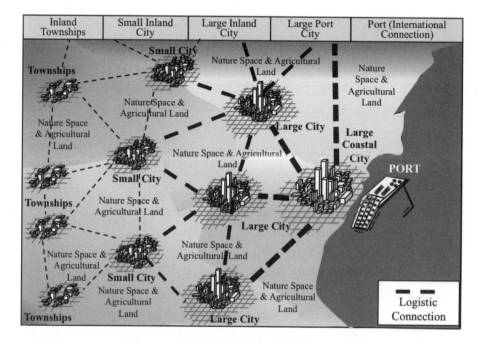

Inland Townships	Small Inland City	Large Inland City	Large Port City	Port (International Connection)

SPIDERWEB-HONEYCOMB SYSTEM

and road connections. This systemic design resembles spiderwebs and honeycombs in nature and is, thus referred to as the spiderweb-honeycomb system.

The spiderweb-honeycomb system design of urban planning would integrate society, industry, and agriculture and allow the blending of human life into the natural world. The population density will be spread out across nature and rural, suburban, and urban nodes. With smaller communal nodes closer to each other, the open land between nodes is freed up for communal, social, economic, and nature activities.

The land can also be utilized as zones for manufacturing and recreation, creating a system capable of responding effectively to the specific needs of each community. As land is more effectively utilized, supply will grow closer to demand, reducing logistical stresses and encouraging entrepreneurship and different forms of employment within the community.

While communal nodes will be self-sustaining, they will also be close to neighboring nodes, permitting easy access and support between communities for larger or more sophisticated needs such as medical care and education. With the potential for different communities to be responsive to each other's needs, the space for creativity and collaboration will expand. As time passes, the people living in these systems will likely gain more confidence in the self-sufficiency of each node, heightening the legitimacy of the supply system.

Living in collaboration with nature, we integrate the benefits of the natural world into the very workings of our own systems, allowing for natural healing and regeneration. The well-being economy will actively take advantage of new technologies to drive clean power, sustainable manufacturing, and industrial activities with better, more attentive approaches to environmental management.

This spiderweb-honeycomb design is more efficient and sustainable than big city configurations. One example can be found in China, which is the comprehensive rail network with an 8×8 grid of main corridors supported by the 4×4 high-speed railroad system that will connect major city clusters, provincial capitals, and cities with population of more than 500,000 by 2030[117] to maximize the connectivity and accessibility of all areas.

This design fundamentally repositions global infrastructure, and its effects will be most apparent in regions of the world with large populations. Because it is still a novel idea, the spiderweb-honeycomb system will require funding, which can come from the reallocation of central funding once certain services have been localized at the community level.

These new infrastructures will precipitate a paradigm shift in our needs and desires as we consciously make different choices to transform a lifestyle driven by the glamor of affluence into a lifestyle motivated by individual and collective well-being. Economic activities will change to correspond to these new desires, becoming significantly decentralized to meet the needs of the individual and communal levels.

New Relationships with Our Environment and Energy

One of the key features of the spiderweb-honeycomb design will be the opportunity for communities to live in much closer proximity to nature. This will enable us to renew our relationships with the environment and to renegotiate what it means to co-habit with the natural world.

Humankind has cut down the trees, overfished the oceans, polluted the land and the air, and depleted the ozone layer—posing a serious threat to planetary sustainability. However, during the Covid-19 pandemic, we witnessed the speed at which nature can heal, repair, and rejuvenate itself as the world was forced to come to an abrupt standstill. All we need is to exercise restraint, and to make mindful decisions to protect the future of our shared world.

In the spiderweb-honeycomb setup, energy production will be more sustainable and dispersed, facilitating effective environmental management. Alternative sources of energy such as solar, hydroelectric, and nuclear power will take over as our primary energy sources, displacing the fossil fuels that have been the main culprit of carbon emissions and other environmental pollutants. Even as the demand for energy will necessarily increase as the size of the global human population grows, we can turn to cleaner sources of energy. Though production costs may be higher initially, technology is evolving and continuously improving the efficiency of energy production and consumption, to eventually produce a net reduction in cost.

The transition into a wholly new paradigm of environmental management is challenging and will take time. However, some countries are already making this ontological leap. Germany, for example, has set their goal of deriving at least 80 percent of its energy needs from renewable sources by 2030 and reach almost 100 percent renewable energy by 2035.[118] As they model the way forward, other countries will soon partake of this new global consciousness. It is consciousness, once again, that will prove to be our solution to the deeply entrenched practices that harm our environment so irreparably.

Living more closely to nature and having access to arable land, we will also develop new relationships with food, which will also significantly reduce our carbon footprint. Being able to sustainably cultivate our own food and increase the proportion of plant-based foods in our diets is not only beneficial for the health of our minds and bodies, but for the health of the planet as well. Shifting away from animal-based foods could add 49 percent more food to the global supply without expanding croplands. This change would also significantly reduce carbon emissions and waste byproducts that end up in our oceans.[119]

Projections have shown that by 2050, plant-based diets will reduce global mortality rates and greenhouse gas emissions by ten percent and seventy percent, respectively.[120] These assertions have been backed up by *Climate Change 2022: Mitigation of Climate Change*, a report from the United Nations' Intergovernmental Panel on Climate Change.[121]

Another area of evident transformation lies in the shift to zero-waste living in a circular economy[122] away from the systems of waste management attached to affluent lifestyles in eras of industrialization. This transformation starts with the individual, as each one of us proactively makes the conscious decision to reduce the amount of daily waste we create through an array of practices, such as saying "no" to plastics, consuming and purchasing items only when we need them, developing the habit of recycling and reusing, and composting scraps to return energy to the earth. In the well-being and happiness economy, we respect Mother Earth and are always aware that our health and enjoyment of life is dependent on her.

In short, changes in worldviews and human desires will produce a chain reaction that can return ecological balance to a damaged planet and restore the well-being of all systems across all scales of life—from ourselves to our communities and humanity at large.

Self-Employment and Entrepreneurship

New employment opportunities will emerge to replace older jobs and outmoded forms of employment. The very concept of employment will shift to accommodate the expansive meanings of work and labor in a new economy of well-being and happiness.

In the new era, we will continually search for more efficient systems of delivery to maximize the value of goods and services and to add value to the economy. As sophisticated robots and artificial intelligence displace manual labor, we will add value in a different way to the system. Tasks that are complex continue to require human creativity, and relationships are not replaceable by mechanization. Humans have many unique and important ways of adding value, such as "creativity, entrepreneurship, vision, collaboration, diplomacy, marketing, supervision, and other higher-order functions."[123]

We will spend time to harness the power of creativity to conceptualize and develop solutions to complex problems. Jobs that do not require innovation or experience—in other words, those that are standardized and require accuracy and speed—will eventually be taken over by machines as creativity becomes our key asset. Radical changes in employment and social structure will result since creative work demands presence and focus rather than fixed 9-to-5 workday routines. The purpose and value of work will be reevaluated and renegotiated, liberating us from the shackles of mindless repetition.

The World Economic Forum estimates that by 2025, eighty-five million jobs may be displaced by shifts in the division of labor between humans and machines, while ninety-seven million new roles may emerge that are more adapted to the new division of labor between humans, machines, and algorithms. New skill groups of critical thinking and analysis, as well as problem-solving, and skills in self-management such as active learning, resilience, stress tolerance, and flexibility will be much more in demand.[124]

In the new era, our work will be concentrated in localized economic activities and diversified away from centralized systems. In many ways, this is about going back to basics. When we cultivate our own food, take charge of our own learning, and realize the value of self-care, the financial burden on the government will be significantly reduced. People will claim the autonomy to create their own forms of employment, becoming self-driven entrepreneurs. It will be liberating for people to fully own the power to decide what we spend our time on, what we plant and cultivate, how we eat, where we live, what we learn, and how to practice self-care. We will choose what work we want to do and for whom, or choose with whom we work. We will be able to achieve a healthy balance between creating, working, living, and playing as we forge meaningful lives for ourselves on our own terms.

Naturally, more opportunities for new start-ups and localized businesses will arise, providing gainful employment to everyone. Entrepreneurs developing services and projects for local communities will be welcomed for their proximity to the market and their first-hand understanding of the community's specific needs. Additionally, this era will witness a renaissance in arts and crafts. Hand-made items rooted in traditional technique and wisdom will be valued, and musicians cherished as essential parts of the communities to which they belong. Focusing on being that informs doing, this era will enhance the meaning of life and give ourselves the space to enjoy the possibility of deep connection with ourselves and with everything around us.

Employment and consumption will be integrated as one holistic economic system driven by communities. Social systems in all corners of the world will have access to these restructured plans for living. Technology will be shared and democratized in a global open platform. Each urban node will create and sustain itself while having access to neighboring support systems through the spiderweb-honeycomb design. Governments will continue to provide employment in areas of services needed to safeguard social stability.

These new forms of employment, tailored to the specific needs of each community, are positioned to serve the market more efficiently from the perspective of relevance, cost, response time, and quality—all by virtue of the new infrastructures of the well-being era. Work will be meaningful, impactful, and value-added, creating innovative solutions around perceived challenges or unmet needs in the market. Everyone will have the opportunity to be stewards of their own lives, taking personal responsibility for their work to serve collective well-being and happiness. Diverse, multifaceted, and enjoyable, work will be integrated into our lives rather than being siloed from it.

While creating new businesses and delivering what we desire with a greater precision and care, the new way of living will attune us more sharply to our true needs and desires. Employment and other economic functions, after all, are closely intertwined with what we desire. With such clarity, we will be able to truly steer our lives in directions that are meaningful for every one of us.

New Technology Powers Media and Social Media

Technology springs from scientific developments and is used to engineer products that meet human desires. Though the speed of technological progress is disruptive, the extent to which technology has been integrated into our lives is unprecedented and would be unimaginable to previous generations. While the purpose of our existence has not changed, technology has expanded the range of possibilities around how we respond to that purpose. Beyond maximizing the efficiency and effectiveness of all manual mechanistic work, technology has also been mobilized as a tool to create the life that we want.

Digital technology has completely altered the way we communicate, collapsing spatial and temporal distances. People can meet one another virtually, playing and learning from the diversity of human cultures. Digital consumption and screen shopping have replaced the physical act of window-shopping. Knowledge and news are accessible and in abundance, democratizing access to information.

Social media has redefined how we relate to and connect with one another. While it can be a powerful platform that enhances transparency, it also poses a security threat, requiring new regulations. The sheer proliferation and inescapability of technology—and social media in particular—means that it is easy for us to become enslaved to it. We must cultivate awareness as a lifelong practice and nurture the wisdom to deploy social media in a way that adds value to our lives and serves our needs.

Virtual reality represents another digital revolution in its ability to create alternate worlds that are totally immersive, stretching our imagination and enhancing our experience. In this new digital realm, virtual reality is reality too; anything we create is part of life. The possibilities for creativity are unparalleled. With all the biosocial and biotechnological aspects of virtual reality integrated as extensions of ourselves, virtual reality demands to be seen as extensions of our physical realities and bodies.

The development of the metaverse expands the scope of digital connectivity, which constitutes a new way of connection that surpasses spatial and temporal constraints in the endlessness of its simulation. These virtual and augmented realities are live, interactive three-dimensional digital universes, akin to an evolved form of the internet where we find ourselves in an immersive game-like world. They can also be testbeds for new innovations before market roll-out and commercialization. According to Piers Kicks, the metaverse is a "persistent, live digital universe that affords individuals a sense of agency, social presence, and shared spatial awareness, along with the ability to participate in an extensive virtual economy with profound societal impact."[125]

All these forms of digitization have also been propelled by the global Covid-19 pandemic. At the individual level, the pandemic disrupted our lifestyles as we shifted to meeting and connecting online and propelling social media forward as the norm of social engagement. Digitization at this level also made it possible to manage the pandemic at national and global levels through sophisticated and efficient health tracking systems. In addition, this same platform has also been deployed to digitize physical notes. China has taken the lead in this regard with e-wallets such as WeChat pay and Alipay taking the country by storm.

These developments will have an enormous impact on our social interactions—how we transact and how we are identified. They will transform the way we communicate or participate in games, sports, education, and social activities. Our digitized identities will serve as the key element for gaining access to goods and services across the world. Like an identity card or passport, our digitized identities will be used to recognize us from a database that consolidates all aspects of our profile, including information relating to health, education, family, and social networks.

Moving Toward a New Economic Paradigm

We have seen that this wide array of material transformations across education, healthcare, urban planning, and technology will arise because of a shift in consciousness. No aspect of human existence will be left untouched by these paradigm shifts. However, everything is essentially a matter of choice—if we are willing to take that inward journey.

Traditional practices encouraging peace and stillness such as yoga, tai chi, and meditation have already begun to gain global popularity across countries with disparate belief systems and cultural traditions. All these practices are paths on the journey of life, founded on the wisdom of Eastern traditions, and leading us toward freedom and liberation. The emergence of these practices, sometimes referred to as *practices of connectedness*, have been a core part of global awakening, and will continue to be adopted as lifelong practices in the new era of well-being and happiness.

With machines and artificial intelligence taking care of most manual labor, creativity will be the most highly rewarded and valued trait in human beings. Across the integrated activities of "working, living, and playing," we will have abundant opportunities to spend time in areas that best suit our creative inclinations. As the new era unfolds, modes of employment will change, and the very concept of work will shift. People will feel more empowered to take ownership of the work they do, creating meaningful lives on their own terms.

In reality, it is our worldview that informs shifts in living, doing and being, while shaping our culture and desires. As economics consists of activities aimed at meeting human desires, it is clear that the economy will shift as a result of a redefinition of our worldviews. The economy, no longer measured by per capita income and GDP growth, will instead be built around maximizing collective well-being and happiness. This new era represents a comprehensive reconsideration of the fundamentals of economics: what it means, how it has evolved, and the extent to which economics is embedded in the systems we live within. A total deconstruction and reconstruction will be needed in this new era as we shift along with our worldviews to the next level of consciousness.

Economics can be said to be the backbone of all social, technological, and political movements, helming other structural changes. Religion, politics, and power all boil down to economics, and economic activity grows from our most basic desires that spring from our worldviews. The well-being and happiness economy will lead integration at a global level, including political systems, governance, business, financial, and public services—all essential pillars of support for the new economy.

CHAPTER 5

A Renewed Economic Model of Social Transformation and Integration

A New Culture Drives the New Economics

Our journey inward will shift our consciousness, worldviews, beliefs, and values informing the desires that drive economics. A new way of living with well-being and happiness as the common objective will shape new economic activities. Market economics will likewise also impact our culture and common worldview. With this commonality as a guide, economics will serve as the lever for the integration of East and West to create a new well-being and happiness economy, replacing the -isms—communism, capitalism, consumerism—that dominate the world today.

This new integrated economic model requires a new playing field with new economic structures.

ETHICS, THE MISSING LINK IN ECONOMIC INTEGRATION

Historical records from the ancient Sumer and Babylonian empires and the rich river valleys of ancient China and Egypt reveal how economics in these early stages of humanity's evolution was aligned with the era's primarily agrarian needs—namely through the management of their crops, livestock, and land. This was designed to serve the individual, familial, and communal needs of wealth generation, inheritance of wealth and properties, and trade within their communities. Self-centered wealth accumulation was inimical to these cultures oriented around the community.

Smith's theory still holds true; it just has not fully materialized. Along the way, invisible hands have become that of those who have the power, directly or indirectly, to manage the marketplace for their own benefit. Rather than serving our needs or the common social good, this economic force is making use of endless marketing to drive consumption patterns.

In the well-being and happiness era, the result-oriented tasks of *doing* must be integrated seamlessly with the ancient ethics of relations driven by *being*. Integrating old and new, where we will have access to the wisdom of our intuition—will give rise to ethical responsibility for our actions. The different forms of economics that served our needs in eras of industrialization— including government economics, business economics, not-for-profit economics, community economics, and individual economics—need to be integrated to serve a common purpose. When everything is integrated as one system of well-being, and individual well-being is dependent on the well-being of the whole, we will invariably act to benefit of the system. We will take personal responsibility for our actions and focus on our own agency; this is what we will do when following our ethics.

Within this integrated economic system, Smith's theory of a self-regulating, self-organizing economy, will finally have a chance of being realized. Ethical stewardship will naturally result in self-directed wealth distribution to resolve the challenges posed by wealth inequality in the era of industrialization. In the new era, the definition of wealth will transcend financial affluence to include freedom of speech and access to opportunities.

The sustainability and growth of all systems will be our central priority as we come to embrace consciousness as the beacon to wisdom.

Intelligence, awareness, and creativity, rather than money and power will become our most precious assets.

These are the tenets that will inform the integration of the well-being and happiness economy—holism, ethics, responsibility. This economy will have flexible, agile, and evolving capital and trade systems, allowing for movements to be constantly calibrated to the next level of systemic coherence.

Regulating the Playing Field

As human beings, we have the power of choice to determine our actions and decisions. We are responsible for creating, maintaining, or disrupting systemic equilibrium, including that of the well-being and happiness economic system. An appropriate form of governance is needed to regulate and control a new playing field for the economic activities to thrive. The sustainability of this new economic system hinges on the strength of its support system; and is thus only as strong as its weakest link.

During the industrialization era, economic activities facilitated profligacy and aided only self-centered desire, with the outcome of concentrating wealth in the hands of an elite group. The growth that resulted from this was narrow and speculative, causing an unstable marketing economy. Clearly, this economic system lacked a moral compass. The world has now awakened to the damage caused by inequity from lack of regulation and has accepted the necessity of setting boundaries for a healthy capital market.

In the well-being and happiness economy, creating true value and wealth creation requires an ethically stable market to be in place to enable us to have the freedom to express love through our creation. Wealth generation will then expand beyond the tangible creation of economic value and integrate opportunities and freedom; it must be led by market needs for everyone to be free to express their creativity and realize the potential for new opportunities. This will form a positive feedback loop as the pool of opportunities perpetually grow and expand the scope of freedom to create.

And it is here, precisely, that governance must come into the picture to safeguard this stable environment. Governance should focus on the integrity of intentions, actions, and behaviors to sustain and add value to a stable, ethical environment in which business can thrive. Transitioning out of unequal wealth will need commitment and collaboration at the highest level. Nation-states and a global body like the United Nations must collaborate to build an environment that facilitates the distribution of wealth and strengthens the stability of their system for business investments. Greater equitability will bring peace and harmony to our world.

By creating these new systems, we will expand beyond the creation of economic value so that everyone can be invested. Greater equitability will bring peace and harmony to our world.

Governments must take the lead in this process of regulating our economy, starting by shifting their modus operandi to a new concept of governance. Rather than acting primarily as a watchdog to impose punitive measures for noncompliance, governments should pivot to become the enabler that builds and sustains a stable environment in which economic activities thrive, with a secondary check and balance responsibility.

This process will expand beyond the tangible creation of economic value to integrate our opportunities and freedom. In this integration, major global economies need to shift to a level playing field and free market. Otherwise unequal competitive advantage will threaten this integration. This process must be led by nation-states; governments should collaborate in the interest of humanity's fundamental commonality. The United Nations must transform into the melting pot for all nation-states to gather, discuss, and collaborate so that they might set new standards and regulations in the new era. While every nation-state plays an important role, the United States and China—which make up approximately 42 percent[126] of nominal global gross domestic product—are especially crucial in enabling this integration.

HOW DO WE DEFINE A GOVERNMENT?

A government represents the will of the people and is responsible for managing an efficient economic and social system that provides goods, services, and security, serving the best interests and well-being of the people. These functions are fundamental for economic stability, security, and prosperity.

Governmental structures and roles have developed with economic evolution. They can be traced all the way back to their primitive incarnations in tribes where alphas emerged to lead the group on hunts and battles. Driven by the needs of the tribe, the leader also consulted with the tribe's wise man or shaman to make decisions that aligned with the natural and supernatural worlds. Over time, as tribes became less nomadic and claimed sovereignty over fixed territories, their governing systems evolved into kingdoms, empires, and republics with increasingly sophisticated laws, structures, and roles.

Religion was closely linked to governmental function for much of human history. For two millennia, religion served as the base on which Europe was governed. In the past five centuries, the breakdown of feudalism, the advent of social movements, and the increasing demand for political transparency within societies led to both the scientific revolution and the industrial revolution. These changes formed the foundation of our modern world.

China had a slightly different history. Feudalism remained strong and society was siloed for much longer periods. Religion never held much sway in China, as there was never an absolute religious creed. Instead, China had Daoism, Confucianism, and Buddhism—life teachings and practices revolving around the relationships between human beings and the cosmos, as well as between universe and nature. These ancient systems of wisdom formed the bedrock of Chinese culture and promoted ethical ways of living in and relating to society, economics, and politics. They are holistic, practical systems that govern life and all the relationships formed within it. This continues to exert significant influence in Chinese society today.

GOVERNING TO SUSTAIN STABILITY FOR PROSPERITY

A prosperous economy can flourish in an environment where stability sustains security, fear dissipates, conflicts are reduced, creativity arises, and growth prevails. This does not mean stagnancy, or an absence of movements or disruptions. A dynamism is an opportunity to create change amidst chaos, because nothing new can emerge without it. Freedom to create can only arise in an environment that is stable. Thus, governing for a stable environment will allow freedom to arise. Creativity will result, and we will collectively prosper and flourish.

In the Chinese world the keyword is stability, which reverberates throughout all systems, starting with the smallest of systems—the Self. The management of *stability for prosperity* constitutes the core of the Chinese economic paradigm and the focus of its system of governance. It is what traverses all systems, whether social, economic, or political. Whereas social stability is derived from a common worldview, the stability of economic systems stems from a collective purpose, collaborative hard work, and fair equitable remuneration for all. The deep systemic thinking of the Chinese, in which individual freedom and liberty must exist in relation to the context of collective freedom and liberty, is worthy of understanding and consideration. If we are to shape this stable environment, a new form of regulation and learning is key.

However, a focus on collective freedom does not translate into an erasure of individuality. A common worldview is a singular worldview with a collective purpose, not a concrete fixed worldview, which is fixed and inflexible. Individually, we maintain our individualities and remain empowered with our unique gifts to contribute to this common cause. We create the conditions of our own flourishing to add value so that the larger system can thrive. In the Chinese world, the keyword is stability, which reverberates throughout all systems, starting with the smallest of systems is the self.

The management of *stability for prosperity* constitutes the core of the Chinese economic paradigm and the focus of its system of governance that traverse all systems, whether social, economic, or political; whereas social stability is derived from a common worldview.

Desires, and talents are fundamental to prosperity, as innovation happens at the individual level. The Chinese system, which is a top-down planned economy, is not without its challenges and flaws; however, it has its fair share of successes. For example, in the areas of poverty eradication, environmental clean-up, and economic growth, it comes as no surprise that China has garnered high satisfaction ratings from its people.

Again, this integration needs two seemingly opposed engines to shift together. On one hand, planned systems must ease restrictions on individual liberty for wisdom to emerge. On the other hand, free market systems should unite for collective benefits so that systems can thrive by integrating the -isms into one economic system so they will expand beyond the economic value and integrate opportunities and freedom. As I have stated, it must be generative and led by market needs so everyone can be included.

INTEGRATING THE CONTROL AND FREEDOM, THE -ISMS, INTO ONE ECONOMIC SYSTEM

The integration of control and freedom as one collective system will free the tensions between the polarities of control and freedom. When love and wisdom are at work, our inner freedom shifts our material worldview, and we act with compassion. Freedom motivates self-management to find coherence in a stable, centralized, and controlled system.

Whereas individual rights constitute the central challenge for a conventional top-down planned economy, a bottom-up capitalist economy must grapple with the equitability and stability of the whole. Although we all yearn for freedom, a membrane will be required to delineate the boundaries within which a system might flourish—so individual and collective freedom—can take place. This is not unlike how the earth has an ozone layer that acts as a membrane for a habitable environment where all life can freely thrive.

The dominant ideas of communism and capitalism as political theories and theories of consumerism established belief systems occupying different forms on the spectrum of positions on balance between freedom and control, individual rights, and collective rights established to suit the varying needs of different eras. However, no system is fully one or the other. The new era will see a formation to varying degrees, where all systems contain different elements of freedom and control and collective and individual rights. Now that a new global balance of systems is slowly emerging, and the formation of a market economy will replace the -isms by integrating through a common worldview the predominantly capitalist system in the West with the primarily planned system in the East. A different lens will result for us to contextualize material freedom in relation to inner freedom as it informs our beliefs, thoughts, emotions, desires, aspirations, and actions.

The trend is already observed in the increased regulations and social controls being adopted by democratic governments in the West, a process accelerated by the pandemic. China's planned economy, however, has blended elements of capital markets into its system. Eventually, East and West will meet and North and South will unite, shifting the previously disparate systems into unification and oneness.

There are several nation-states in the world with planned economies. But the focus here is on the Chinese system because of the size of its economy and population. China's approach to managing its economy differs substantially from a capitalist system. Through its unique socialist market economy with Chinese characteristics, China has created the conditions for a balanced process of wealth creation alongside a more stable environment for economic growth.

The Chinese government has put in place a set of regulations for a stable market environment to safeguard public interest. While the capital market continues to operate freely, strong penalties would need to be imposed wherever there is deviation from the essence of the laws. Much of China's success and unprecedented growth can be attributed to this development, enabling it to simultaneously eradicate poverty. However, they are still challenged by uneven state of development for its nearly 1.5 billion people.

Traditional Chinese has a unique interpretation of democracy; it is *minben* (民本), which literally means "the people as foundation." The spirit of this foundation and its concepts guide decision-making in China, where the interests of the people are of the highest priority. It must be generative and led by market needs so everyone can be included. Under this concept, leaders are elected by the universe. Thus—emperors in ancient China were known as *tianzi* (天子) meaning "son of heaven." Just as leaders have heavy responsibilities, the affluent have the responsibility to ethically steward their leaders. However in modern Chinese, democracy is interpreted as *minzhu* (民主), literally meaning "the power of the people" which potentially sacrifices the spirit and culture of the original *minben*.

Now that a new global balance of systems is slowly emerging, including the formation of a market economy to replace the legitimacy of any earlier system, today's market will be built largely on the trust of the populace in their rulers. It is more imperative than ever for governments to sincerely serve and relate to their people.

For this reason, there needs to be an integration of the *isms* in the common worldview of the predominantly capitalist system in the West with the primarily planned and controlled system in the East. Where one favors individual liberties, the other prioritizes collective interests. The divisions caused by these prevailing worldviews and values have been the source of much instability and conflict. The new integrated system must be founded on a common worldview, a paradigm embraced by all.

No matter what label is ultimately given to this new system, its essential characteristic must be holism, driven by collective social needs for society and humanity. Indeed, the trend is already observable from the increased regulations and social controls being adopted by democratic governments in the West, a process accelerated by the pandemic. China's planned economy, in contrast, has blended elements of capitalism and capital markets into its system. Eventually, East and West will meet, North and South and all will unite, shifting the previously disparate systems into unification and oneness.

There are several nation-states in the world with planned economies. But the focus here is on the Chinese system because of the size of its economy and population. With a domestic demand of around 1.5 billion and contributing to nearly one-fifth of the global GDP, their inclusion is key to this global integration.

Another example is Singapore, which is often regarded as one of the best places in the world to do business. Singapore is an efficient country-state with regulatory and economic environments shaped like a commercial enterprise. With a strong focus on meritocracy, Singapore staffs its political system with highly intelligent leaders capable of engaging and building policies to support a stable and friendly environment for commercial activities. The government engages the business community as co-investment partners, while enabling creativity through incentives. Businesses can thrive in healthy competition since their needs are heard and supported. Singapore's integrated model of economics and governance has evidently been successful—it is another nation-state with high levels of approval from its people.

What will the integration of freedom and control look like? Even as more economic activities are absorbed into the community, governments need to maintain control over several key economic sectors, including education and learning, medical and health care, capital markets, financial systems, logistics infrastructure, environmental management, technology, and research and development. These sectors are all points where a higher level of central monitoring and governance have been needed. They are critical areas to safeguard for social stability, as they constitute fundamental touchpoints through which humanity is cultivated. If left unchecked, they could threaten the common worldview that keeps the well-being and happiness economy intact.

This perception of control will change, as governments will indirectly govern through co-investments with business in these key sectors. While businesses contribute their management competencies to add value to economic activities, governments will establish the ethics of business decisions to safeguard a stable economic environment. This is a way in which control and freedom can be integrated. With the government's presence in these industries, they can stay close to the ground with a finger on the social pulse.

The United Nations can assume a role in this governance system. The infrastructure established since World War II, while noble in intention, has not realized its fullest potential. In the new era, the United Nations must be empowered and serve as the foundation and meeting point for all nations of the world to gather to discuss and address others for the purpose of making decisions, and most importantly be empowered to govern common sustainability challenges. While this new form of government will be more attentive and responsive to social needs, it will also be empowered to govern, as well as serving the needs of humanity's well-being and happiness economy.

However, order in a state of well-being and happiness is equally everyone's responsibility, whether as individuals, businesses, or nonprofit organizations. Collaboration across these different agents will be key in its governance as it oversees value systems and intentions rather than playing the role of watchdog. Responsibility for the authenticity of our intentions ultimately lies within us. With the awakening of inward journeys, we shift our consciousness and become more in touch with our life purpose that guides our decisions and actions. This, then, is our inner authority to freely choose, create, and thrive in the new era of well-being and happiness.

IMPACT INVESTMENT AND ESG

Another form of responsibility binding the investment community that has gained popularity and has gradually taken center stage, is impact investing and investment in environmental, social and governance management, commonly abbreviated as ESG.

Investments today are no longer just about financial returns—their scope has expanded, with impact investing measuring tangible social impact and ESG as a basis for evaluating corporate behaviors. Both are changing the way capital is allocated for investments, reorienting the focus toward ethical business practices and systems.

Even though responsible investing practices began as far back as the 1960s to guide investment decisions, they were limited to the exclusion of certain activities considered unethical or in contravention of human rights. It was not until 2004 that the term Environmental, Social, and Governance (ESG) was formally coined in a landmark study entitled *Who Cares Wins*.[127] Today, it is estimated that ESG investing makes up approximately a quarter of all professionally managed assets around the world.[128]

By integrating a different practice into the investment mindset, impact investment and ESG have the potential to exert a widespread positive impact in economics and to contribute to building sustainable impactful businesses—the missing piece in Smith's theory of moral sentiment. Unlike previous practices of ethical investment and *socially responsible investment*, which were based on exclusion and denying unethical businesses access to capital, impact investment and ESG are generative in nature.

In recent years, the increased emphasis on the need for ESG criteria and impact investment criteria has led to these guidelines being popularly adopted, providing guidance and direction to the economic impetus of many businesses. Being much more intimately linked to a business's true contribution and measured by tangible metrics, these guidelines represent a promising first step toward a better, more equitable future for society.

In fact, many members of the public are now *demanding* that companies must be accountable to ESG and these new criteria. In the well-being and happiness economy, this will be more important, as the basis of valuation of economic activities has been widely re-evaluated to encompass systemic impact with a new set of criteria driven by ethics and values. With the increasing number of people recognizing the ethical challenges that businesses must grapple with, the demand for ethics has heightened, and its integration into the economy has been greatly accelerated.

Business leaders and executives, who are directly responsible for practices and integrating ESG into business activities, require a new system of rewards, remuneration, and recognition that will influence and reshape their practices. In living up to these ESG measurements, they will also shift their consciousness of life, impacting human behaviors and actions in the new era. Rather than subjecting themselves to external forms of governance, businesses are exercising a form of self-governance by embedding ESG within their business decisions to meet new matrices that measure success.

In the new well-being and happiness economy, economic activities will shift capital needs—impact investment and ESG will naturally direct capital allocation where need arises. It is undeniable that the world has achieved unprecedented levels of affluence. According to Statista, global GDP in 2020 was approximately USD 85 trillion, and was projected to grow to USD 127 trillion in 2026.[129] However, agriculture accounts for just over 4 percent.[130]

With self-care and community lifestyles proliferating across the globe, a large sliver of economic activities—such as the cultivation of food, familial and communal support for education, and self-care as the foundation of healthcare—will be managed and provided by the community, which will become significantly more self-sufficient in delivering goods and services for the community. Demands for public spending in these areas would be substantially reduced as they would already be embedded into commercial economics.

The public spending previously allocated to healthcare, logistics, food cultivation, and national security will be substantially reduced. With the increased prominence of ESG and impact investment, capital can now be rechanneled to technological research and development, innovations in infrastructure, as well as clean energy and education in support of the new economic activities. As advanced technologies are applied across all aspects of the economy, there will also be increased transparency, enhanced efficiency, and a minimization of leakages from the system. Savings in these areas will also lead to savings that can be reallocated to further innovate and build the new well-being and happiness economy.

Impact investing and ESG will not only serve to inform the allocation of capital but also facilitate an ethical and secure reallocation of capital to develop new infrastructures, both hard and soft, that are needed in the well-being and happiness era.

Global Trade Integration

Impact investment and ESG will take the lead to direct capital and govern economic activities respectively. Trade systems, especially supply chains, will need to be reconstructed for impact and efficiency. Among the 189 member nations of the United Nations, spread across five continents, several common threads exist along the axes of geographical location, constitutional system, language, and culture to facilitate the process of global systemic trade integration.

Asia Harmonization

The European Union, or EU, came into being to dissolve boundaries of trade, economy, and society among European countries, as well as to facilitate the free movement of people, goods, and capital within their markets. The overarching aim was to bring a thriving and secure marketplace to the region. In a parallel manner, Greater China, Taiwan, Korea, and Japan can be seen as *sibling countries*. They are located close to one another and share a long history, having in common similar languages, traditions, and cultural values, and origins. However, these nations have been divided for centuries by heavy historical baggage, which they must release if they are to collaborate.

China and Japan, for instance, share approximately 70 percent of their written characters, which often have very similar, if not identical, meanings. The dominant ethos in both countries is also one characterized by hard work and a focus on collective well-being. All these factors render these sibling countries especially suitable for integration and have the potential to form a mirror of the EU in Asia. An Asian union, or a "Northeast-Asia Union," could guarantee security, and prosperity would flourish in the region. This union would be a step closer to systemic integration into one global system.

In Southeast Asia, ASEAN,[131] The Association of Southeast Asian Nations, aims to achieve a single integrated market through the process of regional economic integration. Singapore, an ASEAN member, could be a natural melting pot for integration with the Northeast-Asia Union.

HUBS FOR EAST-WEST, WEST-EAST INTEGRATION

English is the *lingua franca* of the world today, used ubiquitously in trade, diplomacy, intercultural communication, and much more. It is estimated that more than 1.75 billion people on our globe speak English,[132] dominating conversational language even in areas where English is not the mother tongue.

The pervasive presence of English, of course, has largely come about through colonization. As England's empire expanded westward to the Americas in search of new land, to Australia and New Zealand for the resettlement of freed prisoners, and to Africa and Asia to trade and offer protection, a common systemic structure was established for ruling the colonized territories. But the empire's influence extended beyond the widespread use of the spoken and written language.

Beyond language, a strong legacy of colonialism exists, consisting of a complex heritage of trade systems, shared traditions, institutions, and systems once implemented to govern these ex-colonies. The primary use of the English language continued long after nations gained independence from their colonial masters. Many postcolonial sovereign nations continued to preserve colonial structures of trade, law, and governance. This common thread is lived out in the Special Administrative Region of Hong Kong, Singapore, Malaysia, India, and parts of Africa, among many others.

From this perspective, Hong Kong occupies a unique position as one of the primary financial and trading hubs through which global systemic integration might be possible. While Hong Kong is part of China, under the one country and two systems policy it retains many features of the Western system instituted by British colonization, such as the British legal system, the commercial contracting system for international trade, the English language, and other long institutionalized holdovers. As China's economy expands beyond its borders, Hong Kong could serve as a gateway connecting Chinese companies to external capitals for products to move out and establish their presence overseas. Hong Kong, fondly known as the *Pearl of the Orient*, is indeed a powerful financial and treasured trade center that could connect China with the external world.

Like Hong Kong, Singapore was colonized by the British and is similarly in a privileged position. It has the potential to serve as a doorway to huge markets in Southeast Asia and Indochina, that is home to a population of nearly 600 million people.[133] In addition, Singapore is the convergence point of cultures and businesses from both the East and West. The multicultural and multilingual diversity of Singapore's social landscape, coupled with its position as a financial and technological hub, has attracted many international companies from Europe and America to set up base in Singapore. Chinese and regional companies are already following suit as many of them established offices and regional headquarters in the country. Because of Singapore's relatively neutral position in the global geo-political system, it is uniquely positioned to be the hub connecting East and West.

On the other side of the world, Great Britain is the natural candidate as the Atlantic hub to bridge West and East. As cousin to both Europe and North America, it possesses a deep repository of knowledge of both hemispheres. Having conquered the largest sea-based empire in human history, it has had a great deal of experience dealing with global affairs around governance and management, including the challenges of cross-cultural interaction.

London, a leading global financial center,[134] is suited to become the point of intersection between East and West. Beyond economic collaboration, other forms of cultural and social exchange between East and West could also take place in London. Such an integration and collaboration would enable these functions to unfold in a mutually beneficial and symbiotic relationship, allowing London to reaffirm its position in the global financial market. London could facilitate eastward investments in Asia through Singapore while accessing the large Asian markets. At the same time, Asia would gain valuable access to Western markets.

INTEGRATING TRADE

These bridges between East and West would facilitate the integration of trade and culture. In the future, Singapore is likely to be the melting pot in the East, integrating ASEAN and North Asia—through Hong Kong as its sub-hub and potentially India. In the Americas and Europe, London is the likely candidate as the Atlantic hub, given its neutrality. Africa will probably use the Atlantic hub, given its existing trade routes and history of European colonization.

New trade initiatives to integrate economic and physical trade will then emerge. For example, the Belt and Road Initiative is a China-led project aimed at revitalizing the old trading land and maritime routes that brought prosperity to all that participated in this network. Drawing from its deep historical experience, the Belt and Road Initiative is China's effort to contribute to global industrialization development by building infrastructure and investments in exchange for access to global market through local and regional cooperation.

According to the World Bank Group's Macroeconomics, Trade and Investment Global Practice, published in April 2019,[135] the Belt and Road Initiative can contribute to a 0.7 percent increase in global income by 2030. More importantly, however, it will enable a more equitable redistribution of wealth. The wide-ranging benefits of this initiative further point to the importance of complementary policies, such as the reduction of border delays and further tariff liberalization. These initiatives will facilitate significant welfare gains for all of humankind.

For centuries, trade was the bedrock of economic and cross-cultural integration. During the Tang Dynasty, the Silk Road connected China with the West through trade, at one point reaching as far west as the Mediterranean sea. Aside from facilitating the transport of high-value commercial products, the trade networks also enabled cultural exchange between East and West. Traders picked up elements of foreign culture and wisdom along the Silk Road and returned to China with fertilized imaginations, new ideas, and philosophies, including religions they had encountered abroad.

Subsequently, during the Ming Dynasty, sea routes were developed as Zheng He supervised and commanded the largest and most advanced fleet of trading ships of the time. He led and completed seven westward voyages, initiating the economic, cultural, and political exchanges as far as the Persian Gulf and East Africa.

Trade routes did not only expand outward from the East. England was a formidable force in this regard. It built trade routes that stretched to the Far East. England's trade expanded the empire to colonized territories linked to England through bilateral and multilateral trade agreements. Sea routes allowed products to be efficiently shipped from colonized states in the Americas, Australia, New Zealand, Africa, and Asia to metropolitan England. Given the immense power exerted by the systems England instituted, these systems would likely continue to be an invisible line of commonality threading through territories all over the world to facilitate global integration in the well-being and happiness economy.

Although trading on these routes brought prosperity and rich cultural exchange and cross-cultural integration through inter-marriages and cross settlements, these collaborations were hardly a bed of roses. Obstacles and challenges frequently eroded the value of these cooperative trade efforts. Traders on land and sea often had to manage life-threatening conditions from robber barons who claimed rights over land and negotiated the hefty taxes and tariffs imposed on cross-border transactions.

In the wake of these faults, today's global trade is designed to have better organization in the exchange of goods and services between countries in order to reach consumers efficiently. For various reasons, trade is now conceived merely as an economic transaction. In different corners of the world, inequalities in wealth distribution are being exacerbated by existing trade networks while large segments of the population do not have access to basic needs for survival.

What is apparent in this new world order is that another form of global engagement and collaboration is possible, one that would expand connection through new infrastructure and redistribute income more efficiently. This would encourage openness and inclusiveness in trade for the betterment of all, foster joint responsibility for sustainable development, and build collective wisdom for creation and innovation. Ultimately, when we achieve this, we will enjoy balanced global development that respects the well-being of every system and our shared planet.

Creating a Single Currency Based on Direct Trade

In the new paradigm, when a common culture drives the development of economics, a reconstruction of the money system will also be needed. Money, in whatever form, is necessary to facilitate trade. There are many perspectives about the origins of money, the roles money played in different social systems, the history of its evolution, and its relevance to today's social, economic, and political systems. This topic has been extensively studied and written about by historians and economists.[136] The intention here is not to argue for or against the system, but to distill the literature about it and suggest a possible framework for money to play an integrating role in the future well-being and happiness economy.

Money started as a system of valuation to facilitate the exchange of goods, balancing the surplus and deficit of needs between two or more individuals or groups. In its beginnings, whether it was in the form of shells, coins, gold, or another currency, money acted as a proxy for the valuation of goods desired by another party. Over time, money's valuation methods increased in sophistication.

As a system, money today is a form of power that separates people rather than bringing them together. It takes different shapes and forms, not equally accessible to all members of society and is now as implicated in politics as it is in economics. As a result, the distribution of power within social systems and between nation-states has become grossly unequal. For example, the use of credit cards and electronic banking systems is not accessible to all. This privilege is closely correlated with one's income level, gender, and geographical location, among other factors.

With the development of international trade, it became apparent that the use of a dominant global currency could facilitate trade. The consolidation of control over the issuance of currencies, uniting the money used in different cities into one common currency under the same territorial rule, reduced monetary fragmentation (Epstein,

2001).[137] Financial systems further consolidated the exchange of different currencies through an international inter-bank system.

A dominant global currency did not come about by democratic selection, where a group of nations voted on which currency should be used. Instead, it naturally emerged from competition; the currency which dominated global trade—as well as the one most stable and resilient against external shocks—would be the most commonly used.

EMERGENCE OF THE US DOLLAR AS DOMINANT GLOBAL CURRENCY

After World War II, the economy of the United States was booming and dominated global trade. With the stability of its economic system and strength of its military set-up, the USD, or U.S. Dollar, gained the confidence of global economic and social systems. It was easily traded, liquid, and could support an extensive banking system to facilitate global exchange. More importantly, it was stable: Under the Bretton Woods Agreement, the USD was pegged to gold at a fixed price, whereas all other currencies were pegged to the USD. Agreement was put together to minimize currency volatility and stabilize international trade. Indirectly, gold was used as a basis of currency valuation.

Upon the collapse of the Bretton Woods system in 1973, President Nixon announced the un-pegging of the USD from gold because of inflationary pressures to print more dollars. Subsequently, international currencies were thrown into a period of open market, self-regulated valuing of currencies; national banks were allowed to choose the currency on which they would base their valuation. From that point forward, social gaps formed and widened as the middle classes disappeared under inflation. The rich were getting richer while the poor were getting poorer.

Until the 1970s, a significant unofficial pegging of the USD to petroleum emerged with an agreement signed between the United States of America and Saudi Arabia to settle the purchase of petroleum in USD.[138] This *de facto* replacement of gold with another commodity, petroleum, has remained unchallenged for decades.

With the impact of China's economy in the global system, and the major economic disruptions occasioned by the Covid-19 pandemic, the stability of the USD and its ability to remain as the one dominant currency for international trade has been put to the test. China continues to grow and impact the system. It is estimated that China will overtake the United States as the biggest economy in the world by 2030. However, due to the vast population of China, more than four times the population of the United States, the difference is very high in terms of per capita income.

Financial systems have also evolved. Valuation has been disconnected from underlying asset valuation—the essence of its original existence. Instead, it has become a weapon of political control, intensifying the unequal distribution of power. Taxes and tariffs, for example, can be imposed to stabilize a system, provide for social needs, and promote harmonious trade, but it can equally be manipulated to build military power or to cushion the decadent, luxurious lifestyles of a rich elite. There is great reluctance among developed markets to find an alternative system which might more efficiently and effectively facilitate trade in this newly integrated world.

We need a new design for currency and a valuation system driven by the economy and free from political control or influence. Its basis of valuation must be transparent and grounded in real assets. Access to this new currency must be freely available to everyone. The goal is less to replace the USD than to set in motion a systemic evolution that will accommodate a new, more advanced and evolved ethical economic model that is free from political manipulation.

A New Well-being and Happiness Currency

Many innovations and breakthroughs have been achieved in recent years. Cryptocurrency, a form of digital currency, has gained traction as a new form of exchange independent of any one group's economic control and is untethered to political sovereignty. The possibility of such a decentralized currency is precisely a result of technological advancements in quantum computing and blockchain technology, representing an innovation in the direction of currency freedom. However, its valuation is based on the supply and demand of cryptocurrency, which so far lacks the solid backing of value-based asset valuation.

After all, the function of currencies is to place a value on the international trade of goods and services. Without an economic system, a currency obviously loses its fundamental reason for existence. At the same time, the surge in the popularity of cryptocurrencies points us to the possibility of freeing currencies from forms of power and sovereignty that distract from their main purpose. If an ethical and transparent valuation system can be embedded, cryptocurrency—or a variation of it—will be a system worth pursuing in the new well-being and happiness economy.

Real value-backed currency fundamentally requires an evaluation of what constitutes real value. Technically, a global master mutual investment fund, with one integrated and transparent system that curtails the prevalence of speculative investments and manipulation in valuation, will allow the possibility of creating value to be stored in the new global currency. The advancements in technology now facilitate the levels of openness and transparency needed in our systems of investment and valuation.

Replicating the concept of a mutual fund, a global master fund would provide the real value needed to back a new global currency. This master fund would pool capital with portfolios balanced by geography, sector, and social needs where investments are valued purely by real value. With ESG integrated into the economic system and enabled by technology, this master fund would have a built-in system of self-governance. Valuation would be transparent, driven directly by the value generated by real asset growth that serves the well-being and happiness economy. This new master fund would become the valuation benchmark backed by real assets and cash flow, allowing for real wealth protection and storing of value.

Real asset growth derived from a well-being and happiness economy will replace gold or petroleum as its peg value. The master fund will store this value and issue units with coupon rates as currency to the global citizen. As members of the global community, we will be able to purchase and dispose these units as currencies to be used in our economic activities. Such a global fund represents an efficient form of storing economic value and will present an alternative to the USD as a global currency.

The investment community of today, with trillions of dollars of assets under management, has the requisite expertise and experience to manage such a fund. A whole new investment system built around this new currency will take over the role of the financial and banking system of sovereign currencies. Nation-states will be likely anchor investors of the global master fund, and their share of the fund represents their sovereign reserves as the fund stores value of the new economy.

This could be an integration that traverses spatial and national boundaries. International organizations like the World Bank and the United Nations need to be empowered to lead discussions on how to implement and transition to such a global master fund.

Integration Needs Technology

Global economic structures of today have been enabled by technology, which has democratized travel, trade, communications, information; transformed organizations, processes; facilitated investments, innovation, and—in short—fueled globalization. The technologies underpinning the fourth industrial revolution are again having a major impact on the way we live. As Klaus Schwab, Founder and Executive Chairman of the World Economic Forum puts it, "The development of emerging technologies has given us the ability to process, store, and access knowledge like never before. These possibilities will be multiplied by burgeoning technological breakthroughs in areas such as artificial intelligence, robotics, the Internet of Things, autonomous vehicles, 3D printing, nanotechnology, biotechnology, materials science, energy storage, and quantum computing."[139] These technological breakthroughs are blurring the lines of digital, physical, and biological spheres.

Many industries are seeing the introduction of new technologies that create entirely new services, improve the efficiency and enjoyment of individuals' lives, and significantly disrupt existing inefficient value chains. Transformation is also coming from agile, innovative competitors who can leverage global digital platforms for research, development, sales, marketing, and distribution. They reap long-term gains in efficiency and productivity. All of this will open up new markets, lower costs, and drive economic growth with high levels of transparency enabling better governance.

During a roundtable at the Tsinghua PBCSF Chief Economists Forum held in Beijing in May 2022, it was suggested that while the focus of competition among big countries is the economy, the focus of economic competition is technology, and the focus of technological competition is innovation capacity. In the face of future development, there is a greater need for stable mechanisms to support innovations in science and technology.

Never has there been an era where technology has had such ubiquity and seamless integration into our lives, and technological development is critical for systemic integration in the well-being and happiness economy. It holds out great promise for a new future. But with greater promise also comes greater responsibility for its use. Without doubt, this breakthrough in technology will enable the integration of the global systems in the well-being and happiness economy. The arrival of modern technology is a mark that the time for the building of this new era is now. Technology's powerful platform for integrating the global systems needed for a transparent and self-governing system that returns the power of choice to all humanity.

It is likely that the breakneck speed of technology's evolution will go on accelerating from here, bringing into being previously undreamed-of possibilities. This presents us with unique opportunities for technology to be integrated with the inward journey and consciousness shift of life. We might imagine the metaverse, in particular, creating a space of healing for our distressed minds and bodies. By allowing our virtual selves to experience bliss and joy in projected futures, the metaverse space might one day be used to release us from the traumas of the past that bind us and constrain our potential. This may sound outlandish; however, it is worth remembering that many of tomorrow's realities will originate in the dreams of today. These brand-new technologies will support the birth of a new era of well-being and happiness.

The New Role of Business

One of the core competencies of business is integration. Business is the most efficient institution to manage and deploy resources in the market economy to meet human desires. It can dance nimbly with the market and has the ability to integrate different capital and economic players. Business is fast and efficient at developing and operationalizing economic activities and can be at the forefront of technological advancement, global integration, and material wealth creation. Business has access to all forms of capital. However, in its current state, it lacks awareness and underutilizes consciousness, whick is the mother of capital.

Consciousness is latent and accessible to all—people only have to make a conscious *choice* to journey into their inner world—its absence is responsible for much of the damage that human society and the natural environment are suffering today because there is a lack of ethical boundaries and accountability for the impact of our actions on the whole system. However, impact investing and ESG, when incorporated in investment management (such as the global master fund), will create a self-organizing economy that redistributes wealth for the flourishing of all.

Although the market economy has created an efficient production and commercial engine, it is also the main culprit behind the sustainability challenges that plague the world today. By prioritizing profit and the fulfilment of short-term desires over all else, industrialization led many of us astray. However, business, which has led us down the rabbit hole, can also lead us out. It is best positioned to be the key integrator of all economic elements—including individuals, nonprofit organizations, and governments—and to coordinate economic activities to lead us out of this thorny predicament.

Businesses have the power to address the world's sustainability challenges. Developing a new consciousness from its global awakening, business can take the lead from here to create an economy driven by meaning and purpose. The competencies of business that caused sustainability challenges are the same competencies that—when combined with a new consciousness in business—can remain relevant in the new economy to create novel models that will ensure the sustainability of the new well-being and happiness economy.

To prevail, checks and balances must be in place to guarantee business ethics. Eventually, new forms of self-governance will be instituted, since only a responsible ethical market economy responsive to social needs will be accepted. All other forms will be rejected by the market. This economic stance would drive changes in all other areas, including politics, technology, society, and the environment.

In fact, businesses are already rising to the challenge. Many companies in the United States have declared that they no longer serve just shareholders but also society as a whole. Investments are shifting in the direction of impact investment—expanding their matrices of success beyond profit to include social and environmental well-being. Businesses themselves are reviewing their models, increasingly engaging in discourse about conscious capitalism and related concepts.

The United Nations' focus has evolved from the eight Millennium Development Goals—which galvanized unprecedented efforts to meet the needs of the world's poorest—to the ambitious and transformative 2030 Agenda for Sustainable Development. This contains seventeen

Sustainable Development Goals founded on a shared vision of humanity and a social contract between the world's leaders and their people. Instead of issuing separate sustainability and ESG reports, businesses can now consider combining them into a "flourishing report," a new matrix to measure business performance.

These are the steps taken to facilitate a new generalized consciousness in business. When energized with purpose while remaining sensitized to external market demands, business will play an indispensable role in the transition. Governments, accordingly, can also serve as facilitators that provide guidance and safeguard the role and purpose of individual businesses. Governments should continue to take responsibility for instituting frameworks and setting boundaries for business. At the same time, they are also investors capable of forming collaborative relationships with enterprises, in which business informs governmental policies and the government has its finger on the social pulse. The market will continue to be best served by a free market economy, guided and governed by the social interests and desires of the market.

When governments and businesses can perform natural checks and balances on each other, a collaborative self-regulating system will be an obvious outcome and a new harmony will emerge.

Corporate Philanthropy Is the Purpose of Business

Corporate philanthropy is being redefined because businesses will gradually launch their own nonprofit activities, socially aware investments, and collaborations. Driven by a new consciousness of love, business management will integrate corporate philanthropy into a practice of impact investment undergirded by the ESG matrix. In this system of well-being, the roles of business, governance, and creating social impact will be infused into a seamless whole; corporate philanthropy will be inseparable from business management.

Investment decisions and strategies will shift to serve social needs, which form the basis of market demand. Being closest to the market, businesses are the most sensitive to its needs. This will inform how they develop appropriate business models and how they do business. Businesses and society can have an interdependent, mutually beneficial relationship. In this new market, businesses would aim to serve human well-being and create wealth at the same time, two functions which should not be mutually exclusive.

This integration has already begun. Corporate philanthropy is now an important form of branding and business credibility, demanded by society and investors alike. What might begin as a reaction to investor demands has instead increased awareness that businesses have their role and purpose as they gradually learn to express love through the philanthropic investments that inform their future markets.

In general, a movement with greater awareness is observable among businesses, as reflected in the 2019 statement by the American Roundtable redefining the purposes and role of business. As these ideas gain traction, nonprofit activities will be stimulated and normalized, and it will become customary for businesses to take on an active role in contributing to social and collective well-being. Businesses must be self-reflexive in interrogating and analyzing their own purpose, defining a wider context for themselves, while providing more meaning and motivation for their staff.

Businesses will redefine branding and, rather than spending money on marketing and self-promotion, will instead channel resources to build loving, caring, and socially invested businesses. Indeed, businesses can be the chief integrator helming the tripartite collaboration between governments, businesses, and nonprofits that will serve both individual and the collective well-being.

Both governments and businesses can fund and integrate nonprofits into their system. ESG will govern how investments are made and the way capital is deployed and invested, including where and how the global master mutual fund will allocate its capital. As in any systemic change, bifurcation will happen where there is a handful of people that have crossed the ontological threshold and can work together to build a new future. Family businesses are best positioned to lead the way and to spark this transformation.

FAMILY BUSINESS HAS A SPECIAL ROLE

In exploring the role of business, we cannot ignore family businesses. Family businesses can be defined as business enterprises owned and controlled by one or more families. According to the Family Firm Institute, family businesses account for approximately two-thirds of all businesses around the world. They generate around 70–90 percent of annual global GDP and create 50–80 percent of jobs in the majority of countries worldwide.[140] Family businesses dominate the business world and have great economic impact everywhere.

But what makes multigenerational family businesses unique is the integrating of family values into the business. Through their direct and indirect involvement, family business owners influence and shape the business culture. Many family businesses naturally consider the long-term implications of their strategy and have family, philanthropy, and business capital allocations—when these different forms of capital are integrated, the system creates impact.

Given these characteristics, the leaders of family-owned businesses could be the pioneering group, the prime movers that tip the system past the point of bifurcation and lead the building of the new well-being and happiness economy. Family businesses can be immensely influential in this new era. They already automatically think long-term, have stable shareholdings and management, and make up the largest share of business worldwide. Additionally, management powers in each family business are usually so centralized that much can be achieved in efficient and effective ways.

Family businesses are also in search of new sustainability models. Many family businesses networks have been formed, and more specialized learning programs on family business are being offered by universities and leadership centers. All of them are in search of that elusive, secret recipe for sustainability and wealth preservation. One example is Family Business Network International (FBN-I)[141] that is leading Polaris,[142] a global movement focused on maximizing economic, social, and environmental impact by incorporating a holistic approach to sustainability.

A new generation of family business leaders will emerge. These leaders will manifest and live within a worldview of values and ethics refined over generations. Every investment decision and business action will carry greater weight. Family businesses, in short, are best suited to helm this area, and are positioned to impact the world. In the new well-being and happiness era, where self-employment and entrepreneurship are dominant, family businesses will model the way in how they operate and set standards, again inculcating and normalizing business ethics.

Shaping a Different Economic Paradigm

What will the future look like, based on this framework? In the quantum paradigm, the future cannot be known in advance because we all have the *choice* to shape it. If we make the choice to journey inwards, we will discover that the freedom of choice is inside us. From this place, everything that seems chaotic represents, in reality, an opportunity to mold the future. Through our beliefs and thoughts, we can create a flourishing future of well-being and happiness that we naturally desire.

This process might occasionally feel isolating, but we must remember that we are not alone. Many other systems are participating along with us in co-creating one Earth in which all beings can harmoniously and peacefully coexist. Just as metamorphosis happens inside the cocoon before the elegant butterfly emerges, most of our transformations must take place within us before we can act. Our inner world informs our way of being. Through our inner journeys, we will be empowered to draw on a deeper authority to act in service of collective well-being. In the new era, those at the helm will become the stewards responsible for how we deploy this power.

Our consciousness and awareness inform how we create and act, and a common worldview will drive the process of bifurcation, precipitating systemic change. Our inner journeys into self-actualization will elevate us to the next level of consciousness to access the power of wishing and being, the energy of imagination and creativity. In place of a scarcity mindset of competition, endurance, and survival, we can opt for a gentler relational energy of rejuvenation and harmony. The choice is ours.

Choice is what we have; we must exercise this power to kickstart our inner journey to access freedom and infinite responsibility. When we reach our deepest self and listen to our true innermost calling, we will align our choices to a common worldview, where commonality is valued and diversity celebrated.

Some people will be at the forefront of this change—they are the quantum leaders, helming the evolutionary process. These are the individuals who have chosen to undertake the lifelong journey of learning. Quantum leadership will emerge to bring the world past the point of bifurcation; their awakening and alignment to a common worldview will inform the energy of collaboration and creativity.

You may wonder how practical this vision is on a global scale. How do we get there? Are there any interim stages? There are many possibilities for how the future will unfold, since it is unknown. But it is certain that education and learning will be key in the creation of a unified human community. Although it is impossible for us to know at present what that would concretely look like, this uncertainty is generative in itself. As we learn to accommodate the discomfort of uncertainty, we can fully claim the freedom to create this future. This, then, is a mindset of abundance and flourishing, constantly seeing possibility in uncertainty and having enough courage to choose a different path, even if it might be unconventional.

In the paradigm shift to the new era of well-being and happiness, several elements of our culture at present will fade away while others will gain ascendance to be attuned to the times. Competition will make way for partnership; relationships and models built on competition will be replaced by models based on principles of healing, reconciliation, and forgiveness. We will observe a shift from greed and scarcity to care and abundance. Our values and perspectives will evolve from self-centeredness to an awareness of collective interest and well-being. Most importantly, no longer will we rely on external forms of authority as we learn to listen to the internal authority that we cultivate and begin to trust our inner sources of intuition and knowledge.

Separation will give way to wholeness; it is wholeness and interconnectedness, not fragmentation, that reflects our true reality. Finally, fragmented organizations with parts pitted against each other will be superseded by structures integrated to serve both those within and without their organizations.

At this juncture lies the *choice* for humanity to come together and write a new story—a story of renewed relationships to self, health, education, learning, family, work, community, environment, and nature; a well-being and happiness economy, of which love is the ultimate expression.

A Vision of the Future Well-being and Happiness Economy

The diversity of our individual constructs, governmental structures and roles, and our economic evolution can be traced all the way back to human's primitive incarnations in tribes where alphas emerged to lead the group during hunts and battles. Driven by the needs of the tribe, the leader also consulted with the tribe's wise man or shaman to make decisions that aligned with the natural world and expanded beyond the tangible creation of economic value and integrated opportunities and freedom. It would have been generative and determined by human needs so that everyone could be cared for.

Fast forward to the era of industrialization when Adam Smith—commonly regarded as the father of modern economics—put forth his vision of economics. He believed that economics, driven by market forces, should be self-regulating and self-organizing. Developing the metaphor of the invisible hand, Smith suggested that public good and social benefits might come about inadvertently because of individuals acting in self-interested ways. He theorized that in a free-market economy, the invisible hand would organically bring about a state of equilibrium without the need for government intervention.

When we make the choice to journey inward, our desires that drive economic activities—which is informed by our consciousness, worldviews, beliefs, and values—will shift. A new way of living with well-being and happiness as the common objective will shape new economic activities. Market economics will likewise impact our culture and common worldview. With this commonality as guide, economics will serve as the lever for the integration of East and West to create a new well-being and happiness economy, replacing the "isms"—communism, capitalism, consumerism—that dominate the world today. This is a philosophy of economics that builds wealth of humanity as the premise to build wealth of nations. It is based on a theory that a shift of consciousness will take us to a level of ethical and responsible evolution—in a new well-being and happiness economy.

This new integrated economic model requires a new playing field with new regulations to direct the capital markets and modus operandi for global trade and economics. Economic activities will restore stability so that all systems can prosper and flourish. Global trade will be reorganized to support these new economic activities while Environmental, Social, and Governance (ESG) will impact investing and become the integrator of current dysfunctional economic models—permeated as culture in the well-being and happiness economy.

The government's role will shift into one of guiding and supporting economic activities to thrive, replacing its conventional watchdog role. Business, whose core competence is integration, will play the role of integrator for different capital and economic players. Family businesses, with their long-term orientation and relational approach to business have the unique ability to lead the way in the negotiation of the continuum of profit and social capital, transaction, and relational connection. This integration of East and West will pivot humanity into a new wea of well-being and happiness economy.

PART THREE

Our Future
Is Now

I awoke to the darkness of my room and looked at the bedside clock. It was six in the morning. I breathed the cool air in, appreciating the stillness inside and around me. With a sense of recognition and gratitude, I realized I was home: at home in myself and in the world. Closing my eyes to meditate, I smiled and laughed inwardly at myself, remembering all the years I had never noticed the coherence and calm that had been within me all along. But now that I have seen what it means to live in a new era of well-being and happiness, I know this for sure: My vision of the future is my experience now.

CHAPTER 6

Discovering One Choice, One World

Awakening

The rise of quantum leadership is now. This is not a theory, but an observation grounded on my experiences and journey. The process of awakening can be likened to the journey of a hero as he embarks on a quest for wholeness and coherence.

The Hero with a Thousand Faces was originally an archetype common in many world myths, first discussed by Joseph Campbell, an expert in comparative mythology. Campbell found that numerous myths centered on the journey of the hero, rather than the person of the hero himself. This "thousand faces" archetype describes a hero who begins his awakening and undergoes a process of transformation, doing things beyond the usual realm of comfort. Importantly, this hero's journey does not take place externally but internally as the hero follows his own calling.

Through the awakening, the hero sees what he was not capable of seeing before; he sees a possible journey in search of oneness, starting from within the individual and eventually uniting all of humanity. It is through this vision that all the heroes will experience a collective urge to act together to forge a common identity that will unify them all. Although they act individually, their decisions are in a common direction.

This chapter is dedicated to the journeys I have undertaken— grounded in my observations and my own experience of awakening.

When we reflect on humanity, we will see that the future is in our hands, and we create our future with our beliefs and thoughts: It is not out of our control. Some might think this is a futuristic dream, but I experience this as the universe calling on us to awaken, align, collaborate, and collectively create this new future.

Whether or not the vision resonates with you, I hope that you will approach it with curiosity and an open mind, treating my personal journey as one that can come to take on a thousand faces across cultures and geographical borders in the new era of well-being and happiness.

Sharing My Story

Over the years, I have come to realize that we are truly the stewards of our own lives and create the destiny we aspire to have. At every stage of evolution, human beings met their challenges and developed creative solutions to make progress. Finding ways to meet basic needs of food and shelter, we eventually transcended fundamental anxieties over our own survival and could begin to live lives of indulgence and pleasure. Moving into the new era of well-being and happiness, more and more of us feel compelled to ask existential questions about the purpose and meaning of our lives. Why am I here? What is my life purpose?

The speed of the development of technologies also tells us something about the future humanity is poised to create. It is now commonplace, and no longer surprising, to hear about great advancements in artificial intelligence. Increasingly, biotechnological interfaces are being integrated into the human body, becoming extensions of flesh and blood. These unprecedented possibilities are manifestations of our creativity: Things that would not have been imaginable decades ago are now unremarkable features of our contemporary reality. But these are precisely the elements that will change our way of living— altering our desires and worldview—to launch us into the new era of well-being and happiness.

New developments in science have shown us that we can create our futures with our beliefs, thoughts, visions, and imaginations; indeed, there is no other way to create a sustainable future. If we reflect on our own history, we will see that we have always been creating our own future. Because the universe is the construct of our minds, and we can use our thoughts to manifest a vision. When we collectively focus our thoughts on a future that will serve the well-being of us all, we will manifest it into existence. In other words, our thoughts inform and shape our reality.

Through the power of belief and thought, we can shift our focus from an exclusive emphasis on willpower—the power of doing—to what I call *wish-power*, the power of being. Instead of being trapped in scarcity mindsets, a state of mind when we compare ourselves to others and constantly subject ourselves to anxiety, wish-power focuses on the possibilities for a new future. With a posture of mindfulness, we liberate ourselves from stress, allowing our true natures to unfold and work their magic. We transform the source of our energy and the way we relate to others. We live our lives according to the quantum paradigm and become comfortable with the truth that the future is unknown. Every moment we choose to create and collaborate and evolve in the direction of coherence.

Of course, to believe in such a future also involves an element of conscious choice. We must all make the choice to believe we will have good possibilities in the future and have faith in a future grounded in benevolence, compassion, mutual benefit, and goodwill before we can imagine what it will look like. It is in this way that we will give birth to the new well-being and happiness economy—the new quantum era.

We are all interconnected, whether we like it or not. The moment we change ourselves we influence the people around us to do the same, and soon the whole system will follow. This is the path of awakening.

All we need, in fact, is to initiate our journey inward to come into contact with the deepest parts of ourselves and to choose ethical ways of relating to others. We condense the butterfly effect within the choices that we make. When we are mindful, we will live our calling, fulfill our purpose, and find our well-being. Of course, this calling that we aspire to must include the specific conditions and demands of the era we currently live in. The calling, then, must be contextualized very carefully in our present.

For this reason, I will share the story of my own journey thus far—of how I came to have the visions, beliefs, and dreams. I want to offer my experiences as learning points for all readers because much of my life has been guided by a fusion of Western and Eastern cultures.

When humans understand the journeys and paths we can choose to undertake, we grant ourselves the gift of freedom. In this journey of exploration into our inner world—through the path of mindfulness—we open ourselves to a holistic world of infinite possibility. When we hear our inner calling, and discover the purpose and meaning of our lives, we are empowered with the authority to create our new future. As in the metaverse, we will be able to create anything and everything purely with the power of thought.

Many have asked me, "Why are you doing this? What if you fail?"

I tell these concerned friends and family, "I cannot unsee what I have seen."

My journey so far, and the choices and discoveries I've made along the way, have opened up infinite possibilities for me and they now inform my decisions and actions. It is my hope that you will find in this story some inspiration, guidance, and wisdom for the paths that you are about to embark upon.

My Journey

My story is one of a Chinese boy who was born into an intersection of cultures. From the beginning, I was exposed to traditions and value systems from both East and West. My family originated in Shanghai, and my cultural roots are Han Chinese. Since I was born into affluence, I never had to worry about financial pressures and difficulties.

And because I was born in Hong Kong in 1957, I grew up in a thriving hub of international trade and commerce.

My family is more Westernized than most other Chinese people and has been highly mobile for generations. When my great-grandfather started the family business during the Qing Dynasty, he had already begun trading with foreigners. My grandfather went to an English Middle School and spoke English fluently. It was rare for a Chinese man in the first quarter of the twentieth century to know the English language so well. He ventured out of China as far as Brazil, eventually becoming a citizen of Brazil. Continuing in this family tradition of adaptability and agility, my father relocated the business from Shanghai to Hong Kong, eventually expanding the family business across Asia from Singapore, Malaysia, Thailand, and China all the way to Japan. Eventually, my father became a Malaysian citizen.

I studied at the University of Michigan and graduated with degrees in naval architecture and industrial engineering—these were forms of knowledge considered necessary for a succeeding generation that was expected to helm the family business as stewards. My generation, similarly, has learned from the experiences of our ancestors. My family is spread throughout the world. Although our family roots are in China and Hong Kong, we are a family of global citizens. Through the family business, I have had countless opportunities to closely collaborate with partners and government authorities across the globe. This has sensitized me to diverse cultures and belief systems. For my family and me, the sheer array of cultural difference across human societies and civilizations has always been a great asset.

There have been periods in my life when I was spending almost 70 percent of my time "on the road." I was once asked where home was for me. My answer, spontaneously emanating from my inner voice, was that "my body is my home." Indeed, my upbringing has allowed me to feel at home anywhere and everywhere, a gift for which I am deeply grateful.

As a baby boomer, I am part of a generation that has likely witnessed across our lifetime the most radical paradigm shifts and

transformations in the history of humankind. While in college I under-
went the hippie phase that was then in vogue. Little did I know how
rapidly the world would change and how abruptly globalization would
take over everything, leading to the dominance of the consumerist
market economy.

I joined the family business in 1977 at the tender age of 20 and
took over as the steward of the family business in 1995. As part of the
fourth generation in the line of succession, I inherited the responsibility
of wealth protection. There is a Chinese saying derived from Mencius,
富不過三代, meaning that wealth cannot be sustained beyond three
generations. This felt like a curse and a challenge at once; I felt the
burden of responsibility to not allow this saying to come true under
my stewardship.

Business success came to me with an almost preternatural ease,
and in ways I did not anticipate. When I was younger, I, too, was
steeped in the materialist mindset rampant in the era of industrialization, and I bought into the ideology of capitalism and globalism. As
an entrepreneur, I certainly contributed my fair share to the sustainability challenges that the world faces today. Looking back, with the
judgment afforded by hindsight, I can see how much of that was a way
of gratifying my ego.

Throughout the years, I had already begun to see how unchecked
economic growth would inflict ubiquitous damage on society. I
witnessed the rise and fall of the Asian economic miracle and the
proliferation of irresponsible speculative activities in an uncontrolled
"gambling" economy. During this period, I saw the dark side of greed
and the desire for wealth accumulation when money is elevated to the
status of an object of worship. For people who view money as the be-all
and end-all, there is nothing in life that cannot be sacrificed. Having
early exposure to the perils of money forced me to give these matters
some deep contemplation.

In a horrifying turn of events, I had been devastated when a staff
member—a colleague—was violently murdered by an organized

gang, a group of fellow humans, as a result of my attempts to institute clean business. This pivotal point in my life affected me profoundly. I took a step back to wonder what the true value of life is and how business fit into that picture. Emotionally rattled, I questioned the nature of business. How could business continue existing as it was and claim to be an honorable institution if it did not cherish human life, the most fundamental and important of all our possessions?

These experiences offered me a cautionary tale, as if warning me against the excesses I might have otherwise succumbed to. Grappling with the burden of being responsible for maintaining and growing my family wealth, I questioned the limits of my philosophy on business and economics. How far would I go for profit? What, really, was the ultimate purpose of business? How would I sustain the family business and preserve the family legacy to pass on to the next generation?

My observations drew my attention to the fact that global sustainability challenges are the result of ethical issues that cause a mismatch between human evolution and our social needs. In other words, our evolution was lagging behind and had to catch up with our changing needs. Businesses are not sensitized to demands that rapidly change. Instead, they continue to doggedly hold onto outmoded business models that can no longer serve the complexities of contemporary reality. When disaster strikes and losses occur, the analysis of exactly what went wrong becomes far more murky. More time is spent fighting fires and managing risk than being alert to the opportunities that come with crisis.

I spent some time researching management models, sustainability, and what it meant to be a businessperson. Not being able to find a satisfactory answer to my reflections from the work of modern management experts, I decided to turn to the ancient teachings of the sages. These concepts have endured for centuries, long after these sages and writers passed. I looked to China, where my family roots can be traced, and delved deeply into the foundations of Chinese culture. I reasoned that there must be something singular that made it one of the longest surviving civilizations in all of human history.

These research endeavors were insightful and taught me many things that I needed to know. However, my real knowledge occurred when I began my journey inward. In fact, this occurred as quite an accident when I stumbled into meditation. I tried the practice purely out of curiosity, not expecting anything to come out of it, but the effects were transformative in a profoundly unexpected way. I connected with the deepest recesses of my inner world and found answers to the existential questions that I had long been asking: What was the fundamental purpose and role of business? Why am I here and what is my purpose and role in this world? What was I born to fulfill? Has such a purpose always been inside me? Have I simply not seen who I really am? Meditation, as the starting point of my inner journey, launched the awakening of my consciousness to a worldview of holism.

What I found was startling. The process was quieting and stilled my mind while I located the answers to my existential questions— those I had been obsessively researching and pondering—latent inside me, waiting to be discovered. There was an inner voice, and it did not seem to be me; I never had such thoughts or such a sense of connection to my inner authority before that would henceforth guide all my choices and decisions. From meditation I discovered that everything I needed to flourish in life was already encoded within me. Rather than casting about externally in universities or management schools for the answers, I had only to look within—to embark on my inner journey. By discovering the way to live, in touch with how relational my reality was, I realized that transformation had to begin with changing the way I see the world.

This reorientation represented nothing less than a total paradigm shift in my life. I was now traveling in a different direction, wandering inward for the solutions to existential mysteries. This change of path precipitated my journey of life and stewardship, through which I sought internal rather than external authority. Attuning myself to my inner voice, I discovered my calling. I saw that it was from my response to this calling that creativity would illuminate my life.

Thus, I awakened to the importance of stewardship in business, which is nothing other than taking ethical responsibility. Having transcended survival mode and reached a comfortable state of indulgence and affluence, humanity needs quantum leaders and stewards who can take responsibility for guiding us all into a new era.

Through the journey of my awakening, my main epiphany was the holism of the quantum worldview and the systemic interconnectedness of its expression. In this worldview, well-being is a state of coherence, manifesting as unity and harmony. Because of this interconnectedness of everything, I understood the urgent need for a unified worldview on which humanity could build common ground—a common purpose and language, to steer us into the era of well-being and happiness.

My crucial discovery was that I needed only to play my role—to do what I was here to do, which was to add value to the system. This also is the crux of my understanding the path for achieving sustainability. With everyone doing their part—making the choice to collaborate and create—real social development can happen; we will all flourish along with the system and be rewarded for our efforts. I decided to ground my business mission on this principle, formulating it in the words: "to serve human well-being and create wealth at the same time."

To this end, I founded a small research center in Singapore in 1995 called the East West Cultural Development Center—today reconfigured as Octave Institute—to conduct timely research on culture and sustainability and to promulgate the wise and knowing theory that we all have a role to play in every system in which we have relationships. Whether these relationships are with members of our family, society, business, or community, we must all find a way to add value for the evolution of the system. If not, the system will wither and disappear, unable to adapt to the changing needs of the times.

My accidental foray into meditation became the unexpected catalyst of my personal journey of transformation. As I came into contact with all the latent wisdom that lay within me, my worldview was shifted. It is this new consciousness that informs all aspects of my leadership and decision-making today. I realize and accept that my future is in my hands to be created; I need to capitalize on my power and steward this transformation.

A Time of Discoveries

On my inner journeys, I also discovered the bridge between physics and metaphysics—the fundamental backbone of the quantum paradigm. This revelation changed the way I perceived religion and triggered a series of deep reflections on the evolution of humanity. My worldview was transformed, and I became attuned to the rhythms of the universe. With more clarity than ever in my life, I saw that everything is life and life is everything. I was—and I am—here to add value to life.

Business, as the most efficient institution to serve human desires, must be oriented by collective well-being as its key priority. Crucially, I made the choice to embark on my life journey and lead my business on its own journey of transformation—to renew the purpose and meaning of our lives. I chose to initiate this evolutionary journey for myself and for the business for which I held stewardship.

Leadership is necessary everywhere, regardless of whether change is cultural, structural, or processual. For me, leadership is an energy, cultivated through inner journeys and explorations. It radiates through a small group of people who have made the choice to awaken to the quantum paradigm. They are purpose-driven, action-oriented, and have the charisma to invite others to participate in the co-creation of a new era of well-being and happiness.

Being the chief steward of a fourth-generation family business, I am fortunate enough to be uniquely positioned to make significant change. I am endowed with sufficient resources to make decisions that will impact the lives of many people. But the important thing is not only my privilege but the choices I have made along the way that were enabled by my inward spiritual journeys. I firmly believe in awakening to the imminent arrival of the era of well-being and happiness, and I have made the conscious choice to participate in the creation of business transformation and to be at the forefront of the global consciousness shift that has already begun.

Relationships in a family business are paramount to its sustainability. With this mindset, I chose to redefine these relationships, starting with my relationship with wealth. I concluded that wealth is a responsibility and an opportunity for stewardship because of the basic principle that "we come from nothing and will leave with nothing." We are stewards, not owners, of this wealth. It was incredibly liberating for me to shift how I conceived of wealth and my role in relation to it, as it made me aware that we all share responsibility for sustaining the continuity of this family business.

I exercised my power of choice in my decision to redefine my family business mandate as one fundamentally grounded in well-being. To me, well-being is the solution that dispels the myth that a family business is fated to collapse and fail after three generations. If we constantly evolve and add value to the larger systems of which we are a part, we are always going to be valuable and relevant. My decision to formulate a *well-being mandate* represents my desire to embrace the process of evolution by building a more expansive vision of family that goes beyond the familial to prioritize practices of sustainability in business economics. Sustainability, in fact, came as a natural byproduct of the desire to construct a full spectrum for the flourishing of life. .

I have chosen to forge a well-being mandate as my offering and my gift for the longevity of this family business. This mandate consists of a set of principles and values informed by a holistic, constantly evolving worldview and view of life. It is my gift to guide the path of leadership beyond this toward a sustainable future for everyone.

I am of the belief that every single individual plays a crucial role in the arrival of the new era of well-being. Our purpose of life is to flourish, to add value to the whole system. Each and every one of us has the power and influence to embark on the hero's journey of leadership and transformation. One does not need to be an academic, scientist, artist, or musician; everyone has the potential to become a quantum leader, partake of the global consciousness shift, and precipitate the process of bifurcation.

After all, one of the central tenets of the new quantum era is the idea that every single part is interconnected in intimate kinship. No system can be well unless every small part within it is well. The human body, with its fifty trillion cells, is perhaps the best and most familiar illustration we have of this truth: all cells in our body must collaborate with one another in an intricate choreography to ensure the healthy functioning of the whole body. Thus, we must understand that each of us is whole, unto ourselves, and that we all have a role to play in constructing and maintaining the well-being for all.

I further realized that family businesses with their global impact and reach can be the fulcrum of business transformation. If family businesses across the globe can make the conscious choice to undertake this journey, we can all be partners in this voyage. Together, we can reach the tipping point and catalyze the bifurcation of business transformation. Because of the prominence and immense potential that family businesses hold, I am invested in the possibility that they will lead the energy for the movement into the new era of well-being and happiness.

This is not a gradual change, but an irreversible systemic alteration—we do not have the option to return to what the world was before. Despite the risk and uncertainty involved, I have chosen to transform my business model into one that serves the new well-being and happiness economy. This model is a live prototype, an ecosystem for life and an infrastructure, containing both hardware and software, to buttress the desires and needs that will characterize the new era. It is for this reason that I created Octave—my leap of faith, my message of hope, my guiding light to an unknown future.

Creating Octave

Octave, a transformational business model to promote global consciousness in this new era, is built upon the belief that well-being is coherent and holistic. It is for this purpose that I decided to establish Octave with new ways of learning, living, and investing. For me, it represents a prototype of the well-being and happiness economy, a whole ecosystem modeling lifelong journeys of learning, the governance of capital by ESG and impact investment and what it means to live mindfully and purposefully. All activities at Octave aim to synthesize the wisdom of quantum science and traditional practices. Through the East-West integration, Octave seeks to learn from the best of both worlds.

The core to the Octave mandate is the creation of a structure and framework to support an era and culture of well-being for the future. This new mandate grounds my family business, most evidently exemplified by the work that Octave does. In its fundamental values and principles, Octave's orientation differs greatly from existing economic and cultural paradigms that measure success by profit and productivity.

Octave is a business that creates the ecosystem of a well-being and happiness economy. It has three key arms:

∞ First is a learning unit that supports learning for the journey inward to cultivate a common worldview and common purpose that will hold future communities together;

∞ Second is an impact investment arm that directs capital and investment toward encouraging innovation in a well-being and happiness economy, and that redefines a new matrix through which to measure investments, incorporating ESG criteria;

∞ Third is a well-being and happiness economic business operation—for a mindful living community.

Octave is a four-layer, five-location infrastructure with an urban center, a sub-urban retreat for cultivating mindful living habits, two vacation retreat locations for recreation and learning, and a mountain retreat for deep and reflective inner journeys. The Octave ecosystem offers a comprehensive prototype of the well-being and happiness economy.

Once tested, this ecosystem at Octave can act as a role model from which larger, more extended systems can be replicated to promote well-being and happiness in economic activities. The dream is for Octave—exemplifying the well-being mandate—to model the way forward by integrating these seemingly disparate functions and spheres into one coherent system. Much of Octave is built on the infrastructure of a school of life and living with the intention to accompany everyone on this life journey and facilitate the emergence of quantum leadership

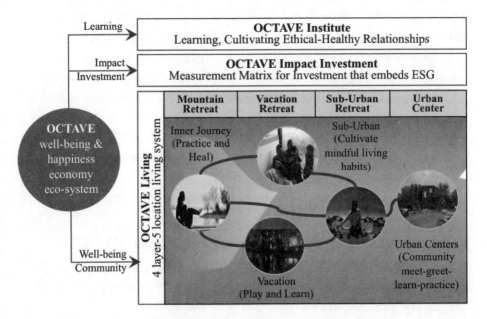

THE OCTAVE ECOSYSTEM DESIGN

in this new era. The hope is for everyone to realize that they have the agency to take responsibility for this shift and become stewards for their families and their communities.

My Calling

Many people have asked me, out of a sense of concern, "What if your Octave prototype fails?" I can understand and sympathize with that impulse. But it is somehow impossible to answer this question satisfactorily. The possibility of failure is, of course, built into the very act of taking a leap of faith. I know that for a fact. I have measured all the risks, and decided that it is still worth my while to do everything in my power to drive the change that I believe in.

I know, deep in my bones, that the time is now. Through my years of experimentation and experience, I have witnessed the beginnings of this transformation to holism and oneness—it is irreversible. The evolutionary energy has already been released into the world, poised to transform all of humanity.

My calling as an entrepreneur and as the steward of a family business is a vocation I have discovered through years of deep listening and inner exploration—it embodies my calling to act. Having understood my purpose and my role, I have made the choice to undertake this inner journey—to exercise my freedom and my power to be a part of this process of transformation. If Octave fails, I have no doubt that alternative models, new innovations and prototypes will rise to take its place.

Perhaps this, then, is my response to the question that so many people have asked. What if Octave fails? If I have learned anything in my journey, it is humility; I am but one part of a larger system that embraces all of us. The future is a vast unknown expanse, and it is not in my power, nor anyone else's, to know what it looks like. I can only take conscious action, with all that I know and value, to bring into being the future that I believe in for the good of all.

Needless to say, I cannot do this by myself, but I am committed to inviting all—regardless of their talents, skills, and preferences—to join me on this journey. It is precisely because I believe everyone has a role to play, and why I have built AITIA Institute and Octave. The former focused on research and quantum leadership, and the latter models a prototype of what a well-being and happiness economy might look like. Through these two projects, working in concert with each other as an integrated whole, I hope to make space for everyone's contributions and to encourage awakening to the unique ways in which we all can add value to the evolutionary process. Here, then, is my response to my own calling—to humanity's calling.

The more businesses that adopt this model, replicating or adapting it to suit their own contexts, the more closely we will approach the tipping point. Whether or not we want to participate in the transformation is the ultimate choice that each one of us can make. The choice is ours to initiate the journey of discovery into our inner worlds, to put a pause on the rhythms of our busy lives and to still our minds for one moment. Observing the core of our being and attuning ourselves to our inner voices, we will find our calling. We will see the world through fresh eyes, as if reborn.

Our participation will be a rebirth—of everything we thought we believed in, valued, and desired. This renewed perception of the world is nothing short of an awakening to the truth of the quantum worldview. Reverberating into our thoughts, desires, values—and finally our actions—this epiphany will shape our culture. From that place of deep connection and intimacy, we will be empowered by our inner being to act in service of the new well-being and happiness economy. The power of our wishes and desires as human beings will inform and provide the energy for the willpower of doing.

Having shared with you my story of awakening and transformation, I invite you to be a co-voyager with me in a journey to forge new paths and territories where humanity has never before set foot. I invite you to make the choice to awaken, to listen, and to act. Every single one of us has a place in the future, a unique way of contributing and adding value to our evolution. Like individual pieces of a puzzle, we only need to discover where we fit into the dazzling, complex, and beautiful mosaic of humanity as it shifts and reassembles itself into new configurations.

Frightening as the uncertainties of the future might be, we must remember that none of us are alone in this. Together, we can bring into being a new order of

> **C**oherence and
> **H**olism, through which our
> **O**uter and
> **I**nner worlds will meet in a dance of
> **C**ontinuous
> **E**volution

In other words, we have the choice to accomplish this! Our choice will set us free and carry us across the ontological divide into the new era of well-being and happiness.

Let us harness the energy of evolution and, united by our faith in creativity and infinite possibility, join the ship with sails aflutter, bound for the horizons of an enlightened future.

Endnotes

1. Ervin Laszlo and Frederick Tsao, *Dawn of an Era of Well-being: New Paths to a Better World* (SelectBooks, 2021), p207.

2. Bruce H. Lipton, "What Controls the Fate of Cells?" (2017). Website: (https://www.brucelipton.com/what-controls-the-fate-the-cells)

3. Albions Butters, *A Brief History of Spiral Dynamics*, Approaching Religion 5(2), (2015), p67–68.

4. Ervin Laszlo and Frederick Tsao, *Dawn of an Era of Well-being: New Paths to a Better World* (SelectBooks, 2021), p82.

5. Theodosius Dobzhansky and Gordon Allen. "Does Natural Selection Continue to Operate in Modern Mankind?" American Anthropologist 58.4 (1956): 591–604.

6. Douglas Kenrick, Vladas Griskevicius, Steven Neuberg, and Mark Schaller, "Renovating the Pyramid of Needs: Contemporary Extensions Built Upon Ancient Foundations," *Perspectives on Psychological Science* 5.3 (2010): 292–314.

7. Yuval Noah Harari. *Sapiens: A Brief History of Humankind* (New York: Harper, 2015).

8. Ervin Laszlo is a philosopher of science, systems theorist, and integral theorist who has published more than 100 books and over 400 papers. A founder of the general theory of evolution and the evolution of holistic consciousness. Website: https://ervinlaszlobooks.com/author

9. Ervin Laszlo, *The Upshift: Wiser Living on Planet Earth* (Waterside Productions, 2022).

10. Ibid.

11. Frederick Tsao, *The Science of Life and Wellbeing: Integrating the New Science of Consciousness with the Ancient Science of Consciousness*, p8.

12. Klaus Schwab, "The Fourth Industrial Revolution: What It Means, How to Respond, World Economic Forum (2016).

13. This quote is attributed to Pierre Teilhard de Chardin in *The Joy of Kindness* (1993), by Robert J. Furey, p138; but it is also attributed to G. I. Gurdjieff in *Beyond Prophecies and Predictions: Everyone's Guide to the Coming Changes* (1993) by Moira Timms, p62; neither cite a source. It was widely popularized by Wayne Dyer, who often quotes it in his presentations, crediting it to Chardin, as does Stephen Covey in *Living the 7 Habits: Stories of Courage and Inspiration* (2000), p47.

14. Ervin Laszlo and Frederick Tsao, *Dawn of an Era of Well-Being: New Paths to a Better World* (SelectBooks, 2021), p167.

15. Ervin Laszlo and Frederick Tsao, *Dawn of an Era of Well-Being: New Paths to a Better World* (SelectBooks, 2021), p43.

16. Ervin Laszlo, *Reconnecting to the Source, The New Science of Spiritual Experience, How It Can Change You, and How It Can Transform the World* (St. Martin's Essentials, 2020), p20.

17. Bub, Jeffrey, "Quantum Entanglement and Information," The Stanford Encyclo-paedia of Philosophy (Summer 2020 Edition), Edward N. Zalta (ed.).

18. 缘起，Pratītyasamutpāda (Sanskrit: प्रतीत्यसमुत्पाद, Pāli: paṭiccasamup-pāda), commonly translated as dependent origination. It states that all dharmas (phenomena) arise in dependence upon other dharmas: "If this exists, that exists; if this ceases to exist, that also ceases to exist." The basic principle is that all things (dharmas, phenomena, principles) arise in dependence upon other things. First seen from Saṃyukta Āgama, one of the four Āgamas as the collection of Early Buddhist Texts.

19. John Horgan and David Bohm, "Quantum Mechanics and Enlightenment, Scien-tific American," 2018.

20. Frederick Tsao, "The Science of Life and Wellbeing: Integrating the New Science of Consciousness with the Ancient Science of Consciousness," p8.

21. Ervin Laszlo and Frederick Tsao, *Dawn of an Era of Well-Being: New Paths to a Better World* (SelectBooks, 2021), p36.

22. James Legge (Translator), The Tao Te Ching, Lao Tse, The Floating Press (2008), 47. Translated Daodejing Chapter 25: 故道大，天大，地大，人亦大 https://www.Daodejing.org/25.html as: "Therefore the Tao is great; Heaven is great; Earth is great; and the (sage) king is also great. In the universe there are four that are great, and the (sage) king is one of them."

23. Rupert Sheldrake. (2019). "Can Morphic Fields Help Explain Telepathy and the Sense of Being Stared At?" 11. 26–33. Mindfield Bulletin, (2019), Volume 11 Issue 1, 26–33.

24. Ervin Laszlo and Frederick Tsao, *Dawn of an Era of Well-Being: New Paths to a Better World* (SelectBooks, 2021), p40.

25. Yun Li, 探源工程实证中华大地五千年文明 [The Research Into the Origin of Chinese Civilization as a Proof of The Five Thousand Years of Civilization in China], Youth and Society, 2018(20), pp7–10.

26. The Maya Calendar and the End of the World: Why the one does not substan-tiate the other, *World History Encyclopaedia*, https://www.worldhistory.org/article/416/the-maya-calendar-and-the-end-of-the-world-why-the/

27. Yang, Ciann-Dong. (2010). A Scientific Realization and Verification of Yin-Yang Theory: Complex-Valued Mechanics. International Journal of Nonlinear Sciences and Numerical Simulation. 11. 135-156.10.1515/IJNSNS.2010.11.2.135.

28. Unfpa.org. 2022. World Population Dashboard | United Nations Population Fund. [online] Available at: https://www.unfpa.org/data/world-population-dash-board.

29. Jurgen Habermas. *The Structural Transformation of the Public Sphere: An Inquiry into a Category of Bourgeois Society*. Cambridge, Mass.: MIT Press, 1989. p3.

30. Inequality.org, a project of the Institute for Policy Studies since 2011, that aims to provide information and insights for readers ranging from educators and jour-nalists to activists and policy makers, https://inequality.org/great-divide/updates-billionaire-pandemic/.

31. Credit Suisse Research Institute, Global wealth report 2021, June 2021, p17, Figure 1, Global Health Pyramid. [online] Available at: https://www.credit-suisse.com/about-us/en/reports-research/global-wealth-report.html

32. Oxfam International, 2020. Time to care—Unpaid and underpaid care work and the global inequality crisis. [online] Available at: https://www.oxfam.org/en/research/time-care.

33. United Nations, Peace, dignity and equality on a healthy planet, https://www.un.org/en/global-issues/human-rights.

34. Patel. (2016). The Path to Printed Body Parts. ACS Central Science, 2(9), pp581–583.

35. Lexico powered by Oxford. https://www.lexico.com/definition/globalization.

36. Global Wellness Institute, GWI is leading source for authoritative wellness industry research, https://globalwellnessinstitute.org/press-room/statistics-and-facts/.

37. Jenna Wortham. *The New York Times Magazine*, "The Future of Work," https://www.nytimes.com/2021/02/17/magazine/wellness-apps.html.

38. "Why you will probably live longer than most big companies," IMD, 2016, https://www.imd.org/research-knowledge/articles/why-you-will-probably-live-longer-than-most-big-companies.

39. Business Roundtable is an association of chief executive officers of America's leading companies working to promote a thriving U.S. economy and expanded opportunity for all Americans through sound public policy, https://www.business-roundtable.org/business-roundtable-redefines-the-purpose-of-a-corporation-to-promote-an-economy-that-serves-all-americans.

40. "Transforming our World: The 2030 Agenda for Sustainable Development," 2015, United Nation, Department of Economic and Social Affairs Sustainable Development, https://sdgs.un.org/2030agenda.

41. Timothy F. Slaper, Ph.D., Indiana Business Review, Indiana Business Research Center, Indiana University Kelley School of Business, Spring 2011 | Volume 86, No. 1, https://www.ibrc.indiana.edu/ibr/2011/spring/article2.html.

42. History of Modern Philanthropy, A Public Charity Dedicated to Providing Philanthropic Expertise, https://www.historyofgiving.org/introduction/.

43. Carnegie Corporation of New York, Andrew Carnegie's Story, https://www.carnegie.org/interactives/foundersstory/.

44. 2017 Cone Communications CSR Study, p9, https://www.cbd.int/doc/case-studies/inc/cs-inc-cone-communications-en.pdf.

45. Graham Allison. "China vs. America: Managing the Next Clash of Civilizations." Foreign Affairs 96, no. 5 (2017): 80–89.

46. Ervin Laszlo, *The Upshift: Wiser Living on Planet Earth* (Waterside Productions, 2022).

47. Ibid.

48. PwC, 2020. China Economic Quarterly Q1 2020, https://www.pwccn.com/en/research-and-insights/china-economic-quarterly-q1-2020-hot-topic.pdf.

49. Edward Cunningham, Tony Saich, and Jessie Turiel. 2020. "Understanding CCP Resilience: Surveying Chinese Public Opinion Through Time." Ash Center for Democratic Governance and Innovation, p3.

50. 2020 Edelman Trust Barometer Global Report, p40, https://www.edelman.com/sites/g/files/aatuss191/files/2020-01/2020%20Edelman%20Trust%20Barometer%20Global%20Report_LIVE.pdf

51. "U.S. Satisfaction Sinks with Many Aspects of Public Life, Gallup," February 2021, https://news.gallup.com/poll/329279/satisfaction-sinks-aspects-public-life.aspx.

52. Ervin Laszlo and Frederick Tsao, *Dawn of an Era of Well-Being: New Paths to a Better World*, SelectBooks, 2021, p37.

53. Eva Wong, *Taoism: An Essential Guide, Shambhala; Illustrated Edition* (March 8, 2011), p23.

54. Roth, Harold. (2000). *Bimodal Mystical Experience in the "Qiwulun" Chapter of Zhuangzi*. Journal of Chinese Religions. 28. pp31–50.

55. Liu, *Ts'un-yan* and Benjamin Penny. *Daoism in History Essays in Honour of Liu Ts'un-yan*. London: Routledge, 2006. p5.

56. Eva Wong, *Taoism: An Essential Guide*, Shambhala; Illustrated Edition (March 8, 2011), p20.

57. CNN, *China's New World Order*, https://www.cnn.com/interactive/2017/05/world/chinas-new-world-order/.

58. Nyree Stewart. (2010). "China is World's 2nd Largest Economy." *Investment Adviser.*

59. "Zhou Enlai (1898–1976) was, for decades, one of the most prominent and respected leaders of the Communist movement." *From Focus on Asian Studies*, Vol. IV, No. 1 (New York: The Asia Society, 1984). © 1984 The Asia Society.

60. Philip Alden Kuhn, [1980] 1990:12.

61. Leften Stavros Stavrianos. *The World to 1500: A Global History* (3th Edition), Englewood Cliffs, N.J.: Prentice-HallV, 1982, p66.

62. Angus Maddison, *The World Economy—A Millennial Perspective*, OECD Development Centre, p263.

63. Mao Zedong, "和英国记者贝特兰的谈话" (*Conversation with British Journalist James Bertrand*, October 25, 1937), Selected Works of Mao Zedong, vol. 2, p354.

64. John King Fairbank, "美国与中国" (*The United States and China*) (World Affairs Press 1999) p208.

65. Xi Jinping's speech at the congress celebrating the 100th anniversary of the founding of the Communist Party of China on July 1, 2021.

66. S. S. Kantha. "Nutrition and Health in China, 1949 to 1989," *Prog Food Nutr Sci.* 1990;14(2-3):93–137.

67. Kishore Mahbubani, "Has China Won? The Chinese Challenge to American Primacy," New York: Public Affairs, 2020, p71.

68. Nancy E. Snow. *The Oxford Handbook of Virtue*, Oxford University Press, 2018, p200.

69. The Chunyun Travel Period, China, 2010, "Largest Annual Human Migration."

70. Confucius, and Legge, James. *Confucian Analects. The Great Learning. The Doctrine of the Mean.* New York: Dover Publications, 1971, p375.

71. Confucius, and Legge, James. *Confucian Analects. The Great Learning. The Doctrine of the Mean.* New York: Dover, Publications, 1971, pp384–385.

72. Jungho Suh, "The Confucian Doctrine of the Mean: The Optimality Principle, and Social Harmony," *Society and Economy* 42 (2020) 1, pp60–61.

73. Martin Albrow, "Nation Shows How to Put Moral Principles into Action," China Daily Global, 2021.

74. Douglas North, "制度，意识形态和绩效"*(Institutions, Ideology and Economic Performance), The Revolution in Development Economics* (Shanghai People's Publishing House 2000).

75. Yang Xiaoming, "奇迹析" *(An Analysis of the East Asian Economic Miracle)* [J]. Nankai Journal, 1997 (1).

76. Klaus Schwab and Thierry Malleret , *COVID-19: The Great Reset* (Chinese version), Citic Press 2020, Preface.

77. *The Complete I Ching—10th Anniversary Edition: The Definitive Translation by Taoist Master Alfred Huang,* pp25–30, Inner Traditions; 2nd Edition, Revised, Two-Color (November 17, 2010).

78. Rupert Sheldrake. Part I—*Mind, Memory, and Archetype: Morphic Resonance and the Collective Unconscious,* Psychological Perspectives (Spring 1987), 18(1) 9–25.

79. *Informal Sociology, A Casual Introduction to Sociological Thinking* by William Bruce Cameron, p13, Random House, New York, 1963.

80. J. Lederach. (2005-02-10). "On Mass and Movement: The Theory of the Critical Yeast." In *The Moral Imagination: The Art and Soul of Building Peace.* Oxford University Press.

81. David W. Orme-Johnson (2003) "Preventing Crime Through the Maharishi Effect," *Journal of Offender Rehabilitation*, 36:1-4, 257–281.

82. Frederick C. Tsao and Chis Laszlo, *Quantum Leadership, New Consciousness in Business,* Stanford University Press, 2018, p121.

83. Beck & Cowan, 1996; Senge, 1993.

84. Barrett, 1998; Mackey & Sisodia, 2013; Pavez et al., 2014.

85. Fritjof Capra and Pier Luigi Luisi, *The Systems View of Life: A Unifying Vision,* Cambridge University Press, 2014, p14.

86. Haigh & Hoffman, 2012; *Honeyma*n, 2014; *Mackey & Sisodia,* 2013; Senge et al., 2008; Waddock, 2008.

87. Ehrenfeld, 2008; Ehrenfeld & Hoffman, 2013; Laszlo & Brown et al., 2014.

88. Dr. Gabor Mate is a renowned addiction expert, speaker and author with expertise in trauma, addiction, stress and childhood development. https://drgabormate.com/.

89. Hölzel, B. K., Carmody, J., Vangel, M., Congleton, C., Yerramsetti, S. M., Gard, T., & Lazar, S. W. (2011). "Mindfulness Practice Leads to Increases in Regional Brain Gray Matter Density." *Psychiatry Research*, 191(1), 36–43.

90. Dorjee Dusana, "Defining Contemplative Science: The Metacognitive Self-Regulatory Capacity of the Mind, Context of Meditation Practice and Modes of Existential Awareness," *Frontiers in Psychology,* Volume 7, 2016.

91. Stephen Parker, in *Progress in Brain Research,* 2019.

92. Frederick C. Tsao and Chris Laszlo. *Quantum Leadership, New Consciousness in Business*, Stanford University Press, 2018, p178.

93. Yang Tianyu and Li Ji Yi Zhu. Chapter 9 Li Yun, Shanghai Chinese Classics Publishing House, 1997, p363.

94. *Diamond Sutra Explained*, Master Nan Huai-Chin, Translated by Hue En (Pia Giammasi), 2004, *Primordia Media, Inc.* pp204–206.

95. Swami Wharvananda, Taittiriya Upanishad, The Ramakrishna Math, 2912, p53–71.
    Norman C. McClelland, *Encyclopedia of Reincarnation and Karma*, McFarland & Company, Inc., Publishers, 2010, p154.

96. O. L. Reiser. "The Evolution of Cosmologies," *Philosophy of Science*, 19(2), (1952), p93–107.
    The physical universe, is the actualized body of the Supreme Imagination, being composed of the cosmic forms that have been crystallized as visions of reality as these have been structuralized in the ever-evolving patterns which are in fact the story of creation, the history of the universe.
    The cosmos is the expression of a Guilding Field, impersonal and non-anthropomorphic.

97. The Smithsonian Institution (the world's largest museum, education, and research complex), National Museum of the American Indian, NK 360°, Living Maya Time, https://maya.nmai.si.edu/.

98. Harper Donald. *Physicians and Diviners: The Relation of Divination to the Medicine of the Huangdineijing* (inner canon of the Yellow Thearch). In: Extrême-Orient, Extrême-Occident, 1999, no21. Divination et rationalité en Chine ancienne. pp91–110, states that in terms of social and intellectual background, the physician-authors of the *Huangdineijing* (Inner Canon), was compiled ca. first century BCE.

99. The Global Wellness Institute (GWI) is a 501(c)(3) nonprofit organization with a mission to empower wellness worldwide by educating the public and private sectors about preventative health and wellness. https://globalwellnessinstitute.org/what-is-wellness/.

100. James Legge (Translator), The Tao Te Ching, Lao Tse, The Floating Press (2008), 130, Chapter 71. 知不知，尚矣; 不知知，病也。 圣人不病，以其病病。夫唯病病，是以不病 https://www.Daodejing.org/71.html as: "To know and yet (think) we do not know is the highest (attainment); not to know (and yet think) we do know is a disease. It is simply by being pained at (the thought of) having this disease.

101. Avidyā 無明 (Sanskrit: अवदि्या; Pāli: अवजि्जा, avijjā; Tibetan phonetic: ma rigpa) in Buddhist literature is commonly translated as "ignorance." The concept refers to ignorance or misconceptions about the nature of metaphysical reality, in particular about the impermanence and anatta doctrines about reality, https://thereaderwiki.com/en/Avidy%C4%81_(Buddhism).

102. James Legge (Translator), *The Tao Te Ching*, Lao Tse (The Floating Press, 2008), 130, Chapter 71, https://www.daodejing.org/71.html as: "To know and yet (think) we do not know is the highest (attainment); not to know (and yet think) we do know is a disease. It is simply by being pained at (the thought of) having this disease that we are preserved from it. The sage has not the disease. He knows the

pain that would be inseparable from it, and therefore he does not have it." 知不知，尚矣；不知知，病也。聖人不病，以其病病。夫唯病病，是以不病。

103.   Yuan, H., Ma, Q., Ye, L., & Piao, G. (2016). "The Traditional Medicine and Modern Medicine from Natural Products." *Molecules* (Basel, Switzerland), 21(5), p559.

104.   The World Bank, Current Health Expenditure, https://data.worldbank.org/indicator/SH.XPD.CHEX.GD.ZS?locations=US.

105.   Eric French, John Bailey Jones, Elaine Kelly, and Jeremy McCauley, "End-of-Life Medical Expenses," Federal Reserve Bank of Richmond, November 19, 2018, page12.

106.   United Nations, Department of Economic and Social Affairs, World Population Aging 2019, https://www.un.org/en/development/desa/population/publications/pdf/ageing/WorldPopulationAgeing2019-Highlights.pdf, page 1.

107.   FoodPrint is a project of GRACE Communications Foundation, which develops innovative strategies to increase public awareness of the critical environmental and public health issues created by our current industrial food system, https://foodprint.org/the-total-footprint-of-our-food-system/issues/the-industrial-food-system/.

108.   Haas R. H. (2019). "Mitochondrial Dysfunction in Aging and Diseases of Aging." *Biology*, 8(2) p48.

109.   Alberts B, Johnson A, Lewis J, et al. *Molecular Biology of the Cell. 4th edition.* New York: Garland Science; 2002. The Mitochondrion, https://www.ncbi.nlm.nih.gov/books/NBK26894/.

110.   Harman Denham, "The Biologic Clock: The Mitochondria?"1972, *Journal of the American Geriatrics Society*, pp145–147.

111.   Stones, R. (2022). In *Thích Nhất Hạnh: Biography*, pp5–6, essay, Independently published. Thich Nhat Hanh (1926–2022) is a Zen master of Vietnamese origin.

112.   Thich Nhat Hanh and Dr. Lilian Cheung, "Savor Mindful Eating," *Mindful Life* (HarperCollins Publishers 2011) p119.

113.   FoodPrint is a project of GRACE Communications Foundation, "Animal Welfare in Food Production," https://foodprint.org/the-total-footprint-of-our-food-system/issues/animal-welfare-in-food-production/.

114.   D. Melé D and G.G.Cantón (2014). "Relational Dimensions of the Human Being." In: Human Foundations of Management. IESE Business Collection. Palgrave Macmillan, London.

115.   United Nations. (1968). "Urbanization: Development Policies and Planning." p3. New York.

116.   United Nations, Department of Economic and Social Affairs, Population Division (2014). "World Urbanization Prospects: The 2014 Revision, Highlights" (ST/ESA/SER.A/352). https://population.un.org/wup/Publications/Files/WUP2014-Highlights.pdf

117.   National Development and Reform Commission, "Medium and Long-term Railroad Network Planning," 2016, pp2–7.

118. "Germany Announces New Plan to 'Turbocharge' Transition to Renewable Energy," *Eco Watch*, April 2022 https://www.ecowatch.com/germany-renewable-energy-transition.html

119. Jalava M, Kummu M, Porkka M, Siebert S, and Varis O (2014). "Diet Change—A Solution to Reduce Water Use?" *Environ. Res. lett.* 9(7):1–14.

120. Springmann, Marco, et al. "Analysis and Valuation of the Health and Climate Change Cobenefits of Dietary Change." Proceedings of the National Academy of Sciences of the United States of America, vol. 113, no. 15, 2016, pp4146–51.

121. Climate Change 2022: "Mitigation of Climate Change, a report from the United Nations' Intergovernmental Panel on Climate Change," https://report.ipcc.ch/ar6wg3/pdf/IPCC_AR6_WGIII_FinalDraft_FullReport.pdf

122. "Sustainable Finance for A Zero Waste Circular Economy," *Zero Waste Europe*, December 2020, https://zerowasteeurope.eu/wp-content/uploads/2020/11/zero_waste_europe_report_sustainable-finance-for-a-zero-waste-circular-economy_en.pdf

123. William Halal, Jonathan Kolber, and Owen Davies. "Forecasts of AI and Future Jobs in 2030: Muddling Through Likely, with Two Alternative Scenarios." *Journal of Futures Studies 21*, no. 2 (2016).

124. World Economic Forum, "The Future of Jobs," 2020, p5.

125. Piers Kicks, "Into The Void: Where Crypto Meets the Metaverse," Jan 2022, Article, https://naavik.co/deep-dives/into-the-void.

126. Investopedia, Economy, "The Top 25 Economies in the World," 2020, https://www.investopedia.com/insights/worlds-top-economies/#citation-94

127. "Who Cares Wins: Connecting Financial Markets to a Changing World," (English). Washington, D.C.: World Bank Group. http://documents.worldbank.org/curated/en/280911488968799581/Who-cares-wins-connecting-financial-markets-to-a-changing-world

128. George Kell. "The Remarkable Rise of ESG," Forbes, *Leadership Strategy*, July 2018, https://www.forbes.com/sites/georgkell/2018/07/11/the-remarkable-rise-of-esg/?sh=67c6ad541695
"Global Sustainable Investment Review 2020," p9, GSIA, http://www.gsi-alliance.org/wp-content/uploads/2021/08/GSIR-20201.pdf.

129. "Global Gross Domestic Product (GDP) at Current Prices from 1985 to 2026," Statista (2022), https://www.statista.com/statistics/268750/global-gross-domestic-product-gdp/

130. "Share of Economic Sectors in the Global Gross Domestic Product (GDP) from 2010 to 2020," *Statista* (2022), https://www.statista.com/statistics/256563/share-of-economic-sectors-in-the-global-gross-domestic-product/

131. ASEAN is a 10-member state of Southeast Asia nations comprising, Indonesia, Malaysia, Philippines, Singapore, Thailand, Brunei Darussalam, Vietnam, Lao PDR, Myanmar and Cambodia, https://asean.org/about-us

132. "Global Business Speaks English," *Harvard Business Review* May 2012, https://hbr.org/2012/05/global-business-speaks-english.

133. ASEAN economic community, https://asean.org/our-communities/economic-community/

134. "Our Global Offer to Business: London and the UK's Competitive Strengths in a Critical Time, p2, the City of London Corporation, https://www.theglobalcity. uk/PositiveWebsite/media/Research-reports/CoL-Our-global-offer-to-business-2022.pdf

135. M. Maliszewska and D. Mensbrugghe, "World Bank Group's, Macroeconomics, Trade and Investment Global Practice," April 2019, pp19–20.

136. Chapurukha Kusimba, When–and Why–Did People First Start Using Money?, *The Conversation,* June 2017.
     Rebecca L. Spang, "The Currency of History," *World Policy Journal*, FALL 2016, Vol. 33, No. 3 (Fall 2016), pp39–44.

137. Stephan Epstein. *Freedom and Growth. The Rise of States and Markets in Europe.* London: Routledge, 2000. "The Late Medieval Crisis as an 'Integration Crisis.'" In *Early Modern Capitalism Economic and Social Change in Europe, 1400–1800*, edited by Maarten Prak, 23–48. London: Routledge, 2001.

138. C. Schenk (2020) "The Sterling Area 1945–1972." In: Battilossi S., Cassis Y., Yago K. (eds) *Handbook of the History of Money and Currency*. Springer, p788.

139. Klaus Schwab, "The Fourth Industrial Revolution, What It Means and How to Respond," *Foreign Affairs*, 2015, https://www.foreignaffairs.com/articles/2015-12-12/fourth-industrial-revolution

140 Family Firm Institute 2017.

141. The Family Business Network (FBN) is the world's leading organization of business families, founded in 1989 and headquartered in Lausanne, https://www.fbn-i.org/about-us.

142. Polaris, "Family Business as a Force for Good," https://www.fbni.org/communities/polaris.

The Chinese Historical Path

Note to the reader about the text in this addendum:

The following diagram on page 227 and the first three columns in the chart on pages 229 to 239 contain text that was translated from the Chinese language and used here with permission from Zhonghua Book Company. The text for the diagram and first three columns of the chart shown here was originally published in Zhongguo Lishi Nianbiao (中國歷史年表) by Chinese Academy of History, Chinese Academy of Social Sciences in 2013.

The fourth column of the chart on pages 229 to 239 contains interpretive remarks about the history of the dynasties is commentary written by the author of this book.

2070–1600 BCE
Xia 夏

1600–1046 BCE
Shang 商

1046–771 BCE
Western Zhou 西周

770–256 BCE
Eastern Zhou
東周

770–476 BCE
Spring and Autumn
Period 春秋時期

475–221 BCE
Warring States Period
戰國時期

221–206 BCE
Qin 秦

202 BCE 8 CE
Western Han 西漢

25–220 CE
Eastern Han 東漢

220–280 CE
Three Kingdoms 三國

265–316 CE
Western Jin 西晉

265–420 CE
Jin 晉

317–420 CE
Eastern Jin 東晉

420–589 CE
Northern and Southern Dynasties
南北朝

581–618 CE
Sui 隋

618–907 CE
Tang 唐

907–979 CE
Five Dynasties and Ten Kingdoms
五代十國

960–1279 CE
Song 宋

960–1127 CE
Northern Song 北宋

1127–1279 CE
Southern Song 南宋

1271–1368 CE
Yuan 元

1368–1644 CE
Ming 明

1644–1911 CE
Qing 清

1912–1949 CE
Republic of China 中華民國

1949–Present
People's Republic of China
中華人民共和國

227

China's Path from the First Dynasty in Chinese History, Established in 2070 BCE, to the Present Government of the People's Republic of China

Year	Dynasty	Remarks	
2070–1600 BCE	Xia 夏	In 2070 BCE, Qi (啟), son of Yu (禹), was crowned emperor, marking the start of the Xia Dynasty	This is the first dynasty in Chinese history.
1600–1046 BCE	Shang 商	In 1600 BCE, the Xia Dynasty was overthrown by Shang Dynasty.	Shang is the earliest dynasty firmly supported by archaeological evidence and written records of that time. The oracle bone script that appeared during this period features the earliest systematic written symbols that have been discovered in China.
1046–771 BCE	Western Zhou 西周	In 1046 BCE, the Zhou Dynasty— known as the Western Zhou— was established after the Battle of Muye.	During this period, productivity increased, agriculture flourished, and culture further developed. During this period, in the reverence, worship and faith in nature, people followed the ways of heaven and created the I Ching, considered to be one of the oldest classical texts in China.

Continued

Year	Dynasty	Remarks	
770–256 BCE	Eastern Zhou 東周	In 770 BCE, King Ping of Zhou, established the Eastern Zhou Dynasty, when he moved the capital to Luoyi. The Eastern Zhou Dynasty was further divided into two stages: the Spring and Autumn Period and the Warring Stated Period. In 453 BCE, the Jin territory was divided into Han, Zhao and Wei. During this period, hundreds of schools of thought emerged, and academics flourished like never before.	After the collapse of the Western Zhou Dynasty, the lords and vassals supported the deposed prince as king, King Ping of Zhou, to establish the Eastern Zhou Dynasty, which was a period of great division with more than 100 vassal states vying for supremacy. In 256 BCE, Qin destroyed the Zhou Dynasty.
770–476 BCE	Spring and Autumn Period 春秋時期		
475–221 BCE	Warring States Period 戰國時期		
221–206 BCE	Qin 秦	In 221 BCE, Qin seized Qi and unified the Chinese empire. King Yingzheng (贏政) of Qin became the first emperor. In 206 BCE, Liu Bang (劉邦) invaded Guanzhong and ending the reign of the Qin Dynasty.	The Qin Dynasty is the first unified, multi-ethnic, centralized and authoritarian feudal state in Chinese history. It introduced a range of reforms, such as standardized currency, weights, measures, and a uniform system of writing.

Year	Dynasty		Remarks
202 BCE–8 CE	Western Han 西漢	In 202 BCE Liu Bang (劉邦) unified the country and became Emperor Gaozu of Han.	There was an interregnum period between the fallen Qin Dynasty and the subsequent Han Dynasty, the Chu–Han Contention between two major powers—Xiang Yu's Western Chu and Liu Bang's Han. The war ended in 202 BCE with a total Han victory.
			Liu Bang then established the Western Han Dynasty and implemented the state policy of light taxation, rest, and recuperation, which led to rapid socio-economic recovery. During the Western Han Dynasty, the "rule of Wen and Jing" emerged, a period known for the benevolence and thriftiness of the emperors, often viewed as one of the golden ages in Chinese history.
			Emperor Wu of Han also implemented the policy of "ban from hundred philosophers, venerate Confucianism," which established the orthodox dominance of Confucian teachings and practices, such as The Three Cardinal Guides and The Five Constant Virtues in Chinese history.
			The Silk Road was established by Zhang Qian's mission to the West during the Western Han Dynasty. It was a period when China's culture began to create more influence outside its borders through trade.
			In the late Western Han Dynasty, with growing political corruption and social unrest, Wang Mang, with the support of landowning bureaucrats, made himself emperor in 8 CE and renamed the state "Xin," which led to the fall of the Western Han Dynasty.

Year	Dynasty	Remarks	
25–220 CE	Eastern Han 東漢	In 25 CE, Liu Xiu (劉秀) became the Emperor Guangwu of Han and continued the state name of "Han," known in history as the Eastern Han Dynasty.	Outstanding achievements in culture, science, technology, and military were seen during the Eastern Han Dynasty. Buddhism first entered China through the Silk Road during this time. After the Han Dynasty, the name Han people (漢人) became a cultural term, defined as people who lived in the Central Plains and believed in the fundamental teachings of Chinese culture. The Han Dynasty further established the national culture of the Han Chinese (漢族), and to this day, the term "Han people" is still used by most Chinese to refer to themselves, while the Chinese language is called *hanzi* (漢字), and traditional clothes are called *hanfu* (漢服).
220–280 CE	Three Kingdoms (Wei, Shu and Wu) 三國	In 208 CE, the Battle of Red Cliff, laid the foundation for the Three Kingdoms period. In 220 CE, Cao Pi (曹丕), son of Cao Cao (曹操), became emperor and changed the name of the state to Wei. In 263 CE, Wei destroyed Shu and Han.	It was a period with a tripartite division of China among the states of Wei, Shu, and Wu, beginning an era of war and conflict that lasted for nearly 100 years.

Year	Dynasty	Remarks	
265–316 CE	Western Jin 西晉	In 265 CE, Sima Yan (司馬炎) became Emperor Wu and established a new regime, renaming it to Jin, known as Western Jin in history.	This was a time of cultural creation, conflict, and integration, when Chinese culture gradually transformed through a fusion of Confucian, Buddhist, and Daoist practices.
317–420 CE	Eastern Jin 東晉	In 280 CE, the Western Jin Dynasty destroyed Wu and unified China. In 316 CE, the Western Jin Dynasty fell. The northern part of China entered the period of the Five Hu and Sixteen Kingdoms. In 317 CE, Sima Rui (司馬睿) established the Eastern Jin Dynasty in the south, and China entered a period of North-South division.	

Year	Dynasty	Remarks
420–589 CE	Northern and Southern dynasties 南北朝	In 398 CE, the Northern Wei Dynasty was established, ushering in the era of the Sixteen Northern Kingdoms in northern China. In 420 CE, the south of China experienced four short-lived dynasties—Song, Qi, Liang, and Chen. These four dynasties are collectively known as the Southern Dynasties.	Although it was a period of civil war and political chaos, it was also a time of flourishing in arts and culture, advancement in technology, and the spread of Mahayana Buddhism and Daoism.
581–618 CE	Sui 隋	In 581 CE, Emperor Yang Jian (楊堅), a powerful minister of the Northern Zhou Dynasty proclaimed himself as Emperor and renamed the state Sui. In 589 CE, Sui defeated Chen Dynasty and unified China.	However, his successor Yang Guang was recorded as a tyrant who did not provide for people's livelihoods. A peasant uprising toppled the Sui Dynasty after a short-lived 38 years of rule. This period saw the birth of the imperial examination system which has contributed to the modern Chinese education landscape structured around the "college entrance examination," and the Communist Party's "selection and appointment of cadres."

Year	Dynasty		Remarks
618–907 CE	Tang 唐	In 618 CE, Li Yuan (李淵) became the Emperor of Tang. In 624 CE, Tang unified China.	The Tang Dynasty was the most celebrated dynasty in Chinese history after the Sui Dynasty, with 21 emperors and a reign of 289 years. The Tang Dynasty extended the great unification of China, ushering in the heyday of feudal economic development based on the foundations built by the Sui Dynasty. The Tang Dynasty was politically enlightened, ideologically emancipated, and rich in talents. It had vast territories, consolidated national defense, harmony between ethnic groups, and effective forms of wealth accumulation. A large number of technological inventions emerged during this period, and gunpowder, one of the four major inventions, was discovered during the Tang Dynasty. The reputation of the Tang Dynasty reached far abroad, and its historical status was so important that in the Ming and Qing dynasties, most overseas people called the Chinese "Tang people." The first and only female emperor in Chinese history, Wu Zetian, also reigned during the Tang Dynasty.

Year	Dynasty	Remarks
907–979 CE	Five Dynasties and Ten Kingdoms 五代十國	In 907 CE, Zhu Wen (朱温) destroyed the Tang Dynasty and installed himself as emperor under the name of Liang. From the end of the Tang Dynasty to the beginning of the Song Dynasty, there were also more than a dozen concurrent states established elsewhere, mainly in South China, known in history as the Five Dynasties and Ten Kingdoms period.	

YEAR	DYNASTY		REMARKS
960–1127 CE	Northern Song 北宋	In 960 CE, Zhao Kuangyin (趙匡胤), launched the Chenqiao Mutiny and established the Northern Song Dynasty.	This is a period when most of the land was reunified, heralding a 319-year period of prosperity.
1127–1279 CE	Southern Song 南宋	During this period, there were other minority regimes in China, such as the Liao and the Jin. In 1127 CE, the Jin destroyed the Northern Song Dynasty. Zhao Gou (趙構) established the state in Yingtian and was known as the Southern Song Dynasty. In 1279 CE, the Yuan Dynasty destroyed the Southern Song Dynasty.	The Song Dynasty represented a prosperous era for the commodity economy, culture, education, and scientific innovation. Woodblock printing techniques, another one of the four major inventions, originated in the Song Dynasty. In addition, the invention of the compass, shipbuilding techniques and canal transportation facilitated advancements in maritime culture. The widespread use of gunpowder gave rise to the world's first primitive cannons. It is estimated that in 1000 CE, China's total GDP accounted for 22.7% of the world economy. (Maddison, Angus. *The World Economy*. Paris: OECD Publishing, 2001. P263).
1271–1368 CE	Yuan 元	In 1271 CE, Kublai Khan (忽必烈) established the Great Yuan.	The Yuan Dynasty was the first unified dynasty in Chinese history that was established by an ethnic minority. During this period, the unified multi-ethnic state was further consolidated, and its territory surpassed that of previous dynasties.

YEAR	DYNASTY	REMARKS	
1368–1644 CE	Ming 明	In 1368 CE, Zhu Yuanzhang (朱元璋) became emperor and the country was called Ming. The Ming army captured the capital and the Yuan Dynasty fell. In 1644 CE, Li Zicheng (李自成) revolted and conquered Beijing. The Ming Dynasty fell, the state renamed as Shun.	During the Ming Dynasty, the monarchy was strengthened in ways never seen before, and the multi-ethnic state was further unified and consolidated.
1644–1911 CE	Qing 清	In 1636 CE, Huang Taiji (皇太極) was crowned emperor in Shengjing and the country was named Qing. In 1644 CE, the Qing army entered Beijing. In 1911 CE, the Xinhai Revolution broke out and the Qing Dynasty collapsed.	The Qing Dynasty took control of Beijing from Shun, and was the last feudal dynasty in China. Through the Kangxi, Yongzheng and Qianlong emperors, the Qing Dynasty gradually recovered and developed its comprehensive national power, economy, and culture, making it a glorious period in China's history. However, the Opium War started a new period in China's history, along with the invasion of the Eight Nation Alliance, comprising of eight foreign imperialist powers. Western science and culture were also introduced into China, allowing the Qing Dynasty to launch a series of reforms and revolutions.

Year	Dynasty		Remarks
1912–1949 CE	Republic of China 中華民國	In 1912 CE, Sun Yat-sen (孙中山) was inaugurated as the Provisional President of the Republic of China in Nanjing.	
1949 CE– present	People's Republic of China 中華人民共和國		In 1949 CE, Chairman Mao Zedong (毛澤東) proclaimed the establishment of the People's Republic of China and the Central People's Government in Beijing.

Index

About the Author

FREDERICK TSAO is a fourth-generation family business leader and Chairman of the Family Business Network's Ambassador Circle. Born in the East and educated in the West, he became chairman of IMC Pan Asia Alliance Group in 1995 and transformed the business from a traditional shipping company into a multinational conglomerate. Fred's research on the subject of consciousness, particularly in Eastern traditional practices, began in 1995. He advocates that business should participate in the transformation and reform of our new epoch. Fred coauthored *Dawn of an Era of Well-Being: New Paths to a Better World* with Ervin Laszlo in 2021 and *Quantum Leadership: New Consciousness in Business* with Chris Laszlo in 2019. He founded the OCTAVE Institute to share a comprehensive, integrated approach to a lifelong pursuit of well-being as his offering to those on this quest.